BEAUTY WITHIN THE BEAST

Raising Orphan Bear Cubs in the Alaskan Wilderness

2nd Edition

© 2002, 2013

Stephen Stringham, Ph.D., Director

Bear Communication & Coexistence Research Program

"Communication is the Key to Coexistence—
Better Armed with Knowledge Than with Guns"

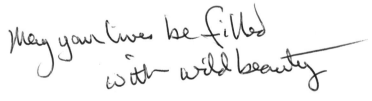
May your lives be filled with wild beauty

BEAUTY WITHIN THE BEAST

For
Jackie, the love of my life
– the extraordinary woman who chose to be my wife and soulmate
-- multi-cultural educator and scholar, loyal friend, wise advisor
and passionate fellow lover of life, learning, and adventure.

Without her support, my wildlife studies would have died long ago;
neither this nor any of my other books could have been written.

Thanks also to rest of my family, including:
Robert and Joyce Stringham
Laura & Brian Lippincott, Helen & Holly Strauss
Jeanette & John Otti, Christine and Valdamir Nicolayeff
whose love, patience and support have allowed me
to extend my wildlife research, conservation, and authoring
beyond the boundaries of political correctness.
Thanks also to
Alatanna, for all the wonderful times.

WildWatch
Publications Division
39200 Alma Ave. Soldotna, AK 99669
wildwatch.llc@gmail.com

© 2002, 2013 by *Stephen Stringham*

Library of Congress Cataloguing-in-Publication data is available on file

ISBN 1-931643-10-5

Search terms
1. Bear attacks – North America – Prevention.
2. Outdoor recreation – North America – Safety measures.
3. Bear encounters
4. Bear viewing – North America – Safety measures
5. Wildlife viewing – North America – Safety measures
6. Black bear – Behavior.
7. Grizzly bear – Behavior.
8. Brown bear – Behavior.
9. Body language – Bears.
10. Aggression – Bears
11. Communication – Bears
12. Wildlife rehabilitation

CONTENTS

Renewal

In part because bears can be so dangerous,
they force you to pay attention.
The awe of being in their presence
strips away the chaos of thoughts and distractions
that normally dominate your consciousness.
They focus your attention on the moment.
They flood your blood
with adrenaline and endorphins.
They introduce you to terror, awe,
amazement and ecstasy.
They connect you to the deepest pulses of life.
This is their gift.
The power to take your life,
or to renew it;
to re-create who you are,
if only for a moment,
and perhaps for a lifetime.

PROLOGUE

I have observed the birth of two bear litters. In the eye of my mind, I can still see the steam rising from the hindquarters of the female I called Soocie as amniotic fluid burst free from her womb and flooded out onto the floor of her den. I recall the gentle plopping sound made by each of three cubs as they slid out of her body onto the cushion of her lower hind leg, and the slurping of her tongue as she gently removed the amniotic sac and licked them dry. Even now, I seem to hear the first mewing bawls of her neonates, surprisingly loud for such tiny animals, and then the lusty sounds of suckling and the gentle rattle of their purrs.

Wildlife Research Institute photo of "Lily" and her cub.

The youngest cubs I have ever held were but hours old, and about the same size as newborn Husky pups–giving no hint of how large they would grow. I felt the cub's warm breath on my lips, their downy soft fur on my cheek, and the coolness of their noses against my own. My hands vibrated with their purrs as they sucked on my fingers, vainly seeking milk that I was not equipped to provide.

I have looked on the eyes of cubs before their eyes have seen the world, when their lids were sealed shut, blinding them for their first weeks after birth. When those eyes opened, in the dimness of their natal den, where the only light was snow-filtered translucence, I saw their obsidian pupils afloat in irises like sky blue pools that would one day turn into amber suns, alight with the intelligence and curiosity that make bears among the most intriguing creatures on earth.

That I would someday acquire three cubs of my own, along with a foxy Goldilocks, came as a complete and wonderful surprise. This is the story of how my new bride, Alatanna, and I raised these cubs, helping them learn to fend for themselves in the Alaska wilderness, and of what they taught us about rapport and coexistence with our ursine kin–about the *beauty within the beast*.

These were experiences I will never forget, experiences filled with high adventure, low humor, and a never-ending series of new scientific insights about bears – experiences which would never have occurred had their mother not raided cabins and suffered the consequences.

Over the months that followed, each new insight revealed by the cubs opened doors to others, increasing our sense of being not merely visitors in the Alaska wilderness, but residents – participants in its cycles of life and death, drawing sustenance from the ecosystems until we too would eventually succumb, whereupon other organisms would draw sustenance from our bodies.

PREFACE

Part I: **Bonding** (Chapters 1–7) tells how Alatanna and I ended up adopting the cubs and our experiences bonding with them as our fear of bears, and the cubs' fear of us, were gradually replaced with trust and affection. Part II: **Preparing for Independence** (chapters 8–14) tells how we helped the cubs master survival skills, while they introduced us to a whole world of new insights into the nature of bears – their aggression, communication, intelligence, curiosity, playfulness and affection.

Where necessary, I have fleshed out my narrative with knowledge acquired from my more recent studies of black and grizzly bear behavior–which continue to this day.

*   *   *

My account is as accurate as journal notes, photos, films, and memories allow, with minor exceptions.

1. Although I took detailed scientific notes, videos, photographs and films, most of those records were lost in a fire. This book is thus based on diary notes and 30-year-old memories. It is as accurate as possible within those limits. Where necessary to assure that readers clearly understand certain features of bear biology/ecology, I have integrated modern knowledge with what was known in the early 1970s. Such instances are usually marked by footnotes – except where a few of the

newer facts (such as about bear diets) are intermingled with older knowledge within reconstructed conversations. I trust that readers are more concerned with accurate knowledge about bears than with the exact chronological order in which all this knowledge was learned.

2. All conversations are reconstructed from what I recall of their content. When I cannot remember the name of a person or place, I use a fictitious one. To avoid confusion, each uncertain or fictitious name is first presented in italics.

3. Likewise, a few names have been changed to protect the privacy of individuals; and some details of my private life have been altered to keep them private.

4. Over the years, I have been helped by numerous biologists employed by the Alaska Department of Fish & Game. Jim Faro, one of my earliest mentors, has become a lifelong source of friendship, insight, and wisdom about bears. At the time I raised the orphans, and for many years thereafter, no government biologist in Alaska knew more about bears than Faro, and my approach was strongly shaped by his. Several other biologists were also of great assistance. After nearly 30 years, I cannot remember exactly who said what or when. So all of them are credited under the fictitious name: Jim Trout

5. My dear friend Tony Zak appears here not only in his own role, but in that of a few other friends whose names I have forgotten.

6. My narrative of bear behavior as witnessed by the couple I call John and Joan Purdy has been filtered through and fleshed out by my own firsthand knowledge.

7. Here and there, I have the altered the geographic range and temporal sequence of events, usually to make the corresponding bear behavior easier to understand. Beyond that, I have purposefully obscured the locations where I lived with the cubs. My former neighbors would not welcome uninvited guests curious to experience the domain of Ontak, Chrislee and Jonjoanak.

8. All figures for bear and salmon body sizes, temperatures and distances are rough estimates.

If you would like firsthand guidance on bear safety, communication, and ecology, you are welcome to sign up for one of my courses or bear-watching tours. Contact me through our website www.bear-viewing-in-alaska.info or by email at gobearviewing@hotmail.com.

Stephen F. Stringham
Soldotna, Alaska, January 2002

ACKNOWLEDGEMENTS

Jane Goodall, Valerius Geist, George Schaller, Robert Leslie, and Jim Faro who led the way.

Lousia Willcox, David Mattson, Tom Smith, Sue Morse, Lee Metzgar, Lynn Rogers, John Rogers, Roger Bon, Skip Richter, Tom Cooper, Clarence Howe, Sylvia Dolson, Lynn Feinerman, Helen Stoltfus, Doug Peacock, Doug Seus, and other colleagues whose friendship and insights about nature have sustained me.

John, Frank, Derek, and Lance Craighead; Chuck Jonkel, Fred Dean, Gordon Burghardt, Maurice Hornocker, Neil Greenberg, John Philpot, Mike Pelton, Robert Ruff, Larry Aumiller, Paul Leyhausen, Konrad Lorenz, Tim Clark, Archie Mossman, Anton Bubenik, Margret Altmann, Peter Lent, David Klein, Dale Guthrie, Tom Stayert, Gene Goselin, Ralph Bellumoni, Ferdinand and Steve Ruth, W. E. Berg, David Henry, Steve Herrero, Cheryl Pruitt, Robert Jordan, Jeanne Ludlow, Harry Reynolds, Dick Sellers, Nikita Ovsyanikov, Ellis Bacon, Tom Bledsoe, Derek Stonorov, and my many other mentors in Western Science.

Stan Price, Charley Vandergaw, Ben Kilham, Charley Russell, Maureen Enns, and Tim Treadwell for their pioneering efforts living with bears.

Grandma Teetzinella, QuisQuiNee, Gordon Belcourt, George and Molly Kickingwoman, Victor Young-Runningcrane, Jess Blackweasel, Michael Jackson, Nels Lawson, Mark Jacobson, Bill Brady, Calvin Wilson Sr., David Rockwell, Richard Nelson, and other mentors in Indigenous Science

My agents Elizabeth Knappman, and Jeanne Toomey.

PART I:

BONDING

Chapter 1
A FAMILY OF BEARS

Moving silently through deep forest shadows, the young black bear climbed up beside me onto the root-mass of a fallen cottonwood. I reached over and gently stroked her cheek at the junction where the short cream-colored fur of her muzzle gave way to the long black fur of her cheeks. A low rumbling purr revealed Jonjoanak's pleasure in this contact – something I could not yet count on with this temperamental cub. Both her siblings, though, were now consistently affectionate after long weeks of effort to establish mutual trust and respect, the key to lasting personal relationships with bears. All three cubs now eagerly accompanied Alatanna and me on hikes where we explored for new sources of food, enjoyed adventures, and reveled in play.

Jonjoanak's gaze joined mine, entranced, as a single shaft of sunlight poured like liquid silver over her sister's dark-brown fur and golden ears. Chrislee had rolled over onto her back, lifted a stick, and begun juggling it with her feet, languidly twirling the branch like a misshapen baton.

Bold, devilish and affectionate, Ontak was my favorite.

Suddenly, their ebony brother interrupted our serenity, dashing by, nipping Jonjoanak's rump, and racing away. Exploding after Ontak, Jon quickly gained on the little male. Ontak leapt onto the trunk of a cottonwood, sank his finger claws into its deeply fissured bark, and hopped upwards.

He was too slow. Jonjoanak arrived, raced up the tree after him, and bit into one of his heels. Hanging on with her teeth, she dragged her brother back to the ground, where they sparred vigorously. This was all in fun, of course. But angry bears have dragged enemies, including people, out of trees in the same way.

Baby-sitter trees usually have rough bark for easy climbing and large limbs for aerial couches; they can be critical for the safety of black bear cubs.

Ontak broke free, ran, and now sought refuge in a birch. Racing toward the tree at full speed, he leapt onto the trunk, landing with his hands five feet above the ground and bounding to the top. Each stride began as he momentarily gripped the trunk with his toe claws, jumped upward, extending his body fully, and wrapped his arms around the trunk. His finger claws dug an eighth of an inch into the thin white bark. Then, with a powerful pull of his arms, his hindquarters were raised and his toes planted firmly again, claws toward the sky, heels toward the ground.

Loose-barked trees like birch and spruce provide an unreliable grip.

Alatanna and I watched anxiously, lips and stomachs tight with dread. The cubs had taken many a tumble from slick-barked trees such as this birch, or aspen. But they never fell from a cottonwood with its heavy rough bark, which is why cottonwood's are favored by black bears as "baby-sitter trees" in this part of Alaska. In other areas of North America, large white pine or hemlock trees are preferred for the same reason.

Secure refuges from which cubs seldom fall are be essential for safe rearing of the youngsters. Loss of such trees to logging, fires, or storms may substantially reduce the survival of black bear cubs. Some baby-sitter trees have been used for generations. Where scarce, they should be protected as a critical habitat component for bears.

Jonjoanak followed Ontak, just a second behind her night dark brother, racing toward the top of the birch. Her dark fur was now speckled with snow flakes of white bark. These had rained down on her as Ontak climbed. The two cubs sparred briefly up where the trunk was little thicker than one of their forearms.

"Tag, you're it!"   Now the cubs' roles were reversed.   It was Jonjoanak's turn to flee. Gripping the trunk loosely, she slid down as smoothly as a firefighter dropping down a stationhouse brass firepole, claws carving long parallel scratches in the bark.

As Jonjoanak neared the base of the tree, the little female turned to check her position, glanced at us briefly, then leapt to the ground near Alatanna and sprinted away. Not to be outdone, Ontak leapt too, from ten feet above, landing on his sister and knocking her over. Laughing gaily at their antics, Alatanna followed along as the youngsters locked together in mock battle and rolled down the hillside through tall fireweed. Pink and greenish-white hellebore blossoms soon spangled their coats like sequins on Las Vegas showgirls.

That the cubs were not really fighting was obvious from their body language and the fact that they were silent except for occasional grunts and grumbles, without any of the explosive woofing, repeated pant-huffing, and jaw popping or moans, growls and roars that often precede or accompany combat. Only in movies and TV programs do bears make such vocalizations during play.

Ontak was ebony; Jonjoanak had black outer and brownish underfur. Chrislee was chocolate brown. (Dianne Owen photo).

As we followed the cubs downhill, Ontak and Jonjoanak joined their sister. Chrislee tussled with them, then scampered up onto a log, coming between the sun and us. Backlit, her chocolate-brown coat was turned into a golden halo of fur surrounding the black silhouette of her body. At this age, the lighter color of the females had nothing to do with gender; it was an accident of genetics. But as bears age, any light-colored collar or chest patch tends to darken. Among both black and grizzly/brown bears, adult males tend to become the darkest of all.

---

* For more information about bear fur colors, see Ghost Grizzlies and Other Rare Bruins. S. Stringham 2010. WildWatch. www.bear-viewing-in-alaska.info.

Ontak broke free of his sisters and raced away through the waist-high grass and blueberry bushes with thumbnail-sized emerald leaves.

The sisters continued wrestling. Standing on hind legs, finger claws raking one another's shoulders, Chrislee and Jonjoanak gently traded swats and bites, each exposing her light pink mouth and tongue, bordered by gleaming ivory teeth. Their lips were as pink as those of a human baby where the flesh was seldom exposed to sunshine, but black where melanin pigment was needed to protect the tissue from ultraviolet light. The nose of a young cub still in the den may be totally pink or even cherry red. But by the time a cub leaves the den, black pigment covers its entire nose except deep inside the nostrils.

Their sparring ended when Jonjoanak bit her sister too hard and the smaller female threatened in response, head low and ears back as she moaned in outrage. Almost half of the cubs' play bouts ended when one cub played too roughly and the victim either retaliated or threatened to do so.

The two females moved apart and began feeding on tiny red bunchberries. Half an hour passed before Chrislee was satiated. She walked up behind Jonjoanak, tossed her head back and forth, then laid one hand over her sister's shoulder, inviting play. Jonjoanak obliged.

As the sisters shoved and chewed on one another's cheeks and shoulders, the ears of both cubs were aimed more or less sideways in the *lateral* position used in many different social and solitary contexts. When Chrislee tripped and rolled onto her flank, however, she was momentarily frightened, laying her ears back against her skull. As Jonjoanak stepped closer, her own ears now

((Lynn Rogers photo)

aimed forward, directly at her fallen sibling, Chrislee's warning intensified; she puckered her upper lip forward and sucked in her cheeks, producing what I called a *long-face threat.*

The bear at left is approaching me in a calm mood. That at right is demanding that I move out of his way. His slow stiff walking gait with elbows turned out slightly is known as a "cowboy walk" because of the similarity to the gait of a bow-legged cowboy. His lowered head and sucked in cheek is called a "long face" threat.

Jonjoanak refrained from leaping onto Chrislee until the lighter-colored cub regained confidence and tucked her chin onto her chest, ears again in lateral position, lip corners curved up playfully in an ursine "smile" much like a dog's, all four hands extended upward. When Jonjoanak did leap, she landed on Chrislee's hind feet, which thrust her into the air and dumped her off sideways.

(Lynn Rogers photo)

While Alatanna remained with the two tussling females, I followed their brother, lumbering under the weight of more than a hundred pounds of video camera and batteries – by contrast to the 1-pound high-def digital camcorder that I now use four decades later.

Ontak raced to and fro among trees and bushes, splashed through a creek, then fought with a stick. Running with a dark yard-long piece of wood in his mouth, he shook his head from side to side as though practicing the neck-snap that many carnivores use to kill small prey, once it has been grasped by the head within the animal's jaws. Sticks and other rigid objects aren't usually shaken as vigorously as floppy ones like a dying ground squirrel or one of my sneakers. Fortunately, none of the cubs had a puppy's fondness for chewing on shoes.

Several times, Ontak slowed to a walk, or stood upright, shaking his head all the harder and batting at the stick with his hands. High above, the sky was bleached by incandescent sunlight. Waves of heat distorted my view of him a mere hundred feet away. He waded into a shadowed creek and dropped the stick. Dancing around his shimmering image were reflections of a pale blue sky and tall dark trees with luminescent leaves.

Older bears also enjoy wading and swimming.

His toy was ignored as the cub sank completely under water for half a minute. First his nostrils emerged, then his eyes. For several minutes, this is all I could see of him.

On surfacing, Ontak shook his head powerfully, clearing his ears of water and sending spray in all directions, showering plants on both sides of the creek and spattering my lens. When I grunted in irritation and pulled out a lens cloth, Ontak glanced toward me with such an air of deviltry I could almost imagine that he'd splashed the camcorder on purpose. Like many bears unfamiliar with cameras, he was sometimes irritated by the "stare" of a lens with a person behind it – which may be one reason why bear photographers are occasionally mauled. Once bears become used to cameras, however, they are typically ignored.

Mouth and back just above the surface, ears in lateral position, Ontak swam around the pool for several minutes. Moving into the shallows, he remained neck-deep, lapping water and panting. But for the camcorder, I would have been right in there with him.

For Alaska, this was unusually hot weather. Even there in the shady brook, the temperature felt above 90 degrees, and the air was clouded by mosquitoes, no-see-ums, white-socks, and other nasty little creatures – just the memory is enough to make my skin prickle.

Ontak nosed the creek bank as though searching for something. "What?" I wondered. His explorations continued underwater, bubbles bursting upward from his nostrils. When his head emerged this time, a clump of glistening emerald moss hung from his mouth. Raising his left hand, he dropped the moss onto the *back* of this hand, then used it like I might have used the palm of my own hand to hold the underwater plant for closer investigation. It may have tasted foul, for after nibbling a few pieces, Ontak shook his head as if to rid his mouth of it, then lowered his right hand back into the water, where the remaining moss gently washed free and floated away.

Ignored, but not forgotten, the stick had floated a few body lengths beyond the young bear. He bounded downstream with a high rocking horse motion that lifted his chest half out of the water with each bound, bursting with that magical exuberance of young animals and children.

Catching up with the stick, Ontak made no effort to retrieve it, but instead just followed it at the current's pace, batting the toy now and then, knocking one end underwater as the other end rose into the air. Each time, he lunged to catch the upper end of the stick before it sank again, or the stick was shoved down, submerged completely in the coffee-colored muskeg water, then released so that it popped to the surface again with a splash. Chin on chest, ears forward, the cub walked upright, right hand held higher than his left, poised to strike. "Go get 'em, Tiger!" I called in encouragement.

It was usually with just his right hand that Ontak swatted the stick. Occasionally, though, he threw his whole body into the attack, landing on the stick with both hand and a mighty splash that drove the stick completely underwater. The stick jammed into the muddy bottom, hidden by the silt-clouded water. "Where did it go?" his expression seemed to say. Initially just curious about the disappearance of his toy, Ontak reared up again and looked around for it. Nothing. Dropping down, head dipping underwater, he looked there too. Swirling silt still masked the stick. Again, he stood, ears now laid back, cheeks sucked in, upper lip pursed and chin dropped onto his chest in *long-faced* irritation.

Frustrated and angry, he flew into a tantrum that would have done justice to any two-year-old kid, slapping the water repeatedly with his right hand, then with both hands alternately, as he whipped his head from side to side, as though semi-playfully shaking an opponent. His turbulence popped the stick free and it bobbed to the surface.

Ontak's ire disappeared as suddenly as it had begun. Curiosity took over. Ears returning to lateral, then forward, he cautiously approached and gently nosed the stick. All okay. His hand rose a few inches above the toy, hung briefly suspended, then slapped down suddenly, hitting the stick so hard that it flipped over, the far end rising into the air, then dropping to bonk him on the muzzle. Ouch!

Leaping back in surprise, the cub shook his head. Ears back again, lip puckered, he stalked the toy, pounced, and killed the wooden demon.

A light breeze had been blowing all morning. Now it strengthened, swaying the tall green horsetail stems and brown willow canes that lined the creek bank near where I sat. Ontak turned to watch. Standing, he hooked a springy cane a dozen feet from me and pulled the cane to the water's surface. The cane slipped free and snapped upright, whipping back and forth. Again, the cub grabbed the willow under the claws of one hand and pulled the cane down. Now the cane was released on purpose while the cub watched it intently, like a cat mesmerized by the sight of feeding birds. Again and again, at least twenty times, this maneuver was repeated with variations. Different stems were tried, some of which were extremely springy and whipped powerfully. Others just broke or were pulled out by the roots.

Now Ontak remembered his floating stick. Looking around frantically, he turned and bounded downstream, arms reaching far in front, chest pushing a sparkling six-inch bow wave. He caught up with the toy a hundred yards farther on, at a spot where flotsam and froth gathered in the small eddy below a half-sunken cottonwood. Keeping my eye glued to the camcorder to capture the action, I followed along on the creek bank. Grasping the stick in his jaws, the small black male lunged up the sheer rocky bank, then slipped and fell back into the water. Drifting downstream in the current a dozen yards, the cub tried again, with better luck. After shaking himself dry, spraying water all around him, Ontak found a sunny spot where he plopped onto his back. Relaxing his jaws, the cub took the stick in his hands and held it aloft. Using both hands and feet, he twirled the stick slowly, dropping it often, then retrieving it lazily with outstretched hands or jaws.

Finally tiring, Ontak dropped the stick behind his head. Drowsily, he arched his body, looking back upside down at the stick as he handed it into his mouth. Biting down on the toy, Ontak rolled to his feet. The stick was carried to a shady spot and dropped. Scratching the ground listlessly, Ontak's claws slowly removed the sun-baked duff of dead vegetation and warm organic soil on the forest floor until he reached cool, moist mineral soil. The cub plopped down, belly and groin pressed against the soft, refreshing earth. Chin resting on the stick, he was soon asleep.

While engrossed with Ontak, I had lost track of his sisters. Once they arrived, with Alatanna in tow, they quickly succumbed to the afternoon's heat, stretched out on their backs in the shade of a thick log, legs splayed, hands beside their ears, muzzles pointed toward the sky, snoring lightly.

Alatanna and I relaxed out on the heavily shaded end of that same log. My back leaned against its root-mass while she cradled in my arms with her head against my chest. Watching the cubs deep in slumber, I pressed my cheek against my bride's corn-silk hair, intoxicated by its floral scent.

It was the finest morning we had ever spent with our adopted youngsters. That I'd finally been able to videotape the cubs was just icing on the cake. What mattered most is that, after nearly a month of effort to tame our little foundlings, while building trust and respect, we had finally been accepted by the cubs as members of their rollicking, insatiably curious, and sometimes ferocious family. The amount of effort and patience required had been phenomenal. But such are the joys and challenges of parenthood–or, in this case, *bearenthood*.

Goldilocks and the three bears – no fellow ever had a nicer family.

Alatanna

ENCHANTED

Alatanna and I had met the previous summer when I was studying grizzly bears on the Alaska Peninsula, in the region between Katmai and Lake Clark National Parks and Preserves. My research focused on bear body language – on the system of postures, gestures, and vocalizations by which bears inform or manipulate one another. The ability to recognize a bear's mood and intentions can greatly reduce the risk of disturbing bears or of being injured by them during close encounters.

One key to understanding signals that bears display toward people is understanding their meanings when displayed toward other bears. I had therefore divided each week into two three-day work periods, one period to be spent near Czar Lake Lodge* documenting bear–human

* I've long forgotten actual names of the lodge, river, lake, etc.

interactions, and the other period to be spent far into the backcountry documenting bear–bear interactions where the animals were much more numerous and free from human disturbance.

A few miles from Czar Lake, up Wolf River, I found a good observation site. The river cut through a gorge, the walls of which rose steeply for a hundred feet, then sloped away more gently. The brink of the cliff provided a clear view of a large gravel bar with water shallow enough to make fishing easy for bears. I set up camp there and succeeded in filming several confrontations over which bear would utilize a given fishing site, as well as a variety of more peaceful interactions.

Three days later, pleased with my progress, I headed back toward the tent-cabin I had been assigned along Czar Lake. I stunk like a goat and badly needed to shower and relax. After a single day off, I would again observe bear-human interactions near the lodge for three days, then head back upstream.

Walking the path down Wolf River, about a mile above Czar Lake, I saw a woman on the trail ahead of me, walking in my direction. Between us was a log bridge spanning Bath Creek that drained into Wolf River. Just before reaching the bridge, she turned and climbed a path beside the creek.

I continued past the bridge perhaps fifty yards before curiosity got the better of me. I hiked back to the path she had taken, then up it until I saw her a few hundred yards ahead, climbing with quick graceful steps. This was one foxy lady!

She stopped beside the creek and slipped off her outer clothing. Betraying no sign that she saw me approaching, she stepped gingerly into the water and out of sight, on her way to the thermal area for which Bath Creek had been named.

I didn't want to be pushy. But I had to see her again, if just for a moment. Reaching the spot where her clothing was piled, I found shirts and jeans from several people. I had no swimming suit, but didn't mind getting my jeans wet. Stripping off my shirt and boots, I waded into the creek. Downstream maybe twenty yards, I saw five people lounging in steaming water where the creek was warmed by a hot spring.

Getting there was an ordeal. Above the hot spring, Bath Creek was so cold that every muscle in my belly and chest tightened like a fist, making me gasp for breath.

Each of the people sat on or against a boulder, where they could lay back easily in comfort. But there was no free boulder for me. In fact, the only open seat was beside the woman I had followed up the slope. That bold, I was not.

In the Alaska bush at that time, where men outnumbered women a hundred to one, and pretty women were scarcer than egg-sized gold nuggets, many guys found talking to a pretty woman harder than facing a belligerent moose or grizzly. I was no exception.

I knelt at a spot where the hot and cold currents ebbed and flowed. One moment I was boiling, the next freezing. *On average*, I may have been quite comfortable, but that's not how it felt. I could never relax; the temperature could shift abruptly at any moment.

Suddenly, a plume of hot water roasted me, and I stood up with a gasp. Conversation ceased, and everyone burst out laughing.

The blond goddess took pity on me. "I wondered how long you would last out there," she laughed. "Here, sit next to me; best seat in the house." That it was... that it *surely* was!

She told me that her name was Alatanna and introduced her girlfriend Rhoda and their companions.

I stayed maybe fifteen minutes, intrigued, but too tongue-tied to talk, for fear of sounding like a jerk. I finally fled, hoping to meet the lady again under more auspicious circumstances.

I waded back upstream through the icy water, chilling rapidly. Covered with goose bumps and shivering, I had no sooner stripped off my jeans and underwear to wring them out than I noticed that I was not alone. Fifty yards away, a roly-poly platinum-colored sow grizzly was gorging on bright–red berries. Another blond – just what I needed.

She gave no sign of aggression, or of even being aware that I was nearby. But nothing unnerves me quite as much as meeting a grizzly in my birthday suit.

Slowly, not wanting to attract her attention, I picked up my jeans with the toes of one foot, then backed into the creek. Once there, I sat down, slipped on my pants, then floated downstream to warn my new companions.

"That's probably just Old Gertrude," Alatanna laughed. She had known this sow for years. The bear usually ignored them and their clothing unless someone was carrying food – someone like me. After three days in the backcountry, I still had a small bag of trail mix in a pack pocket. Oh well, not any more.

Gertrude's coming broke the ice between the group and me. But I was still so nervous that I kept quiet, unaware of how much my silence intrigued Alatanna. She was used to men who monopolized conversations.

I was smitten. Alatanna seemed to sparkle with gay energy and warmth. The ring of her laughter, the flirting tilt of her head, the glint of her sparkling sea-green eyes enchanted me. When she focused on me, I felt like the most important person in her world. I felt the glowing warmth of a fine spring day after a long cold winter. When she turned away, blizzards swept back through me. However much I wanted to think of myself as a man of the world, and despite having grown up with four sisters, I had no idea how to cope with beautiful women.

Finally, as the evening grew dark, the group rose to leave. I got back to the clothing first. Sure enough, my trail mix was gone, but nothing was damaged. The bear was apparently familiar with zippers, for she had opened the pack pocket as neatly as a person would have done–my first hint of how dexterously bears can use their finger claws.

As we walked down the trail, Alatanna's friend Rhoda came up beside me and began chatting. She was much like my sisters. Suddenly, as if a dam had burst inside me, I relaxed. Talking to Rhoda was easy, and I was soon chattering away. Funny stories kept springing to mind. We laughed most of the way back to the lodge.

That, however, was nothing compared to the laughter I heard a week later, when I came back out of the hinterland to give a lecture at the lodge about my previous studies on moose.

The talk went well as I showed more than a hundred slides, mixing humorous anecdotes with scientific information on the ecology of these giant deer – focusing on how mother moose raise their calves, and how their populations are impacted by trophy hunting so intense that it eliminates most fully mature bulls. I also told of rearing two orphaned calves.

Calf about one month old and one year later.

After the question–and–answer period, as I was boxing up my slides, a woman's voice came from behind. "That was a good talk. You sure know a lot about moose. But actually, I thought you were a bare biologist."

I had several slides balanced in my hand and didn't turn around. The voice, stifled with barely contained laughter, continued. "I'm sure Gertrude was impressed. There's nothing she likes better than bare biologists."

Several seconds passed before the name Gertrude struck a chord of memory, and I understood the pun; not "*bear*" biologist, but "*bare*" biologist. Gertrude was the tolerant grizzly I met in the buff at the hot–spring. I whirled around and nearly bumped into Alatanna and Rhoda. They burst out laughing. They had loved my stories about raising the orphaned calves, especially when I told of having to feed the foundlings and clear up their messes every couple of hours around the clock.

"A man doing woman's work!" Alatanna kidded me. "Maybe we should call you 'Mother Moose,' " I smiled weakly, hardly thrilled with the nickname.

Rhoda came to my rescue. "Better yet, `Pappy Moose.' "

They turned and walked off, glancing back just long enough to make sure I was watching.

After my third and last visit to the backcountry, I returned to Czar Lake Lodge where I met Alatanna again. With a picnic supper of foods unlikely to attract bears, we returned to the hot–spring. We ate, then slipped into the soothing water, resting side–by–side at her favorite spot.

Before coming to Alaska, Alatanna had studied acting in New York. Professionally, she was a third generation lineal descendant of Stanislavski – a protégée of the Master's own protégée. She had been a rising star of the Broadway stage who seemed destined for great things – until the demands for sexual favors become unavoidable, a price she found too steep to pay.

Hours passed as conversation eventually ceased and we let bliss overtake us. Occasionally, our hands or feet touched, then moved away. Finally, I summoned the courage to hold her hand. Gradually, our shoulders slid together until her head rested on my shoulder, and my head leaned against hers. The scent of her hair made me feel like I had been drinking champagne.

Above us, the mist began to glow. In the distance, out of sight, the sun was setting. It turned the steam around us into an enchanted veil of rose translucence. I squeezed her hand and felt her answering grasp.

Finally, as the forest darkened, we rose, dressed, and started hiking back to the lodge. Although pretty much at ease with bears this close to camp, neither of us wanted to run into a grouchy individual. This was just the time of night when the more wary grizzlies, especially the giant males, started using the trails.

Back at the lodge, when it came time to part, we hugged tightly, clinging together for an eternity. Then someone emerged from the building and walked toward us, breaking the spell. I took Alatanna's face in my hands, shivering with excitement and fear. My lips pressed gently on her forehead. She hugged me tightly, then turned and walked away.

That was my last evening at Czar Lake. The next morning I would catch a plane to Katmai National Park to begin the next phase of my pilot study on grizzlies. As much as I wanted to stay there with Alatanna, I had a commitment to the National Park Service, which I could not break.

WILDERNESS WINTER RHAPOSODY

In mid-September, Alatanna and I performed what we called our "Indian wedding" ceremony that bound us together romantically, if not legally.

We had all the love in the world, but almost no money. Nearly broke and unemployed, without job prospects before spring, we were beginning to despair of finding a way to stretch our meager savings that long. Then my friend Cliff Wright saved the day by offering to let us use his cabin deep in the Wrangle Mountains, at the border between Alaska and the Yukon Territory, in what is now the heart of the Wrangle/St. Elias International Park. Living off the land, in one of the most awesome environments on earth, we not only survived, but thrived.

Cliff Wright's cabin lies in the heart of what is now Wrangle-St. Elias National Park. These mountains feature dozens of mighty glaciers, rivers of ice that are sometimes over a mile wide and many miles long.

Alatanna quickly won the trust of several squirrels.

First dusting of snow, late September. (*Cliff Wright photo*)

The first snow melted and we had two weeks before the first big dump, which lasted until April. At 60° below zero, without a breath of wind, the land was soon covered with frost flowers several inches high. (*Cliff Wright photos*)

WEDDING

In May, we returned to civilization and were married officially. My golden–haired bride was radiant in an exquisite white satin dress, its shoulders covered with flowery brown silk – the product of many long winter nights with needle and thread, working by the flickering light of a kerosene lantern.

A justice of the peace spoke the official wedding words. He had arrived among us an intrusive stranger, imposed on us by the legal system, yet quickly became a delightful friend. In those days, while Alaska was still a frontier, bonds formed or broke quickly.

Teetsineela, the old Cherokee woman who adopted me as her honorary grandson and began teaching me about wildlife from a Native perspective – which is radically different and more profound than I had ever been led to believe – the subject of a future book **Becoming Bear.**

Tony Zak

After being pronounced man and wife, we held a spiritual ceremony. In place of a priest, our ceremony was conducted by the man whom we thought of as our "tribal" elder, Tony Zak. Although reared in the coal mines of Pennsylvania, with little formal schooling, Tony had a great love of literature and poetry. His renditions of Robert Service verses were unsurepassed.

Now, at our wedding, Tony's deeply moving words were followed by a recording of *Wilderness Rhapsody*, a piano piece I had composed for the occasion.

Alatanna made her wedding dress by hand,
in the dark little cabin by lantern light.

In lieu of an alter, we used a set of moose antlers and a rose bush -- representing, Zak quipped, the union of Pappy Moose to his wilderness rose. Another friend called it the marriage of horney to thorny.

Among our guests was Sam White, a giant of a man in more ways than one. Now 84 years old, this distant relative of Alatanna's, was Alaska's first game warden and one of our most reverred bush pilots A few months thereafter, he traded in airplanes for another kind of wings.

(To learn about him, read **Sam O. White, Alaskan: Tales of a Legendary Wildlife Agent and Bush Pilot** by Jim Rearden, 2007)

Intoxicated with love, we spun romantic fantasies of what our future would hold, and of the children we might someday have – never dreaming that parenthood of another sort was just weeks away, or of the tragedy that would orphan three lovable young bear cubs.

Bridal suite. Our first home as man and wife was a tent I made from a sheet of clear polyethylene plastic. Beyond providing shelter from wind, rain and some bugs, it gave us a panoramic view of wilderness and wildlife, sunrises, sunsets and brief starry nights.

Chapter 2
MARAUDER

Early June

If ever the road to hell has been paved with good intentions, this was just such a case. A few years before Alatanna and I wed, another couple befriended a juvenile female black bear. Initially attracted to the garbage pit behind the cabin of John and Joan Purdy,* the young sow soon found meat scraps left on the porch for their cocker spaniel puppy. The bear returned the next day; then again, and again. Soon, the Purdy's cabin became a regular stopover. It lay within the sow's permanent domain, and was probably close to where she had been raised. Daughters commonly inherit part of their mother's domain or stake out new domains nearby.

Always shy, the sow seemed friendly. She was a fascinating, welcome guest, whom they called Doddy in honor of Joan's aunt Dorothy. Her visits were awaited eagerly and enjoyed immensely. Even the puppy soon became accustomed to the bear. Growling was gradually replaced by friendly barks, submissive whines and tail wags.

Although Doddy weighed no more than John, thick fur made her seem twice that big – at least 400 pounds, he guessed. Exaggeration heightened the Purdys' awe at having this wild carnivore so readily accept them as neighbors. Her fangs and two-inch claws could have easily torn them to shreds; her massive carnassial teeth could have crushed their bones. But, in fact, the only things torn and crushed were the apples, melons, and other goodies provided by the couple. Soon Doddy became confident enough to take snacks from their hands. Attempts to pet Doddy were instantly rebuffed, however, as the bear opened her jaws toward them to avoid being touched, or shook her head to break contact.

---

* I repeat their story as best I can recall it – remembering the skeleton of events and fleshing them out from my own knowledge of bear behavior.

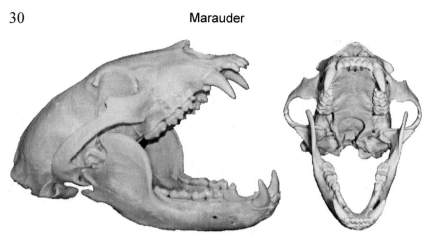

Black bear skull

Joan and John thought Doddy was tame. They were wrong; she had simply lost her fear of them. Like most black bears, she was not aggressive by nature. She remained an entertaining companion throughout that summer, when succulent herbs, berries, and salmon were abundant.

That winter, while Doddy was in hibernation, the Purdys left too, taking jobs in town. A couple of years passed before they returned. Just as they remembered Doddy, she remembered them and their goodies.

The spring that John and Joan came back, wild foods were not yet abundant, and Doddy was no longer alone. Waddling beside her were three tufts of fur, each with gray–blue eyes, ball-shaped head, tea cup muzzle, and cigar-sized legs.

At birth, each cub had weighed less than two pounds, about the size of a newborn German shepherd. Like puppies, the cubs were blind for the first weeks, with limited ability to hear or smell or crawl. Mostly, they just whimpered when cold or hungry, purred while nursing, or slept.

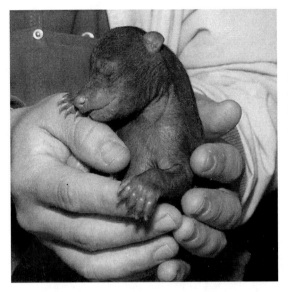

Day-old cub (left) and 2-week old cub (below). (Photos courtesy North American Bear Center)

For the first month after birth, each cub's legs had been all but useless. Each infant crawled by pulling itself along with its hands. Only as winter waned and the time to emerge from their den emergence neared, did the cubs begin walking.

This delayed maturation of the legs may be an adaptation to keep cubs from straying outside the den while their hibernating mother is too drowsy to keep track of them. Once out in the open, a cub could quickly fall victim to weather or predators.

When not sleeping, cubs remain fully alert and active from birth. Their mother hibernates lightly to conserve energy. Her body temperature and breathing rate don't fall as far as those of a male, so that she remains alert enough to care for her cubs. Even a mother sharing her den with yearlings continue to produce milk and allow the youngsters to nurse. Mothers are also alert enough to detect anything approaching, even through powder snow, sometimes from hundreds of yards away.

The function of hibernation is to cope with food shortages. Bears can seldom kill prey while fighting their way through snow. Also, little of the high quality forage bears eat is available during winter. Staying active during that season uses more energy and nutrients than can normally be replaced by feeding.* Hibernation lowers the rate at which fat reserves are utilized so that these reserves can sustain the bear all winter long, and often through early spring.

A sow's energy demands accelerate as soon as she and her cubs emerge from the den and begin traveling, while she produces increasing amounts of milk that is over 25 percent fat. Meeting these demands requires energy-rich nutrients; but few are available from spring forage. Most sows continue losing weight until berries or salmon become abundant in early to midsummer. Doddy would have been no exception.

---

* In some areas of Alaska, thermal springs draining into rivers keep the rivers from freezing. Any surviving coho salmon thus remain accessible to bears into early spring, enabling some of those bears – mainly big males – to shorten hibernation by two or three months. Bears living on coasts with rich arrays of intertidal invertebrates may also stay active all winter.

Coho salmon

Doddy–Day 1

It was thus in a very different mood from the earlier year that Doddy returned to the Purdy's cabin. With three cubs at her side and no rich natural source of calories, she was eager for the fondly remembered snacks that her human hosts had provided in the past.

(Sue Mansfield photo)

(Dianne Owen photo)

The first time Doddy arrived, she took her family straight to the garbage pit behind the little cabin. Once those tidbits were consumed, Doddy visited the cabin itself. John and Joan were delighted to see their wild friend again, and entranced by her cubs, who were far too shy to come closer, although they often stood on their hind legs and watched the couple intently.

The few apples and other treats that Joan could afford to give the bears were little more than appetizers. The Purdys were now unemployed and no longer had a dog. No dog, no dog food. Nor did they have any more boxes of overripe fruit, which John had previously obtained free while working at a grocery store.

Doddy eventually wandered back to the garbage pit and the humans left, on their way to town for the day. That evening, when they returned, John and Joan found that their cabin had been raided. All their food had been eaten. The place was a shambles. Obviously, the culprit was a bear. But they could not believe it had been Doddy, not gentle Doddy. *She* would never do such a thing. It must have been another bear.

Doddy–Day 2

After they had restocked the cabin, it was raided again. Still, they refused to believe that Doddy was the marauder.

Doddy and her cubs wrecked havoc at the Purdy's cabin – whose entrance was blocked with two logs, in a futile attempt to keep the bears out. Chrislee stuck close to her mother. Chrislee and Jonjoanak are barely visible in the tree above Doddy's head.

All doubts ended that night. They heard something banging around outside the cabin. Apprehensively, they peeked out to investigate. There were Doddy and her cubs. When the Purdys tried to scare them away by yelling and throwing pots and pans, Doddy stood her ground and threatened them in turn, leaping forward a few paces in so-called *hop charges* that often ended with a powerful slap to the ground, a vivid warning of what could happen to them.

Finally, around 2 A.M., Doddy left, and the couple fled into town. When morning came, John called the Fish & Game Department to report the incident, begging for someone to come out and shoot Doddy.

However sympathetic the state biologists were with his problem, they were not willing to kill the bear. Having no rifle or any experience using one, John did not dare try killing Doddy himself. Fish & Game recommended that he buy metal hinges and hasps to replace the leather ones currently supporting the cabin door. Once the door could be locked, and the window barred, they felt Doddy should not be as much of a problem, especially if the Purdys quit feeding her and hauled out their garbage each day.

Returning to their cabin that evening, John and Joan found that Doddy and the cubs had been back again. The bears had dragged their remaining food outside and consumed it. They had pulled out a backpack and managed to unzip all but one of the pack's pockets; that pocket had been ripped open at the seam. Indoors, Doddy had pulled food out from under the table, with minimal disturbance to anything else. Amazingly, a carton of eggs had been knocked off the table, yet landed right-side up. Rubber bands around the egg carton had kept it from bursting open and the eggs from breaking. Apparently the unbroken eggs had not been recognized as food, for the bears left them alone.

Doddy–Day 3

In the morning, Doddy and her cubs returned once more. The bears arrived while John and Joan were having a bitter argument. Joan was fed up with the tiny dark cabin and with Doddy's raids. She had been offered lucrative work as a secretary on an Alaska Pipeline construction project and wanted to take the job. John had not been so lucky; if Joan accepted her job, he would be left behind.

They were screaming at each other when the cabin door opened. Doddy stuck her head in cautiously, spooked by the argument, but drawn by the odor of corned-beef hash cooking on the little wood-burning stove.

So engrossed were John and Joan in their fight that they paid Doddy little heed. She sniffed the pan of hash, burning the tip of her nose. Her head jerked back and her eyes blinked. That food was *hot!* But its aroma was irresistible to both mama and the cubs. Whereas Doddy was cautious, her cubs were bold. One reached past Doddy, hooked the pan's handle with its paw, and flipped the food onto the floor. Instantly, commotion erupted as all three cubs lunged forward to eat, bawling and swatting one another as they fought for a share, only to be swept aside by their mother's four–inch wide paw and warned by the gurgling moan in her throat.

Hardly aware of what he was doing, John redirected his rage toward the bears. Grabbing a cast-iron frying pan off the narrow board counter, he swung with all his might, spanking Doddy's rump, and yelling at her to "Get out!"

With cubs to protect, the famished sow whirled around so fast that John hardly saw her blow coming. Doddy rose slightly and swatted his shoulder, knocking him to the floor. Standing over him, she huffed and salivated heavily, drool raining onto John's chest. Her jaws snapped together rapidly, again and again, so hard that her teeth popped like stones being pounded against one another. So terrified by the "jaw pops" that he was babbling, John lost control of bladder and bowels – something, he wrongly believed, that might have convinced Doddy that he wouldn't taste good. She finally turned and claimed the hash.

Trembling with fear, Joan and John retreated the few remaining feet to the far corner of the cabin, huddling there under a small table, their sole chair held up for protection, its legs extended toward the bears, lion–tamer style.

Moments later, the cubs abandoned their attempt to steal scraps from Doddy and began searching for other goodies. One cub's upwardly exploring paw found the edge of the board counter on which Joan prepared meals. His claws dug into the wood, and with a leap, the cub was crawling up onto the counter. His siblings quickly tried to follow suit, bawling in frustration.

The counter was too small to accommodate three cubs of about twenty pounds each. One was knocked to the floor, landing on its back and bawling loudly. Instantly, Doddy responded. Lunging at John and Joan with her nose low to the floor, Doddy batted the chair from John's hands, confronting the humans from just an arm's length away, ears back, pant-huffing, jaws popping, irises forming a golden brown band around each narrow black pupil.[*]

> * Pant-huffs are deep rapid breaths (two to three per second), each ending with a loud exhalation. They are usually preceded by one or two louder explosive exhalations called "woofs." Pant-huffs may be followed by or interspersed with jaw pops (one to five per second). Pant-huffs mean to bears about what stress-barks mean to dogs.

Quickly, though, Doddy recognized that her cubs were safe and the people intimidated. Forelegs still stiff and pigeon-toed, she turned away from Joan and John toward the counter, again popping her jaws, but less violently, less rapidly this time. Woofing explosively with fffhhh!!! sounds, she stood upright. Resting one paw on the counter, she reached toward a shelf laden with canned goods. With a sudden angry sweep of her paw that ended in another woof! and a lip-puckered glare at the humans, Doddy cleared the shelf. Cans, jars, plates and cookware were swept from the second and third shelves too, crashing onto the floor. Jars burst into glass splinters, spilling jams and other preserves that the cubs quickly lapped up, somehow without slicing their tongues on the glass. Doddy was experienced with cans and knew enough to bite into them, breaking the walls to provide a grip for her claws so that she could rip the cans open.

Also dumped onto the floor were bags of flour. One landed on a cub, drenching it in white powder, which stuck to the food already gooped on her fur. Sneezing and shaking its head, the cub jumped away fearfully – right up against Joan's legs. She screamed and the cub yelped. Fortunately, Doddy was too busy feeding to respond.

Eventually, nothing but smears were left of the Purdys' food supply. Their entire cabin was a shambles. Doddy and her cubs had reached under the bed and pulled out everything stored there, tearing apart not only boxes of food, but clothing and other possessions.

Appetites satiated, at least for the moment, the bears became more playful. All three cubs climbed onto the bed and wrestled there. They shredded both down sleeping bags, filling the cabin with a blizzard of tiny light feathers. Then the blankets were pulled off the bed and the foam mattress ripped apart.

No longer so fearful of the humans, the cubs investigated Joan and John again and again. Stalking forward stiffly but cautiously, a cub would approach to within a couple of feet before taking fright, woofing and darting away – only to return a few minutes later, glaring balefully with nose pointed toward the floor, cheeks sucked in, upper lip puckered, moving just a bit closer than the previous time.

Sometimes the cubs' moments of fright alarmed Doddy, triggering her to lunge at John and Joan once more. Yet no matter how fiercely she bawled, or how hard she slapped the floor in front of them, Doddy never touched the people. Highly dramatic threats are seldom followed by attack. Their purpose is to intimidate and win without having to risk injury in a fight.

By late evening, there was nothing more to eat, and nothing new to investigate or play with or mutilate. Doddy left first, soon followed by her three youngsters, all of whom were by now coated with sticky food, flour, and down feathers.

Until then, Joan's tears had flowed silently, lest they provoke the bears. Now her sobs grew stronger until her whole body shook as she huddled against her husband. Arm curled around her, John remained silent, still deep in shock. More than an hour passed before they dared emerge from their illusory shelter beneath the flimsy table. Although the food was gone, the bears might come back at any moment. They had no gun. There was still no way of locking their door. The only thing to hold it closed was a loop of cord that could be hooked over a nail sticking a couple of inches out of the door jam.

Neither the leather hinges nor latch string could offer much security – as proved true later that night, about 2 A..M.., when the bears returned. Bathed in sweat from the hot weather, John had been too scared to sleep. When he heard Doddy scratching around outside the door, he prepared to take shelter. The only refuge within the cabin was under the bed. He tried to arouse Joan. She moaned but refused to wake up. Curling up tightly, she seemed to withdraw all the farther into traumatized unconsciousness. By now the door was banging back and forth as Doddy struggled to get in. Pushing Joan closer to the back of the bed, against the wall, John lay in front of her. He covered both of them with the remnants of their blankets and sleeping bags, along with whatever else came to hand.

Finally, Doddy hooked the base of the door with the claws of one paw and ripped the door off its leather hinges. She and her cubs entered, ignoring the hidden people. Maybe 'out of sight' was 'out of mind' during the half-hour it took the bears to lose interest again and leave.

Doddy–Day 4

The following day, the bears rummaged around outside a couple more times. On each occasion the cubs entered the doorless cabin alone. One cub climbed atop the counter and found items John had piled there. These were swept off the counter and landed on a sibling, who bawled in fright. Doddy burst into the cabin and looked around, again huffing, popping her jaws, and stamping her forefeet on the floor.

Stiffly, Doddy stalked forward to the bed where John and Joan were still hidden under blankets, suffocating in heat and fright. Doddy's cheeks billowed out as she woofed explosively and lunged the last few feet. Rearing up, she swatted the bed–frame so forcefully that it broke. The covers fell off John and Joan, exposing them to full view of the bear just a yard away, her forequarters still elevated above the bed. Then Doddy's head turned sideways. slowly and dramatically profiling the massiveness of her jaws, which she chomped repeatedly. She turned again to glare at the people briefly, gold-rimmed black pupils looking as sharp and hard as her canine teeth. Only then did she drop back down to the floor and shoo the cubs ahead of her out of the cabin.

From the time Doddy had first entered the shack over thirty hours earlier, John and Joan had lived in terror, not daring to leave the cabin, even to use the outhouse. Now, they realized that they had nothing to lose. The cabin offered no real security; it just trapped them right where the bears wanted to be–like "sausages in a box," as Joan put it.

Waiting until the bears had been out of sight for a couple of hours, the Purdys fled.

Doddy–Day 5

I first learned of the Purdy's plight the following day when I found a note from John begging for my help. While waiting for him to call again,

I got back to work, chipping away at my mountain of data on grizzly behavior from the previous summer. Watching bears and filming them was exciting at times. Their fights are brief but awesome. And there is nothing more entertaining than having a ringside seat to a litter of playful cubs or to a couple of well-fed young boars sparring. It is incredibly heartwarming to watch a sow nurse cubs while listening to the rumble of their purrs. But aside from such high points, bears spend most of their time feeding or sleeping. Observing them catch salmon got rather old after the thousandth fish, and watching them eat berries or snooze could narcotize a speed freak.

Yet if watching bears sometimes became boring, that was nothing compared with the tedium of listening to field recordings of my own minute-by-minute descriptions of the behavior, then transcribing these verbal notes onto paper. Listening to myself talk was pure torture; so much for a career in politics.

When John called back, I welcomed the interruption. He launched directly into a tale of woe about a marauding bear that had ransacked his cabin and threatened to kill him and his wife.

Concerned for their safety, I listened sympathetically. It was past noon by then, so I used the break to eat, holding the phone's mouthpiece up near my forehead so that John would not hear me chewing.

Boiling with frustration and desperation, John was barely coherent as he described the series of raids by a mother bear he called Doddy. Slowly, the bits and pieces of his story began falling together. He and his wife Joan had fed Doddy through one summer, a couple of years earlier, when natural foods were abundant. But they could not afford to sate her appetite during the current lean times when she had three cubs to support. Doddy had taken matters into her own "hands," destroying just about everything John owned.

He begged me to kill the bears.

I didn't know what to say. Sure, he'd had a tough break, but my job was protecting animals, not killing them. True, I had hunted for meat while living in the bush during the previous winter, where groceries came only by plane once every month or so, and starvation was all too easy. I would kill game to survive. But I despised killing, and the idea of doing it for "sport" just nauseated and angered me. Also, I had no experience in wildlife damage control.

I suggested that John get help from the Alaska Department of Fish & Game. Even if I wanted to get involved, the Wildlife Protection officers wouldn't appreciate intervention from a civilian.

John admitted to having already called them and being turned down; they said he'd made the mess and he'd have to clean it up.

Like the guys at Fish & Game, I had no interest in getting involved. I already had more than enough on my plate, or on my desk anyway: a couple of hundred hours of voice tapes to transcribe; dozens of rolls of movie film to splice, edit and analyze, some of it frame by frame; hundreds of hours of office work staring me in the face. I had to finish that before I could get back to observing bears. I also had more grant proposals to write. Half the summer could be gone before I got back into my field research. I really didn't need any more interruptions. And I certainly didn't want to kill any bears.

Nevertheless, I was worried about the fate of Doddy's cubs. John had a couple of neighbors within a mile radius and both hated bears. Doddy had visited their cabins too – a transgression she survived only because no one was home. Sooner or later, though, her luck would run out. Most likely, her cubs would be shot as well, if only out of fear that they would also grow up to be marauders. When it came to bears, most people believed "better safe than sorry."

The cubs were doomed unless someone convinced the authorities that the cubs would never bother anyone again. I could try to do that, while arguing that the cubs could be a source of important scientific insight. If I could save their lives, maybe they could help save human lives – including my own – by contributing critical knowledge about bear communication and aggression.

*   *   *

I explained my thinking to John. He shared my determination to save these cubs. To help, he made an offer that I couldn't refuse. Alatanna and I could move into his cabin. We could live there and use it as a base for

(Dianne Owen photos)

rescuing Doddy's cubs – if they survived. Not only was Joan ready to leave for her new job on the North Slope, but John had landed employment in town that provided living quarters. The Prudys would move as soon as John recovered the remains of their possessions from the cabin. Even knowing that this might bring me face to face with Doddy, I agreed to help.

Chapter 3
CONFRONTATION

Doddy–Day 6

Determined to save Doddy's cubs, I needed to consult with Fish & Game about dealing with their marauding mother. Fortunately, I would not have to travel by bicycle anymore. In the three weeks since our wedding and my first meeting with John at his cabin, Alatanna and I had finally scraped together enough money to buy a pickup truck. It was an ancient Ford, the pale blue color of a hot cloudless sky. I called it the *Blue Mustang* after a horse I had once admired – a bucking horse which this pickup tried to imitate on rough roads, due to worn-out shocks and busted leaf springs. Worse, the truck drank almost as much oil as gasoline. No matter; it was a mighty improvement over bicycling.

It was a muggy afternoon, so hot that the air had a slight tang of turpentine and other aromatics distilled by sunshine from conifers. I drove with the windows open, elbow hanging out as air blasted through the cab, evaporating my sweat but providing little coolness.

Outsiders imagine that Alaska is cold even during summer. Far from it. With sunshine almost around the clock, the temperature in the countryside was often in the 70s or even 80s during the first half of that summer.

I parked the battered Ford in front of the Fish & Game office. Stepping inside was like stepping into a walk-in cooler, so chilly that goose-bumps popped up on my arms.

The dark–haired receptionist was no warmer. She had piercing eyes that warned me not to waste her time. If she could smile, I saw no trace of it; or of any other emotion except irritation.

"Is Jim Trout* around?" I asked, trying in vain to break the ice.

"Probably in back." She shoved a phone jack into the proper socket. "Who may I say is calling?"

---

* "Jim" is a composite of three ADF&G biologists, none named "Trout."

"Steve Stringham."

At that time, Jim and I barely knew one another. But we were fellow alumni from Humboldt State University, with friends in common. More important, he was well respected as a game biologist and manager; a good man to handle ticklish public issues such bear banditry.

The secretary looked up at me again, face still as deadpan as those of the moose and deer whose heads adorned the walls around us.

"He will be right out. Please wait here."

I looked around. No chairs. I leaned against the edge of a table stacked with pamphlets. Most contained fishing and hunting regulations. Others gave instructions for identifying various kinds of game animals, or for cooking them.

Hanging in the foyer above the entrance was a Dall ram with horns that curled nearly one and a half times around. It dwarfed the biggest ram I had ever seen alive, which had a single full curl that most hunters would have considered quite a trophy.

Jim emerged from a nearby hall. "Hi, Steve. What's up?" he smiled, reaching out to shake my hand. His grip was strong, his gaze steady and clear as it scanned my eyes and face.

Behind him, high up on one wall, were enormous antlers from moose and caribou, with huge, heavy brow tines. Lower down were mounted heads of Sitka deer from Southeast Alaska.

"Bit of a bear problem, Jim. I guess John Purdy has been talking with you about it?"

Jim nodded, leaning casually against the counter. Above calf-length black hiking boots and dark jeans, Jim wore a red-checked cotton shirt. His jaw was heavy below a thick, dark mustache – a solid, dependable guy who enjoyed helping people.

"Sure. Sounds like it's his own fault, from what I can tell." Jim asked questions, probing and weighing my reactions. He was astute that way, a good communicator.

Jim invited me back to his office. I followed him through hallways hung with the heads and pelts of a wolf, a wolverine, and other furbearers – all dwarfed by the grizzly hide I had seen in the foyer. That beautiful

Toklat blond bear must have stretched ten feet from nose to tail. What had he been like alive? What they had all been like before someone poached them? That was how several of these trophies had ended up in the hands of the Fish & Game Department.

Jim's office was crowded with books, boxes of scientific journal articles, and file cabinets of field data and bureaucratic paperwork.

As we walked in, his phone rang. Cradling the phone on one shoulder, Jim pulled open a file drawer and thumbed through worn file tabs.

Respecting his privacy, I stepped back out into the hall. Nearby was a room crammed with audiovisual equipment and educational props. Out of curiosity, I took a closer look.

Hanging on one wall were boards showing a series of jaws for each species of big–game animal. Each series began with the jaw of an infant at the top, dropping to very old adults at the bottom.

Labels and arrows pointed out clues for estimating age from the number and type of teeth present, and from their degree of wear. Like humans, animals do not have all their teeth at birth. As the jaw lengthens, more teeth grow in and milk teeth are replaced with permanent teeth. Biologists know within a few months the age at which each tooth is added, enabling them to distinguish a six-month-old bear from a yearling, for example. As an animal ages, its teeth wear down. Most bears in a region suffer wear at about the same rate. So wear can yield a rough estimate of age. More accurate aging requires pulling a tooth, cutting it crossways to make a thin slice, then counting its annual rings–analogous to tree rings.

"Steve!" I turned around. Jim waved me back into his office.

Having already talked with John a couple of times, Jim knew the situation. He plunked down in his chair and lifted both heels onto the edge of the gray metal desk, typical government-issue furniture. The room smelled of dust, metal, and old cured animal hides.

Draping myself over a thinly padded chair by the door, I explained the problem in more detail. Jim listened patiently, then interpreted the situation from a Department perspective. "It's legal to kill a bear in defense of life or property. But, first, every effort should be made to end the problem nonviolently. John can begin by eliminating garbage from around his cabin and securing the window and door. When the bears come around, scare them away by walking toward them in a tight group, yelling and waving your arms. If that doesn't work, try gunshots. But fire into the ground, not the air. Bullets that go up, eventually come down. They can kill someone."

My chair was of the same genre as Jim's desk and very uncomfortable. I fidgeted, trying to find a bit of foam to cushion my buttocks.

What Jim had said about violence being a last resort made sense. I understood his skepticism about anyone teaching Doddy to avoid cabins. Even if she learned to avoid John's cabin, she would probably still raid others.

I explained that I had no interest in being the one to kill Doddy. But if someone did, I would be glad to rear the cubs so that I could study their behavior.

Jim warned that the standard procedure was to kill the cubs too. He was interested and sympathetic, but cautioned that the Department took a dim view of anyone rearing bears, except in captivity where escape was impossible. These cubs were already following in their mother's footsteps as marauders. The last thing anyone wanted was three more problem bears who might someday become dangerous.

"Let me tell you how we see things, Steve. Around here, berries are the main summer food for black bear sows. Sure, there are plenty of salmon for bears with access to a river or stream. But grizzlies and big boar black bears tend to dominate the good fishing sites."

As Jim talked, he leaned back farther in his chair, rubbed the fingers of both hands through his hair, then linked both hands behind his head. Beyond him, outside the window, I could see a mountain ash tree covered with bright blossoms. They were crawling with bumblebees.

Jim continued, "One of our guys, Dave Hatler, recently finished his master's thesis on how black bears respond to failures of the blueberry crop. Famine sends bears far and wide in search of alternative foods. Many become desperate for nutrition – so desperate that they raid garbage dumps, garbage cans, homes, and campsites. The same thing can happen when the salmon run is poor."

A gray Canada jay landed on the mountain ash; then a second jay. A screaming match started. One bird flew off, chased by the other.

Jim's secretary tapped on the door frame, then handed me a stack of papers, which I passed over to Jim. Dropping them into his in–box, Jim continued.

"Sooner or later, Steve, scavenging bears come face-to-face with people, people who don't want their property damaged or their food taken. Confrontations occur. Bears learn that they can intimidate people. Occasionally, someone is injured. Rarely, someone is killed. More often, it is the bear that suffers most."

I understood what he meant, having had long conversations with Dave Hatler about his findings, and about those of Chuck Jonkel in Montana. The impacts of famine are compounded by the impacts of bears killed as marauders. Then that impact is compounded by especially high numbers of bears killed by hunters during famines. Starving bears not only hang out closer to people; they are less wary, more visible. Like a one-two-three punch, famines decimate bear populations. Meanwhile, the famished bears like Doddy create minor havoc, at least until the year's blueberry crop ripens or the bear obtains access to salmon.

The sun had dropped far enough to peek past the corner of Jim's window. Its rays pierced the glass like lasers, burning my eyes. To see Jim, I had to use one hand to block the light; only his silhouette was visible.

I agreed with Jim about the need to break the cubs of marauding, protesting gently that death was not the only solution.

Seeing how the light was blinding me, he turned and lowered a shade, throwing the room into relative darkness. I blinked as my eyes readjusted.

He settled back in his chair again, motioning me to continue.

I promised Jim that if the mother bear was shot, I would be willing to take her cubs to an uninhabited coastal island or deep into the Wrangle Mountain wilderness where Alatanna and I had spent the previous winter, and where there were few other people. I would raise them to live like fully wild bears, eating natural foods, not garbage or handouts. In short, I would do for these cubs what Joy and George Adamson had tried to do with Elsa and other orphaned lions in Africa. Since bears are less social than lions, these cubs should face less difficulty than Elsa had with social integration. Rearing bears this way had already been done by Robert Leslie with three orphaned black bears in British Columbia with fair success.

Jim pursed his lips and looked at the ceiling, mulling things over. Finally, his gaze dropped back down to me. He was skeptical, but commented that rearing the cubs in a remote area might be worth a try, in the event that someone was forced to kill the mother bear – which we both hoped would not happen.

It was 4:30 P.M. when we wrapped things up, quitting time. Jim walked me out to the Ford.

"You've got to remember, Steve, that the Department gets dozens of people each year asking for permits to keep wild animals, especially orphans. Most of their justifications and their plans sound great on paper. But all too often, follow-up investigations reveal serious mistreatment or neglect. And most hand-reared cubs eventually become dangerous. At least ninety per cent of the time that we issue permits, we end up regretting it. So don't expect that you'll have an easy time getting one, despite your credentials, even if you believe you can guarantee you'll keep the cubs far from other people. The Department doesn't like taking chances when they don't have much to gain if you succeed, but plenty to lose if you screw up."

The nearby mountain ash buzzed with dozens of bumblebees. I had seen them from Jim's office where their sounds did not penetrate. Now, outside, I was surprised by their loudness.

Clouds had drifted in. The temperature had dropped to the low 80s. Maybe it would rain.

* * *

Taking my rifle, several gunnysacks, plenty of rope, and two packboards, I picked up John so that we could retrieve his gear from the cabin. As we drove, he told me more about how his problems with the marauding bear had begun four days earlier.

Eventually, John asked, "Why did Doddy change so much since her first summer with us? She was so tame, so friendly! Now she's a fiend. What happened to her?"

The Ford had seen much better days. It rattled and clanked so loudly that John and I could barely hear each other talk, even after we closed the windows.

"For one thing," I explained, "she is now eating for four."

The air tasted like dust and engine oil. The Naugahyde seat cover felt hot enough to fry bacon.

"Second," I told John, "you no longer keep a pan of dog food outdoors for Doddy. That alone could be enough to frustrate her. Third, Doddy has only been out of her hibernation den for a month and is starved from fasting all winter."

"But, what's the problem?" John asked, sweeping his hand across the windshield to indicate the birch-spruce forest through which we were driving. "There's plenty of food out there. Hundreds of kinds of plants, tons of grass and leaves, and so on. What more could a bear want?"

"Actually," I offered, "bears need a lot of calories in their food, to store fat for hibernating. That's why they home in on sugar, starch, and especially fat. At this time of year, plants don't provide much sugar or starch; and Alaska plants never provide much fat, although new growth of sedge and some leaves does provide some protein."

With the windows closed, there was a lot less noise as well as a lot less ventilation. The truck quickly became a furnace. We opened the windows again.

I slowed as the dense upland forest thinned out, giving way to a broad low bog; the only trees were spindly black spruce, few more than fifteen feet high. The bog was covered with a thick mat of emerald sedgegrass and low brownish shrubs; the chartreuse leaves had just broken free of their buds. A few weeks earlier, this bog had still been frozen.

I pointed to the sedge. "When that sedge-grass first sprouts, it's full of protein. One kind of sedge growing on the coast is up to 20 percent soluble protein. Here it's probably lower, but still fairly good food for bears."

"Again, what's the problem?" John repeated, slightly exasperated.

"Sedge meadows aren't very common. They don't offer much cover, which makes bears – especially sows with infants – nervous about feeding there during the daytime. And, as sedge matures, its nutritional value drops rapidly."

John nodded, shifting the wing window on his side so that it directed a strong blast of air across him.

I continued. "Bears tend to lose weight from the time they quit feeding in the fall, throughout hibernation, until berries ripen and salmon arrive during the next summer. Foraging on low-energy vegetation like this, between den emergence and summer, just slows their weight loss."

I stuck my left elbow out the window. Wind whipped the hair on my forearm, making it ripple like a field of golden wheat.

"I still don't understand why Doddy doesn't just eat grass and leaves, like moose do," John questioned. Can't bears eat just almost anything?

"Actually, no. The only reason moose and certain other hoofed animals – ungulates – can thrive on a diet of grass and twigs is that their digestive systems are specifically adapted for this."

We were out of town now, on a gravel road. Away from all of the concrete and asphalt, the air temperature dropped several degrees. A red Oldsmobile had pulled up close behind the Ford, anxious to pass. I dared not drive over 35 mph with an engine that leaked oil so rapidly.

Through the trees beyond John, I caught glimpses of a wetland surrounding a small pond. Two white adult swans were dipping their heads underwater, possibly hunting for snails or clams. Small black birds flitted among the reeds.

We came to a wide spot in the road. Slowing, I pulled over and waved the red Olds past. Instead of a "thank–you" wave, the driver left only billowing clouds of dust in his wake. We raised our windows, but not fast enough. Dust drifted into the Blue Mustang's cab.

Up ahead, a pickup was approaching rapidly, trailing a huge dust cloud. For now, we had to keep the windows closed, despite the heat.

Later, when the dust subsided, we opened the windows again, practically gasping for fresh air and any trace of coolness.

The road was narrow, just two thin lanes, with a deep ditch on each side. Serving as catch basins for moisture, these ditches were choked with the new growth of fireweed and other plants that would start flowering over the next few weeks. Drainage off the adjacent hillsides concentrated enough moisture along the ditch to support a lush strip of water-loving willow and alder. New alder leaves were narrow and light green in color, but already corrugated like corduroy. As the leaves matured, they would broaden and darken like old jade.

* * *

Finally reaching the trailhead, I parked the truck. Even after I switched off the ignition, the engine whirled, sputtered and backfired before it quit. We pulled backpacks out of the truck bed and hiked toward the cabin.

Without the truck's movement creating a breeze, the air seemed hotter. We perspired heavily. I wrapped a bandanna around my head to absorb sweat, grinning sympathetically as John did the same.

In the distance, a bald eagle soared, riding air currents beyond the ridge we were climbing,. With luck, the eagle would soon find the carcass of a salmon that had spawned and died, or one slow and weak enough to be easily killed.

Arriving at the cabin that afternoon in early June, we found the yard strewn with just about everything John and his wife had once owned. Pots, pans, and bits of paper or plastic from food packages littered the ground. A pair of pants had been carried into a tree where they flapped in the wind like drying laundry.

Dozens of food cans were scattered among the bushes and indoors, crushed and punctured by bite marks, some still leaking contents that had dried into a crust on the can, floor, counter and walls. Flour, cornmeal, and other drygoods coated the cabin's dirt floor. Feathers from the down sleeping bags and chunks of foam rubber from the mattress were everywhere indoors. The bears must have had a dandy time.

We gathered up the few possessions that were worth keeping and hauled them to my truck. Cleaning up around the cabin took hours more.

It was evening before the last trash was packed into gunny sacks. Although still far above the true horizon, the sun was low enough to shadow the southeast-facing slope where the cabin lay. That lowered the temperature into the 70s, and a river–cooled breeze moved over us down the valley. It was the first time I had been comfortable all day.

We were only halfway down the trail when Doddy appeared with her three cubs. They had probably caught our scent or heard us, then come to investigate in case we had a fresh supply of food.

(*Diane Owen photo*)

Boldly, Doddy walked right up to us, head at shoulder height, ears forward, lips closed but not puckered, as the tip of her pink tongue flicked in and out several times a minute. The cubs came too, scattered among the trees and brush. They were hidden from view except when their huge ears, bright brown eyes, and inquisitive noses stuck up amid the ranks of lavender fireweed blossoms to watch us.

Doddy's patience soon wore thin. When we failed to offer snacks, she tried circling to get closer to the gunnysacks of trash tied to our packboards. These smelled of garbage and Doddy had no way of knowing they contained only debris that she had already worked over thoroughly. The only way to appease her was to open the bags so she could check them out. While John removed his packboard, I kept my rifle trained on Doddy, who paced back and forth, forelegs stiff, muzzle down, lip puckered, ears back. She was in a foul mood and potentially dangerous.

As John dropped his sack to the ground, Doddy hop-charged forward with an explosive woof, spreading her hands and slamming them down on the bag, taking possession. I had hoped to open the sack first, to empty it onto the ground so that the sack itself would not be ruined. Doddy had no such compunction. When pawing the burlap bag with just her right paw did not open it, she planted the left paw firmly on the bag and pulled sideways with the right. This time the bag was ripped apart and its load of trash quickly scattered.

Finding no food there, Doddy turned to me. I was too stubborn to surrender my bag. I had just spent an hour picking up this trash and was not anxious to repeat the process. Having to regather John's load would be bad enough.

As Doddy circled me, I turned to keep facing her, rifle held low, centered on her chest. With the second bag of trash still on my back, I thought it was safe from her. I had forgotten about the three cubs until something grabbed me from behind. A cub had reached up and snagged the bottom of the burlap bag with both hands. As he tried to rip the sack off me, he pulled me backward. Stepping back to catch my balance, I tripped over the cub and fell, nearly landing on the youngster.

In the moment between falling and realizing what had happened, I was terrified, thinking I was being attacked. I would have shot any bear I could see. However, Doddy was out of sight long enough for me to realize

I was safe. John said that she had jumped away from me as I fell and that her cubs had scattered in other directions.

Emboldened by my fall, Doddy now started toward me more confidently, ears back and head lowered with her face slanted at least 60 degrees below horizontal – a bear's way of signaling "Back off!"

Rolling to my feet, I pulled an air horn from my belt. I had bought it the previous summer to deter grizzlies that I encountered on the Alaska Peninsula. Designed as a boat foghorn, the gadget was powered by some kind of pressurized gas – Freon as I recall – which chilled the can and the air around it whenever the button was pushed to emit a deeply pitched "wwwaaaannnhhhhh." Unfortunately, the sound did not drive Doddy away; it irritated and perhaps frightened her. She became all the more threatening, popping her jaws with such force that her teeth clacked like hammered stones.

Rather than risk being mauled, I surrendered the bag of trash and left it with her as we hiked rapidly out of sight down the trail, then raced the last half-mile to my truck.

Even before we reached the Blue Mustang, we knew Doddy and her cubs had been there too. The ground around the old Ford was thick with debris. All the loads of trash that we had cleaned up so laboriously at the cabin and hauled to the truck, then dumped into its bed, were now strewn outside once more.

Chapter 4
ADOPTION

Cubs–Day 1

Two nights later, I shot Doddy while she was raiding the cabin. Taking that responsibility was the only way I could see to save her cubs from the same fate.

Standing over her body, I recalled with sorrow how beautiful she had been; beautiful, wild, and dangerous. Dangerous mainly because people had made her so; killed for the same reason. With rare exceptions, nearly *every fed bear (is eventually) a dead bear.**

I was sad, I was angry; yet I was also hopeful. If Doddy had lived, there would have been no way to prevent her cubs from adopting her bad habits of seeking garbage and handouts, taking by force of intimidation any food that people would not surrender willingly.

Freed from her bad example, however, her cubs had a chance – but only if any addiction to human foods and contempt toward people could be eliminated. Just how that could be done we had yet to learn.

First, though, we had to get the cubs out of harm's way. They no longer trusted people, and fled when Alatanna and I approached. In order to overcome their fear, I decided to use Doddy's pelt as bait to lure the cubs toward John's cabin – which he and Joan had abandoned to us. We all to happy to leave left the plastic tent in which we had been living and have a home with solid walls and roof, even if the floor was dirt.

As Alatanna and I approached the cabin, the cubs caught our scents and began tracking us. They were seldom visible; but their mournful bawls testified that they were keeping within a hundred feet of us. After putting our packs inside the cabin and securing its door, we crossed the narrow valley separating us from the cubs, threading our way between nearly impenetrable thickets of chest-high willow.

---

* Especially during famines, food provided to bears in the wilds can lure them away from towns where they would otherwise cause havoc. This is known as "diversionary feeding."

Travel up the far ridge was easier. This was a parkland of scattered jade–green spruce and white aspen. Around the trees was a rich palate of bright colors and fragrances: fields of lavender fireweed dotted with white yarrow, yellow pineapple plant, orange *soma* mushrooms, and red lingonberries that were backed by deep-green leaves the size of my fingernail.

Higher up the ridge was a scattering of pinkish-white paper birch, one of my favorite trees.

Birch

I have a particular fondness for birch bark.
For the way it grows in sheets
that can be peeled away to make canoes and baskets.
For the way these sheets split lengthwise as a tree grows.
For the way the edges of these splits peel away
in ultra-thin layers that curl back
like sheets of paper left too long in hot sun.
Curls that crumble as my fingertips brush them.
Curls that blaze instantly at the touch of a match flame,
starting fires which have kept me alive in winter camps
when the chill factor was nearly 100 degrees below freezing.
Winter, eight months of it each year in interior Alaska.
Winter, recently dead, and soon to be born again.
But not this day,
which was already in the mid-80s by late morning.
A day when the only snow to be seen
was the blizzard of tiny flakes of birch bark
loosened by my wandering fingers
as they brushed this trunk or that – connecting
me with the land and its life through this sense of touch,
more intimately than through sight and sound and odor.
Moments of intimate serene peace and beauty,
while the heat and bugs faded from awareness;
while Doddy's tragedy could be forgotten.

My momentary serenity within this low boreal jungle was shattered once more by the loud bawling of Doddy's three orphans, their voices clawing at my conscience with their pangs of fear and loneliness. They would soon die unless Alatanna and I could win their trust and become their foster parents.

It was now noon, and our time for helping the cubs that day had run out. Alatanna had to get to her job; I had chores to do. After spreading Doddy's pelt out on the ground as a rallying point and security blanket for the cubs, we left behind a big pot of oatmeal laced with honey.

Cubs–Day 2

That first pot of cereal had been eaten. The following morning we left another, sweetened with honey, raisins and applesauce. The cubs would still not let us near.

Cubs–Day 3

I decided to take matters in hand more decisively. As much as I would have loved being patient and letting the cubs come to us of their own accord, even if it took a week or two, I knew that they could easily fall prey to a person or to one of the wolves or lynx that lived in the area. If they would not come to us willingly, I would capture them with the help of John Purdy and Tony Zak.

We spread out and climbed the hill, legs brushing through herbs and grasses that had been lush and succulent mere weeks before, but now rustled and crackled with sun-baked brittleness.

Warned by the sound of our approach, the cubs scattered ahead of us, darting in and out of sight, black blurs that revealed themselves only momentarily, not letting us come close.

Finally, one took refuge in a spruce. My lips pursed as the cub raced up the trunk toward the pale blue sky. "Now I've got you, you little imp."

For the first ten feet above the rocky ground, the spruce's trunk was bare except for its rough, tightly scaled bark. Within seconds, the cub had shinnied over that and reached the lowest branches, none thicker than my pinkie finger. Using the branches as steps and handholds, the cub rapidly wove its way upward until it was lost from sight, more than thirty feet overhead.

If this cub wouldn't come down to me, I'd have to climb up to him. That would require the tree climbing gear I used when felling trees – which was stored in the pickup a mile away at the road.

While Alatanna and Tony stayed by the spruce to keep the little bear from escaping, I ran for my gear, hoping to make the round trip within twenty minutes. Even at 10 A.M., sweat rained off me, attracting a cloud of biting insects that kept pace no matter how fast I ran, both going to the pickup and returning to the cabin.

Ducking into the cabin's cool dark interior, I grabbed a hand-towel and used it to wave away the bugs until I reached the creek and could wash myself in its sweet earth-cooled spring waters.

"Better use some of this," Tony suggested from behind me. He had walked down to join me, offering a bottle of Off, the most effective

Wolf stalking a grizzly cub as Momma appears to protect her youngster.
(Kent Fredriksson photo)

brand of insect repellent we had. Despite the abundance of wee beasties flying around us, his forehead and face were relatively free of welts.

Slopping the bug dope over my neck, hands, and face, I took care to avoid areas from which sweat could carry the repellent into my eyes and burn them. Mosquitoes still buzzed around me, while other, less visible insects crawled through my hair and beard. At least their numbers had thinned out enough to be barely tolerable – something to be thankful for.

Back inside the cabin, Tony made sandwiches for all of us while I dressed in leather clothing and strapped on the climbing belt, draping the attached rope over my shoulders. We hiked back to the ridge where the cub was treed. Tony carried a sack of sandwiches and a six-pack of cold Cokes. Not lunch, breakfast; our first meal since the stew he had cooked for us twelve hours earlier. I had already grabbed my first sandwich and was stuffing it down as fast as I could bite and swallow, almost ecstatic with the flavors of baked ham, rye bread, and mustard.

"You sure you really want to do this?" Tony asked, his deep voice grinding like chunks of gravel being ground underfoot. "You don't have to impress us."

I chuckled to myself, knowing he spoke more from concern for Alatanna than for me, sympathizing with her nervousness about how she'd fare if I was injured. I was sympathetic, too, of course, but not worried. I had climbed trees this way countless times, and had never needed more than a few Band–Aids to patch up my dings and scrapes.

Reaching the spruce, I reiterated my determination to catch the cub. Alatanna finally agreed.

I sat down and strapped on the J-shaped climbing spurs. The touch and odor of their smooth, weathered leather straps and pads was always reassuring.

John helped me stand. My original estimate of twenty minutes to get the climbing gear and return had stretched into an hour. But Alatanna's continued presence at the base of the tree had kept the cub from escaping.

Together again now, heads back, we studied the boughs far overhead until we could distinguish the cub whose round, dark face was visible as he watched us intently.

Many times before, I had seen cubs take refuge in a baby-sitter tree like this. The same nervous woofs, pant-huffs, and jaw pops that sows used to warn off intruders also served to send their youngsters scurrying into the treetops. Then momma bear usually fled, whether for her own safety or to distract pursuit from her offspring.

Later, when the danger was over, she would return and grunt-gulp to call them back down again.*

---

* Each grunt or gulp is a discrete call lasting no more than ¼ to ½ second. When combined, they serve to solicit close contact, as when a mother bear calls her cubs. A grunt is made with the vocal cords and has an "unh" sound; the grunt of a bear is very similar to that of many other species, and to the sound a human makes while lifting a heavy load or when slammed in the stomach with a football.

A bear's gulp also sounds something like that of a human; producing this sound makes the laryngeal area of a bear's throat bob up and down strongly. One colleague, Terry Debruyn, suggests that the gulp is sometimes combined with a cluck (which he calls a "click"), but I don't recall ever having observed this. A bear's cluck sounds very much like that of a rider urging a horse to move faster. A person clucks by pressing the tongue against the roof of the mouth, and keeping the tip there while the rear part of the tongue is pulled down to the floor of the mouth. Whether a bear produces this sound in the same way is unclear.

I had tried to call the cubs with grunt-gulps; but at that stage, my renditions were either too poor or we humans were just too frightening to this cub. Over the next few months, I became more skilled at making these sounds. Despite any errors in my utterances, the cubs learned to respond appropriately, much as they did to purely human signals.

Above me, tree branches were densely packed. In the best spots, I could weave between them; in the worst spots, branches had to be broken away or cut to make room for my passage. The three-inch saw blade on my Swiss Army knife took several minutes to cut through a two-inch branch. More than two hours passed before I got within a body length of the cub.

As I approached, the tyke stayed in place, watching me calmly. I reached up and petted him gently. He licked my fingers and pawed them softly. The rough black skin of his hand tickled my fingertips. Although no doubt frightened by recent events, the cub did not try to flee or to defend himself – until I made the mistake of grasping him by the scruff of his neck and pulling him loose from the tree, so that I could stuff him into a gunny sack.

The "sweet, cuddly" cub twisted around in the loose skin of his neck, chomped down on my wrist just above the glove, and began chewing. I let go and jerked my hand back. With a quick lurch, the small animal sped up the spruce to where its trunk was about the same diameter as my wrist. I couldn't follow.

A cub at the top of a conifer can be impossible to reach. (Courtesy of the North American Bear Center).

Six feet away was another, larger spruce, reaching twenty feet higher. If I could climb it, I could come level with the cub, then reach back across to this tree and nab the "wee" bear, which was the size of a big tomcat.

Descending my tree so that I could climb the other one, I got halfway to the ground before Tony yelled out that the cub was following me down. The tyke looked as though he was ready to leap from about twenty feet up. Falls that would kill a person may not faze bears. I have watched other cubs leap from such heights and land like beanbags, then spring up and run away with no evidence of injury. To stop this cub from leaping, I shouted and climbed back up toward the animal. He retreated ahead of me.

To keep the cub trapped above me while I moved to the adjacent tree, I had to take a more direct route. I rocked my tree back and forth until it swayed across such a wide arc that I could grab the end of a branch from the second tree. Pulling the two trunks to within three feet of one another, I hooked one knee around each trunk.

I planned to let loose of the smaller tree and end up in the larger one. But as soon as I began to relax the force holding the two trees together, they sprang apart, stretching me between them, hanging on to each with just one hand and ankle.

Even with me spread-eagled, the tree trunks still leaned together a bit. Their efforts to straighten out exerted strong, unrelenting pressure that threatened to tear me off of one or both trees. Before that could happen, I let go of the smaller tree and whipped my body toward the larger one, getting both arms around the trunk just enough to slow my fall as I crashed downward through the branches, ripping strips of hide off my belly and chest, as well as nearly gouging out an eye on the stub of a broken branch. The mauling I'd feared from the cub was being delivered instead by the tree.

My recollection of those seconds is tinged with surreal tongue-in-cheek humor. *By the time I came to rest, the tree seemed to have taken on a more russet tinge, as though sprayed with ketchup. My heart was firing at the leisurely pace of a machine gun, while my adrenal glands spurted fight-or-flight hormones like a fire hose. Below me, Tony and John were cursing while Alatanna screamed, all sure I was about to land on top of them – which I would have preferred, of course, to hitting the hard stony ground. For now, though, I was hugging the tree.*

Chest burning with pain, I shinnied up the trunk of the larger tree until I was level with the cub in the smaller spruce. Repeating my earlier maneuver, I swung the taller tree back and forth until I could grab a branch of the shorter one and pull the two trees close together. Carefully, I straddled both trees again, hooking one knee around each. Lower down, where both trees were thicker and stronger, I had not been able to control straddling both and had felt like I was being drawn and quartered. At this height, though, the trees offered little resistance.

Out of my shirt came the burlap bag into which I planned to stuff the cub. Until I came close, the little male cub seemed to ignore me, as though sure I could not reach him. Now he watched me intently, upper lip puckered forward, cheeks sucked in, ears back, woofing and pant- huffing to warn me away.* When I tried to pet the cub, I was

---

* The pant-huff of a bear is somewhat similar in rhythm but not in meaning to the pant-hoot of a chimpanzee.

---

greeted with his gaping, tooth-filled mouth and snapping jaws. I would have loved to give him time to calm down, but felt impelled to rush ahead and capture all three cubs that day before a lynx or wolf got them. Folklore holds that most large carnivores relish cub meat.

I grabbed the cub by the nape of his neck, pulled him off the trunk of the smaller tree, then held the burlap bag underneath so that I could plop him inside.

Unfortunately, a burlap bag does not hang with its mouth open, but shut. Keeping it open was not easy with one hand while the other supported a twenty-pound, furiously struggling, clawing, biting bear cub.

Then, too, I was now ten body lengths off the ground, stretched between two trees that were once again swaying in the wind. Though they had started swaying in unison, their rhythms differed. Sometimes they would swing left together, then right together. At other times, they swung toward one another, then apart, nearly tearing me loose.

Just as my legs started to slip and I had to reach out with my right hand for support, the cub twisted around and planted his paws in my face. His claws dug in, climbing my lips, nose, and eye sockets, gouging pockmarks into my face to match those on the tree trunk. The cub's finger claws penetrated my face and scalp, leaving a scar that is still visible on my forehead.

Instantly, I lost all interest in keeping hold of him. Seizing his opportunity, the young black bear lunged out of my grasp, over my head, and up the spruce above me. The cub climbed to where the trunk narrowed to the thickness of my bicep. I could no longer get within three body lengths, which must have suited the young bruin just fine. Admitting failure, I retreated to the ground.

Once again, we had run out of time and had to attend to other responsibilities. On impulse, I picked up Doddy's hide and carried within a hundred feet of the cabin, then spread it on the ground beside a pot of oatmeal. Hopefully, these would draw the cubs to us.

Cubs–Day 4

It was nearly 7 P.M. before Alatanna and I got back home. We were rewarded with the sight of all three cubs napping on the ridge in front of the cabin, stretched out on their mother's pelt – until they detected us. Like mist on that hot evening, they disappeared into the surrounding foliage. Out of sight, but not out of mind, their cries evoked a powerful sense of how much they mourned the loss of their mother and the rich milk she had provided.

Knowing that the youngsters would be hungry, we had hauled in more food for them: a couple of gallons of Karo corn syrup, as well as boxes of powdered milk, lard (bear milk contains at least 25% fat, lard would help us mimic that), raisins, prunes, oatmeal, and cornmeal. Alatanna cooked up three gallons of mush in a washtub. I hauled the steaming food up the ridge and set the tub down beside Doddy's pelt. Returning to the cabin, I was no sooner indoors than the cubs came to dinner.

All three cubs could have easily fed from the yard wide tub. Instead, warfare immediately broke out, each cub battling to monopolize the syrupy mush. The pan was tipped over and the cereal spilled across the ground. Three writhing bodies quickly smeared the food over more than a hundred square feet of grass and brush. Only then did the cubs calm down and start to feed – as though the battle's entire purpose had been to spread the food out until each cub could dine in splendid isolation from the others. That their black and brown pelts had turned gray made us wonder whether any of the cereal ended up *inside* the cubs.

Once again, rather than further spook the little ones, we decided to leave them alone and let nature take its course. Hunger, we hoped, would eventually lure the cubs to the cabin. Sure enough, before the night was out, their heads had popped in through the open door several times, and one cub had tried to raid our pantry before my movement scared her away.

Cubs–Day 5

Around 5 A.M.., we put out more food for the cubs, then jogged a mile to the truck, hurrying so that Alatanna would not be late for work. She loved the early morning shift because it left her afternoons free for fun – which she usually spent with friends until she could catch a ride.

Each morning, I dropped her off at the home of Jake, her boss. Each evening, Jake either brought Alatanna back to his home or dropped her off at my office, depending on where the Blue Mustang was parked. Riding with him saved Alatanna a buck a day in gas at a time when every dollar was tough to come by.

My work required me to perform a variety of statistical tests on my behavioral data. This necessitated a computer, a device which I was just beginning to "master." For anyone who could touch-type, there was not much trick to punching hundreds of data cards and feeding them into the IBM reader; it was just pure tedium. Writing down the proper programming code in Fortran was the real challenge. I had reached an impasse and had to hunt up a colleague to help me find the error – probably an extra space or one too few, or maybe a period or semicolon out of place. Even the tiniest error gridlocked a program in those days. One who has never faced those frustrations will find it hard to fully appreciate the wonders of modern operating systems and application software, which do 99.99% of the work for you.

After returning to our cabin that evening, Alatanna and I prepared yet another huge tub of cereal, laced with powdered milk, lard, dried fruit, and Karo. This was not left beside Doddy's pelt, as had been done previously; and I didn't repeat my mistake of putting out only one source of food. Rather, I dumped the cereal into three widely spaced bowls, hoping that this way each cub could eat her fill without having to fight for a share – getting more cereal into her tummy and less onto her fur.

The cubs were nowhere in sight, and I hoped they were not watching. Instead of rejoining Alatanna in the cabin, I crawled under Doddy's pelt so that my scent could mingle with hers – although, admittedly, it would take an acute sense of smell to pick up either of our odors over the stench of rotting flesh on the underside of Doddy's hide. Rarely have I ever undertaken professional duties with less enthusiasm.

Ranchers often trick mother sheep or goats who have lost their young into adopting orphans by tying the dead youngster's pelt to the orphan. As soon as the mother associates the orphan's scent with that of her own youngster, or has thoroughly anointed the foundling with her own odor, she mothers it as though it were her own young, even after the pelt of her dead infant has been removed. I hoped that the same thing might work in reverse with the cubs — that they would gradually associate my scent with Doddy's and transfer their bond from her to us.

I had tried to talk Alatanna into taking over for Doddy as surrogate mother. Not a chance. Her response to the idea of being draped with the rotting bear hide left much to be desired. She would help; but "bearenthood" would be solely my responsibility.

To facilitate establishing the association between Doddy's scent and mine, I avoided using any insect repellent, for it would alter my odor. I made that decision despite the abundance of mosquitoes and other voracious bugs.

My judgment of both cubs and insects could not have been more mistaken. It took the cubs almost an hour to return, and then they came with great reluctance, obviously spooked by my presence. Although I was completely covered by the hide, they knew I was there. Instead of nuzzling the hide and lying on it as they had before, each cub made short rushes toward it, swatted the pelt, then dashed away while looking back toward it. The oatmeal was ignored.

Though cub appetites were curbed, bug appetites became ravenous. Never in my most feverish nightmares had I dreamed that biting insects would be highly attracted to a bear, with its seemingly impenetrable barrier of fur. I had not taken into account the raw, bloody, gooey flesh exposed on the underside of the hide and now smeared all over me. The pelt was surrounded with a thick cloud of mosquitoes, no-see-ums, white-socks and other starving stingers that made quick work of me.

Attacked by both cubs and insects, I finally gave up and fled. At that point, I must have already had several hundred bites, with more to come – many many more.

Imitating a mother bear's clucking grunts as well as I could, I rose to my hands and knees, with the hide still draped over my head and back. Quickly, I crawled downhill, hoping the cubs would follow. No such luck; instead of following, they ran for the woods.

The heck with it! Throwing off the hide, I stood up and beat my own hasty retreat, running for the cabin. Bear blood and rotting, gooey slime covered me from cowlick to boot sole.

Alatanna saw me coming and caught a whiff of the powerful bear odor. She barred the door, refusing to let me inside until I had washed. "All of you," she demanded through the door. "Peel off that godawful putrid clothing and use the soap I left outside for you."

I didn't smell *that* rank. But rather than argue, I grabbed the bar of Fels Naptha soap and dashed to the creek. Swiftly undoing my heavy climbing boots and then my leather pants and shirt, I rolled around in six inches of creek water, soaping body and hair thoroughly despite the scarcity of suds produced in such cold hard water. Then I rolled and splashed for the several more minutes needed to get the worst of the soap off me.

The remainder of this story is best told with a dash of humor that is less exaggerated than you might think:

Sprinting back to the cabin, I found its door still barred. "What now," I demanded. "Get rid of the bugs!" she yelled.

Bugs? What bugs? Looking down, I could not see a single mosquito, no–see–um, or white–socks. Not a single one. What I could see was a writhing mass of something grey that covered me as completely as a sea otter's pelt.

Running one palm over a thigh, I scooped up a handful of wee beasties that turned into a handful of blood and guts when I crushed them – my blood, their guts. By the time I had scraped off the worst of them and sweet-talked dear lovely Alatanna into letting me inside,   I was ready for two pints of whole blood. No bartender, make that three; and one for the road.

In the hour and a half I had been out of the cabin, I had acquired over a thousand identifiable bites. We counted them! The top layer of bites was pretty distinct, with one tiny bump here, one there, and so on. On the middle layer, though, a lot of the bites ran together.

As to the bottom layer, those closest in: well, those could not be counted at all–although they could sure be felt. Itch. ITCH!, ITTTCCCHHH!!!!!!! For the next few days, scratching was utterly, unendurable ecstasy.

*   *   *

I had no sooner dressed in a fresh shirt and jeans than I went to fetch Doddy's hide and stretch it out in front of the cabin, draped over a log.

Through binoculars, we watched all three tykes return to the oatmeal and devour it swiftly, clearly ravenous for more.

Cubs–Day 6

It was morning when we fed them again. Just before driving Alatanna to work, I carried the cereal pot uphill, then left a trail of cereal puddles leading down to the cabin. The cereal pot, still holding six inches of food, was left beside Doddy's pelt which I laid out inside the cabin, leaving the door open. With luck, the cubs would return, enter the cabin, feed, and fall asleep inside.

For once, our plans worked . When we returned that evening, sneaked up to the cabin, and peered in the window, all three youngsters were fast asleep on top of Doddy's pelt.

We had brought packages of discarded fruit from the grocery store where John had previously worked. Removing the plastic wrapping, we tossed this food onto the ground outside the cabin, then retreated into the surrounding forest to watch what happened.

Quickly the cubs awoke, apparently aroused by the scent of food. Soon, all three were fighting over the goodies. By the time the food ran out, our patience had too. Rising from our hiding place, we approached the cabin and cubs – who disappeared into the high grass and shrubs.

Cubs–Day 7

Come morning, Alatanna and I left another trail of cereal puddles leading into the cabin, where Doddy's pelt again lay. This time we did not leave. It was Sunday, Alatanna's day off from work at the café. I rigged a string running from the door across to the bed, where we sat hidden under blankets. An hour passed before the cubs entered the cabin. They immediately gathered on their mother's pelt, whimpering and bawling. (Bears emit a variety of bawls, expressing moods as diverse as distress, anger, and possibly despair. As though to purposefully confuse matters, all of these very different signals are called "bawls".)

Yanking the cord, I slammed the door shut, trapping all three cubs inside the cabin with us. They erupted like Roman Candles on the Fourth of July, bursting across the cabin and bouncing off the walls for several panicked minutes as they sought to escape.

Fortunately, this wasn't winter, when the stove would have been blazing, for the cubs not only smashed into it, but they bowled it over, strewing ashes across the floor and filling the cabin with a blizzard of soot.

Finally, all three cubs came to rest in the corner of the cabin behind what was left of the flimsy sheet-metal heating stove. It was the only object in the cabin which provided even a meager physical barrier between them and us, yet left us in plain view of them – for the covers had fallen off of us when I pulled the cord to close the door.

We remained still, occasionally glancing at the cubs, but never staring at them. In such a tense situation, prolonged eye contact would have seemed threatening.

Soon the youngsters were emboldened enough to stiffly stalk around the cabin, each with its upper lip puckered in irritation. Then, within the hour, their playfulness returned along with their curiosity and hunger. We tolerated their demolition of our food stores so as not to spook them again.

Finally, all of our food was gone, inside their bellies or coating their fur. Their long guard-hairs were speckled with dry oatmeal flakes and cornmeal, as well as with Karo that they had broken out of its bottle. Our three little bandits plopped down behind the potbellied stove and fell asleep, stretched out on their backs, with their own distended potbellies as tight as drumheads, rising like tiny hills above them.

Chapter 5
TEMPER, TRUST, AND RESPECT

Mid-June

So far as we knew, Doddy had started her brief marauding career with raiding John's cabin. There had been no prior reports of other cabins in the area being raided so far that year, and all of the local raids occurred within a period of less than one week. So if Doddy had soon found enough natural food and quit raiding, her cubs might not have bothered anyone's cabin ever again – we had no way of being sure. Fish & Game clearly didn't want to take that chance, however slight.

To keep the cubs alive, I would have to develop a reliable alternative way to prevent further marauding. Making sure the bears never got human food was supposed to be vital. According to conventional wisdom:

Once a bear is exposed to human food – once it is "food conditioned"— the bear is addicted. The only way to prevent the bear from seeking human food again, and taking it by force, if necessary, is to instill such intense fear of people that the bear will ever after avoid people. Hunting bears is the best way to instill such fear.

That notion is to some degree supported by the experiences of Drs. Peter and Gertraud Krott who raised (uncaged) brown bear cubs that did become food raiders who were the bane of local residents.

Nevertheless, just the opposite experience was had by James Capen (Grizzly) Adams in the 1800's and by Robert Leslie in the early 1900's. Although some bear biologists have questioned Leslie's credibility because he had not even completed college at the time he reared black bear cubs in British Columbia, his observations of bear behavior were so astute that I tended to trust him. I know of no prior publication of the insights Leslie shared on bear communication signals – insights that agreed almost exactly with what I was observing. One could argue that none of Leslie's cubs was ever out on his own during a famine that could have driven him into becoming a raider. Yet there was also no proof that hand-reared cubs would be any more likely than mother-reared cubs to become raiders.*

Good science consists of testing assumptions, not blindly accepting them. With this much room for doubt, I believed that the cubs deserved a chance to live and we deserved a chance to determine whether orphans could be safely raised. My challenge would be figuring out how to do that; and I would seek advice every place I could. Meanwhile, judging from the experiences of Leslie, the best way to control aggression by my cubs seemed to be instilling not fear, but trust and especially respect for us – a process I call *acclimation*.

By that time, we had named the cubs. Ontak was the coal–black male who had redecorated my face while we were in the tree. The chocolate–brown female was Jonjoanak, and the lighter–brown female, Chrislee. Unlike Joan and John, who had called the mother bear Doddy, we did not give the cubs human names. Whatever Joan's Aunt Doddy had been like, she could not have closely resembled a wild bear. Calling her Doddy may have been one reason why Joan and John mistakenly thought she was tame.

The first stage in development of the cubs' trust for us had been voluntarily coming to the cabin for security and food. Allowing Ontak and his sisters to continue taking refuge with us turned out to be a vital second step in winning their trust. They used our cabin much like wolves and many other carnivores use a den, even though a den is not something the cubs would have needed had Doddy survived. Cubs and their mother abandon their winter den as soon as hibernation is finished. Rarely has any of the many bear litters I have watched retreated into any kind of a

---

* Three decades after I raised these three black bear cubs in Alaska, Dr. John Beecham, senior bear biologist for Idaho, reviewed all available literature on raising and releasing bear cubs on this and other continents. He too found no evidence that properly raised cubs are any more likely than mother-reared cubs to become raiders; and there was no evidence that they became dangerous to people. One type of proper rearing is the "bear-enting" method pioneered by Leslie and me. (Beecham, J. 2006. Orphaned Bear Cubs: Rehabilitation and Release Guidelines. Report to the World Society for the Protection of Animals.)

den for shelter from weather or refuge from enemies. Instead, they usually reacted to any potential enemy by fleeing or taking refuge in a tree. Sometimes the mother black bear joined her cubs in the tree. More often, she left them there while she defended access to the tree, or more often fled from it, as though to draw the "enemy" after her, much as a mother grouse does by pretending to have a broken wing.

During the day, I could likewise send Ontak and his sisters up a tree easily enough by imitating bear danger signals – for instance clapping my hands loudly to simulate jaw pops – and yelling "tree!" But I didn't know how to keep them aloft while we were asleep or gone. The cubs usually came down on their own initiative within an hour, then returned to foraging and playing. I doubted that they were wary enough to avoid being ambushed by another bear, or a wolf, wolverine, or lynx – all of which had left spoor within a mile or so of the cabin. Even moose could be lethal, and they were everywhere. Our presence provided a vital zone of relative security for the cubs, and the cabin was a safe haven in which they could sleep and rest.

Hoping for an easy meal, this wolf stalked a grizzly cub. But upon being discovered, the cub confronted the wolf and intimidated it.

A tougher challenge would be breaking the cubs' associations between food vs. people and their homes. Hence, we fed them indoors only during the first few days when that was the only place they would trust us. As soon as we could move around outdoors without spooking them, nearly all feeding was done there. Later, once we were sure they were receiving adequate nourishment from natural forage, fish, and game, we would quit supplementing their diet in hopes of permanently weaning them off of human food.

Although accomplishing all this was reputedly difficult, if not impossible, we were encouraged by the fact that the cubs continued to forage for at least ten hours out of each twenty–four, despite their wariness of being out in the woods without Doddy.

Just as they seemed bolder inside our dark little cabin than outside, while outside they seemed most confident when the light was dimmest, and especially during our brief "night" of dusk fading into dawn. That was when they wandered farthest from the cabin on their own.

After their unaccompanied foraging trips, all three youngsters usually returned quietly and bedded down together indoors on their mother's pelt, behind the pot–bellied stove. The pelt was their security blanket. After sleeping several hours, they ate anything we offered, then interspersed additional naps with foraging nearby until dusk approached once more.

Discarded stove that I salvaged and repaired for the cabin.

I was less worried about any so-called addiction to human food than about potential aggression against people, whether to obtain food, to exert dominance, or to defend themselves against someone who surprised at such close range that they dared not turn their backs to flee. Over the week that they had accompanied Doddy in raiding this cabin, they had threatened Joan and John on several occasions. This "habit" had to be broken, or the cubs might become dangerous as they grew larger, stronger, and more assertive. Although neither Doddy nor they had ever harmed anyone, even threats frighten most people so much that the offending bear will be killed.

Our worries about the cubs eventually posing danger initially seemed fully justified by the fact that, from the first day they were with us, they had foul tempers and always fought over the food we provided. Only after reading Jane Goodall's book *In the Shadow of Man,* about the effects of providing bananas to chimpanzees, was I reminded that even normally peaceful animals can be "provoked" into aggression if they have to compete for a scarce but highly prized resource such as certain foods or mates. Bears of any age may fight over salmon or carrion; yet even the most aggressive adults normally spend no more than a few seconds a day fighting. Cubs fight more often, but seldom harm one another. They are no more "inherently" violent than puppies and children.

On the cubs' third morning with us. I awoke to the bangs and clangs of cubs rummaging through our kitchen, looking for food. The cubs' keen noses had detected breakfast – three bowls of cornmeal mush, laced with milk and Karo. I had prepared it for them the previous evening, then stored until breakfast on a high shelf where it could not be raided. Quickly hanging the bed's mosquito netting out of reach, I took their bowls outside, where they dug into the sweetened mush with all the dainty restraint of adult bears feasting on a putrid moose carcass.

The only way to keep cubs from fighting over food was to serve their meals in separate pans.

At left, Ontak battles with Jonjoanak. Initially, all the cubs were fed on the ground. But we eventually discovered that Ontak was best fed on the roof of the cabin's porch. Not only did this keep him separated from his sisters, but this was his favorite resting spot.

Having three separate bowls avoided the usual battle temporarily. While they ate, each threatened the others with head down, ears flat, mouth agape and upper lip puckered. Then Chrislee snuck over and began lapping up the last of Jonjoanak's meal — whereupon Jonjoanak whirled and attacked Chrislee. Suddenly, all three cubs were fighting — roaring, biting, swatting, and dodging with far greater speed than they used while sparring. As abruptly as the battle had started, it ended with all three cubs standing with heads bowed and mouths agape, moaning or "pulse-bellowing" (a deep-toned pulse with a beat frequency a little slower than that of purring) which conveyed threat rather than contentment. Finally, they separated, as each cub stiffly stalking back to its own bowl.

In an irrational effort to bring peace, I gave the youngsters a treat — their first taste of canned peaches. They were ecstatic! They gobbled up the bright golden fruit so fast that they nearly choked, each trying to finish her own treat and then to steal her sibling's. Jonjoanak bowled Chrislee over and got her little sister's peach — as though in payback for Chrislee's theft of a bit of Jonjoanak's mush. The second time I passed out the syrupy fruit, I protected Chrislee until she managed to swallow her goodie — whereupon she and her sister together tried to steal the remainder of Ontak's peaches.

As bad as it was trying to pass out food bowls without getting caught in the middle of a spat, this was nothing compared with the challenge of bottle-feeding. At the time they were orphaned, the cubs were still supplementing plant foods with their mother's milk. We tried to replicate that with homemade "baby formula" as soon as the cubs would approach and touch us freely.

During that first week, Ontak was the least aggressive cub, despite my attempts to capture him in the tree a few days after his mother died. We started bottle-feeding with him. After heating water on a fire in the yard, Alatanna waited until Ontak was alone in the cabin, then joined him with a pan of warm water. Quickly mixing in powdered milk, she poured it into a baby bottle.

"Ontak," she cooed, sitting down on the edge of the bed. Initially, she was ignored as the cub hunted around the cabin for a tidbit of his own choosing. But Alatanna persisted. Blond hair bound up in braids that hung over her shoulders, she leaned over toward him, making kissy sounds. Their similarity to sucking sounds was probably accidental, but certainly appropriate. Moose calves beg their mothers to nurse them by making sucking sounds. I think I have heard grizzly cubs do the same thing. Anyway, Alatanna's "kisses" caught Ontak's attention, but did not lure him into trying to nurse. Finally, she squirted milk onto the little male's muzzle. *That* did the trick!

Licking his muzzle, the cub walked up to her and nosed the bottle, then bit down on the nipple. Instead of sucking, he tried to pull the bottle out of her hands. She held on, and the nipple popped off the bottle. Milk cascaded over the cub, which seemed to suit him just fine. He eagerly lapped it up. Still dripping from his milk bath, he came looking for more.

Meanwhile, Alatanna retrieved the nipple and replaced it on the bottle, which she refilled. She again offered it to Ontak. When he tried to bite the nipple, she pulled the bottle back a few inches, speaking baby talk and telling him to be gentle. Instead, he reached out with his right hand and curled it around her hand, pulled the bottle to his mouth, then bit down on the bottle and pulled it away from her. He laid the bottle onto the back of his left hand and held it down with the right one as he investigated it. Quickly detecting that milk dribbled only from the rubber nipple when he bit there, he used the claws of his right hand to pop the nipple free from the glass bottle. Once again, the floor was flooded with milk, which he licked up.

This was not what Alatanna had bargained for. Three cuddly tykes she would have enjoyed, but our triplet hellions kept her upset and her eyes often brimmed with tears of frustration. She rarely fed the cubs again until they were tamer, a few weeks later.

When I offered the bottle to Jonjoanak, she turned away as though it was offensive. Squirting milk from it into her mouth cured that, but led to worse problems. Now understanding that the bottle contained milk, she stalked over and batted it out of my hands. The bottle didn't break on the dirt floor, but I was unable to retrieve it before her teeth shredded the nipple.

We tried again the next day with a new nipple. By then, all three cubs understood what was going on and we could not separate one from the rest to feed it. Anytime I got one alone and started to nurse her, the others stalked over with head low, lip puckered, and/or jaws gaping to roust their sibling and usurp the nipple. Three cubs fighting for access to our single baby bottle quickly proved too hazardous to continue. From that point on, for the next week, all their milk and other food was offered in bowls, and only outdoors.

*   *   *

No matter how tolerant the cubs were of our proximity indoors – where they still spent the hottest part of each day – they remained wary of us outdoors. When we tried to approach, they fled up a tree, or climbed from a tree onto the cabin. The two females usually perched on a big horizontal willow limb that overhung the cabin; Ontak found refuge on the roof.

With its shingles of corrugated sheet metal, the roof resounded when walked on or pounded. This was especially true of the porch roof, which was shingled with flattened Blazo gas cans and resounded like a giant bass drum. Occasionally, when especially huffy, Ontak slammed his hands down on the thin metal roofing. He quickly learned that his actions produced the most horrendous racket when he pounded over the porch; thereafter, he seldom pounded the roof anywhere else. Apparently, he deliberately chose that spot to maximize the intimidating quality of his threat display.

This was similar to what Jane Goodall observed with a chimpanzee she called Mike in the Gombe Stream Reserve of Africa. The fuel cans he used for aggressive displays were not flattened on a roof, but in their original intact shape. One or more cans were banged together against the ground, or thrown ahead of Mike as he charged and screamed. This so thoroughly intimidated his peers that he quickly dominated them. Ontak's displays intimidated shy little Chrislee, but not his bolder sister Jonjoanak.

*   *   *

Sometimes, instead of climbing a tree or racing into the forest when spooked by Alatanna or me, an anxious cub fled back inside the cabin. When one of us came inside to join her, the cub was initially apprehensive. A few minutes with the door shut, though, was all it took to calm her.

I had to wonder whether it was the darkness, the closeness of the room, or some other cue that had such a calming effect. No doubt, the cubs remembered the security of their natal den, and may have reacted to the dark little cabin in much the same way. Given the readiness with which I had seen fox and wolf pups retreat into a den for security, I suspected that many species of denning carnivores felt more secure in small dark spaces. If fear of such places could be called *claustrophobia*, I supposed that preference for them could be called *claustrophilia* (*philia* comes from the root word for *love* in Latin or Greek). When observing other black bears, grizzly bears, moose and deer, I had noticed how they too were much less apprehensive in dim lighting. For this, I had coined the term *umbraphilia* for *love of shade* or darkness (*umbra* being the root word from which *umbrella* is derived).

About the same time that I reared Ontak and his sisters, fellow biologist Gordon Burghardt reared two orphaned black bear cubs in Tennessee. These tiny females were named Kit and Kate. From the time he adopted them, in the month of April, the twins "preferred dark places. This was not just an escape reaction, but a true preference. For instance, they soon learned to open and climb inside the clothes dryer, kitchen cabinets, and the clothes hamper. They would play or relax in these situations, which indicates a lack of fear. If frightened, ..., they would run and hide in dark places." [1]

The same psychology may explain why my youngsters did most of their roaming without me during the twilight between sundown and sunup – sometimes staying out for several hours, but at other times coming and going repeatedly.

They had long since learned how to open the cabin door, which was still on its original leather hinges. All a cub had to do was hook the bottom of the door with a paw, pull the door inward, then hop through before it swung closed and slapped the cub on its rump. The first few times a cub got slapped, she glared at us belligerently. Soon, though, the cubs got the hang of things and began to treat the swinging door as a toy.

*   *   *

It was Alatanna who finally broke through the cubs' mistrust. Or, more precisely, it was the lure of the fish she provided after spending a few days with Tony catching salmon.

To my surprise, all three cubs vastly preferred their fish cooked. Wild bears normally have access only to raw salmon, which they eat in enormous quantities. I would have thought raw fish would be preferred, but our three youngsters had other ideas.

Not only did they prefer their salmon cooked, but they would eat it only while fresh – freshly thawed, that is. They disdained any fish that had sat around overnight. Only when famished, and then with displays of bad temper, would they eat fish which had been caught or unfrozen for more than half-a-day.

This too was quite different from what I have seen with fully wild bears. Even if those animals preferred fresh fish, putrid ones were often eaten, especially by low-ranking individuals, mostly adolescents, who could not get access to good fishing sites or who lacked fishing skills.

They had to subsist on scraps left by their more successful elders. Even when wild bears had only sun–*ripened* fish to eat, I saw no recognizable sign of irritation or distress as they fed.

Given that the dead fish seemed to have been in just as bad shape as the live ones, it was not clear why the high-graded carcasses were of any interest. Perhaps these adolescent boars had been getting enough fat, but still needed protein for building muscle. On the other hand, some bears may tire of the flavor of fresh fish and thus eat carcasses for variety, much as people eat cheese. Limburger and some other "stinky" cheeses smell very much like rotting meat, perhaps because the same microbial by-products are produced in both foods. For bears, as for humans, liking the flavor of rot may be an acquired taste.

As to my own cubs' irritation with carrion, perhaps bears are not so different from people in one respect: those used to getting just want they want are angered by having to settle for second best; but those usually lucky to get scraps may be delighted with second best. *Best*, like *beauty*, is in the "taste" of the beholder.

*   *   *

Winning the trust of Ontak and his sisters was much harder than I had anticipated, but still nothing compared to curbing their aggression. Not only did the cubs fight each other for food, but it was no small chore keeping them at bay while we prepared meals for them. During the first few days that the cubs shared our cabin, they would approach us no closer than a few feet. Then suddenly one day, as I prepared their supper, they began crowding around me. From then on, we could seldom get their food, or our own, served before a cub managed to hook the food bowl with her paw and dump the contents, leading to a mad scramble as the three youngsters fought for a share.

They were especially determined the first time they smelled roasted salmon. The first batch of fish entrails that Alatanna brought home drew the cubs immediately. Each one quickly polished off about four pounds of the raw offal. Once the cubs seemed satiated, Alatanna pulled out a pair of eight inch king salmon steaks for our own supper. With outdoor temperatures back up in the 80s, it was too hot to cook inside the cabin. As usual, I built a small fire out in the yard, then laid a grill across several soot-blackened rocks the size of my head. On the grill, I laid out the reddish-orange steaks, dashed with salt and pepper.

As soon as the fatty skin around each steak started sizzling, I found myself having to fight off all three cubs. The odor of roasting salmon was the spark which set their appetites ablaze. This was the first time all of them had ever come up to either of us outdoors, so at first I did not try to discourage them from crowding around me. When one cub tried to snag the salmon steaks, however, I lost my temper, shouting and shoving the cub away. Immediately, the other two cubs came to her aid.

This was far from an attack, but neither was it playful. The cubs bawled in fouled tempered frustration, lunging and swatting at me time after time. But for my leather pants and shirt, they might well have drawn blood. To rescue the steaks, I grabbed the hot grill with leather gloves and stood up while all three cubs tried to climb me like a tree.

I couldn't walk with three twenty-five–pound cubs hanging on, digging their claws into my clothing and skin. Holding the grill and steaks aloft in one hand, I peeled cubs off with the other hand. I finally made it inside the cabin. Before I could set the steaks down on a high shelf, though, a cub tripped me. Lightning strikes little faster than hungry bears, and the steaks were gone before I could lift my face off the dirt floor to see what was happening.

Angrily, I slammed the cabin door, trapping all three cubs in there with me. I had had enough of their nasty tempers and aggression. The violence of their competition over food was perhaps to be expected and tolerated within limits, given that I had seen mother-reared cubs do the same thing when momma provided a salmon. Alaska bears have just a few months each year to consume their annual diet. But I had little patience with unprovoked belligerence toward Alatanna and me.

Folklore held that this was typical of bears; hence the term "bearish" temper. But was it really inherent and permanent, or could it be alleviated? Had it been exaggerated in these cubs by the trauma of their mother's death, coupled with their confusion and loneliness, and by the way we fed them?

Inherent or not, the time to start breaking the cubs' bad habits was now, before they got any larger and stronger. I was determined to win their respect in the only way they seemed capable of understanding – through force.

Behaving toward the cubs as if I were a predator – stalking them or attacking without warning or provocation – would, of course, have done no good. The idea that hunting bears reduces their aggressiveness toward people has always struck me as not only a bit self-serving for bear hunters, but illogical. Hunters are predators, and the way an animal defends against a predator is to flee or attack. I didn't want the cubs to do either.

Rather, I wanted them to submit to Alatanna and me. This is not something we could expect if they perceived us as predators. Any form of submission toward a predator would be suicidal. We could expect submission only if the cubs treated us with the same kind of respect they would show toward a higher-ranking bear, trusting that we would not attack them without provocation, as predatory or bully bears do, but apprehensive of provoking us by breaking our rules, and afraid to be so aggressive that they would elicit harsh reprisal. I wanted them to treat all people as social superiors – affectionate superiors in the case of Alatanna and myself, slightly grouchy superiors in the case of friends such as Zak, and belligerent superiors in the case of anyone else.

How might a bear expect a belligerent superior to act? The best examples I knew of at that time came from observations by Maurice

Hornocker, a member of the Craighead research team which had studied grizzlies at Yellowstone National Park. Some of those bears, especially boars vying for top rank, were extremely aggressive and prone to attack any victim that failed to treat the dominant with proper respect – for example, one which came or remained too close, failed to defer on a trail or at a fishing site, failed to surrender food, or didn't otherwise exhibit appropriate submissive behavior. Although a naive bear might not always know why it was attacked, it could learn over time. I suspected that the reason for most attacks was fairly obvious to any well-socialized victim.

I could not expect proper submission from our cubs until they knew our rules. Anything a dog could learn, a bear could probably learn too, but likely much more quickly. Judging by that standard, these cubs probably knew quite well how they had transgressed. What they lacked was not knowledge of the rules, but respect for them, and for us.

I had read that sows discipline their cubs with swats and nips. If necessary, I was prepared to be equally severe. Nevertheless, my temper cooled quickly, and my attempt at domination took a somewhat gentler approach. Grabbing Jonjoanak, the meanest of the three, I pinned her with my left forearm jammed into her mouth. My arm was so thick compared to her mouth, and the leather sleeve of my welding gloves so heavy, that she could not sink her teeth into me. Then I sat across her hindquarters, pinning them so that her hind claws could not rake my belly. With the cub virtually helpless, I stroked her tummy, head, and flanks. So far as I could tell, I was causing her no pain beyond mere discomfort, and the caresses would have been loved by a dog or by any of the other bear cubs I had handled in the past; yet she struggled furiously. Meanwhile, her siblings kept lunging at me and swatting, or grabbing my back and attempting to bite it. After half an hour trying unsuccessfully to dominate Jonjoanak, I tried the same thing on Ontak and Chrislee, with equal futility.

As I later discovered, I was making a fundamental error. Since the cubs had not yet bonded with me, they interpreted punishment as attack and responded defensively. Surrender to a dominant animal is safe only if surrender inhibits further aggression, not if it increases the victim's vulnerability to violence. During intense confrontations, a subordinate bear remains on guard, ready to defend his life. I have seen the same thing among canids that were bitter enemies, including wolves from different packs. As a general rule, I would not expect a wolf to submit to such an enemy from outside its own social group except as a last resort; for instance, by rolling over onto its back and perhaps urinating on itself. Trapped wolves sometimes do that or cower in helpless terror when approached by a person; but I have never seen a bear do so.

In highly social species such as dogs, wolves, chimpanzees, and tightly knit human groups, each individual not only depends on group membership for its well-being; it contributes to the group and may be valuable even to those individuals which can dominate it in a fight. A dominant may serve its own interests by halting attack on a subordinate soon after the opponent submits. Among bears, however, the subordinate is likely to be valuable to the dominant only in a few situations: if the subordinate is (a) the dominant's own offspring or other close kin; (b) a potential mate; or (c) an ally in combat or in excluding other rivals from the dominant's domain. Such alliances are common among siblings who remain together for a few years after being weaned and dissociated from their mother. Other bears, including adult sows, also team up, but much more rarely. In any event, I could not expect my cubs to surrender until they trusted me not to take advantage of their vulnerability to harm them.

We had already made a lot of progress in winning the trust of Chrislee and her siblings; for instance, by letting them take refuge in and around the cabin with us. But further progress could depend on fulfilling their deep craving for reassurance and affection. The more I watched sows with cubs, the more I realized that most discipline was exerted with threats or by refusing incentives such as food, play or affection – thereby manipulating a cub's emotions. Disciplining cubs with restrained bites and swats was actually uncommon, and was sometimes followed by displays of reconciliation and affection (although not so elaborately as among wolves and chimpanzees). A "stick" works best in combination with a "carrot." I began using that same tactic with these cubs.

It was my perception, as well as that of Bob Leslie and bear trainers Doug Seus and Wally Naughton, that the more violently cubs are disciplined, the more violently they will eventually compete with the "bearent" for dominance. Gentle, firm, consistent discipline tends to inhibit both violence and power struggles. This is especially important considering a person's own vulnerability to even a small bear. With bears, as with people, excessive punishment or permissiveness are equally harmful.

Indeed, having once proven to the cubs that I was far stronger than they were, I did not have to repeat the demonstration so aggressively. It was sufficient to occasionally overpower them gently during play, by rolling them onto their back and holding them there briefly.

When a cub persisted in biting, I taught it the folly of this by squeezing its cheeks between its molars. It could not bite me without biting its own cheeks. Ouch! Within a few hours, each cub understood that biting hurt and they seldom did bit us again.

As the months passed, I never tolerated threat without responding in kind, quickly followed by reassurance. I retaliated against swats and nips with loud violent threats; for instance, by banging pots and pans together while I stomped toward the offending cub – quickly followed by a peace offering. The fact that we reassured the cubs quickly after any discipline probably contributed heavily to strengthening the bond between us; conversely, I suspect that the *relative* scarcity of such reassurance from one bear to another contributes to breaking of social bonds and to bears' so-called "asocial" nature. Among wolves and chimpanzees, the victim of an attack often pleads for reassurance as soon as an attack ends, and the victim and aggressor are commonly back on friendly terms within a few hours.[2] I have rarely seen anything equivalent to that among bears, except occasionally with a mother and her cubs.

The more I studied Ontak and his sisters, as well as mother-reared bears, the more I was struck by similarities and contrasts with large primates. Years of observation had been required before Jane Goodall, Dian Fossey, or Stewart and Jean Altmann could more than glimpse the complexity of social organization among chimpanzees, gorillas, and baboons, respectively. I thus saw no reason to expect to discern the real intricacy of ursid social relationships without a comparable effort – a prediction which has been well confirmed by subsequent research.

I was also struck by the challenges of close association of people with large primates. Like bears, both chimps and baboons are highly attracted to some human foods, and to our endless variety of novel objects – attractions which sometimes lead to marauding and threats, mainly among the animals themselves, but occasionally against people. This was natural, but no more tolerable with chimps than with bears. Like Goodall, I had to keep exploring new ways to minimize this, a need of which the cubs soon reminded me yet again.

Noting how much Ontak and his sisters had been attracted to the cooked fish, Alatanna had boiled a dozen salmon heads. She called me when the meat was ready. As soon as I opened the door, the cubs burst out into the yard where the fish heads were waiting. There, our three little monsters took out their remaining aggression on one another in a free-for-all.

Although there were plenty of fishheads for each cub to eat its fill, stolen fish, like stolen fruit, were apparently the most attractive. Alatanna had already pulled three fishheads from the pot to cool. She now tossed the largest of these to Jonjoanak, who ran off and began eating. Chrislee did the same, but was seen by her larger sister, who immediately abandoned her own fishhead and raced over to steal Chrislee's – whereupon Ontak stole Jonjoanak's first prize. Still gripping Chrislee's fishhead in her jaws, Jonjoanak raced after Ontak, butting him with her head and battering him with her paws until his jaws opened and disgorged her fishhead. Even with two fishheads, Jonjoanak was not content to eat them. Anxiously biting into both fishheads this way and that, until she could carry them together, Jonjoanak hurried over toward the cookpot to usurp the whole batch of heads.

The rest of the fishheads were still resting in very hot soup, but Jonjoanak would not be dissuaded. When Alatanna raised her hand to keep the aggressive cub at bay, Jonjoanak swatted Alatanna's arm so hard that she left scratches that were soon lined with blood beads. Dropping the first two fishheads from her mouth, the chocolate-brown female plunged her jaws into the pot to steal another head, then whelped in pain when her mouth was burned.

Ontak took advantage of the situation and darted in beside his sister, snatching one fishhead off the ground, then boldly sticking around to try stealing the second one too. His pain-angered sister whirled and bit down on his neck, violently whipping her head back and forth as her claws sunk into his face and shoulders. The loose skin of his neck allowed him to twist around and flip upside down until he could use his toe claws to rip at his sister's throat, which was fortunately well protected with thick fur and skin. We had witnessed many fights between the cubs before, but never anything so savage.

Breaking apart, the two cubs stood four-footed, partly facing one another a yard apart, faces vertical, noses pointed at the ground, mouths open, roar-bawling furiously. One fishhead was under Jonjoanak's belly, the second between the two cubs. Ontak raised his head with gaping jaws and suddenly they were blurred in battle again, rising up on their hind legs, with each cub's jaws clamped onto the cheek or jaw of its opponent, whipping their heads back and forth.

Lunging forward, Jonjoanak pushed Ontak over onto his back and drove her head in under his chin, trying to bite his throat. Ontak's toe claws raked her belly, doing no obvious damage, but pushing her back, even as he protected his throat by using his hands to shove her chest and head aside. Turning to bite one of Ontak's hands, and inflicting enough of a wound that he limped for a week afterwards, Jonjoanak exposed her own throat.

It was not Ontak whose teeth sunk in there, however, but Chrislee's. Throughout the several seconds that the fight had been underway, this smallest and most timid of the cubs had just watched tensely from the sidelines, standing guard over her own fishhead. Now, as her siblings' thrashings brought them within range, Chrislee did not grab her own prize and retreat, but attacked, biting her sister on the side of the head, just where it joined the neck. *

Not sensing that Chrislee was an ally, Ontak now bit and clawed at both sisters, who quickly turned on him in tandem. As all three cubs rose up onto their hind feet, teeth and claws locked into one another's fur and flesh, they toppled over into the cookpot. Jonjoanak landed with her back in the scaling liquid and screeched, breaking loose from her siblings and whirling to stare balefully at the overturned pan, face once again vertical, ears flattened, upper lip puckered.

Her siblings had also been splashed with the hot fish soup. They fled, then turned to face the fireplace again. With their heads initially high and ears forward to appraise the situation, both cubs then lowered their heads and stalked forward with stiff forelegs, bawling warnings to one another. There they remained for the next quarter-hour, standing guard over fishheads that initially burned their mouths and paws. As the fish gradually cooled, each cub took more bites, gingerly at first, shaking his head when its mouth was burned, then eventually eating ravenously.

By the time those fish heads were consumed, all three cubs were in gluttonous agony. For the first time since we had adopted these youngsters, they came to us outdoors for comforting, resting contentedly on our laps as we stroked their distended bellies.

---

* Although I have never seen one cub inflict a serious bloody wound on another, even an injury (e.g., a paw bite) that just impairs the ability to escape from predators or follow momma across a stream, could reduce the cub's chances of survival. All else being equal, the risk of injury and the certainty of competition from siblings would tend to reduce cub survival rate. Whether these detriments are outweighed by benefits remains unknown.

I should have anticipated that feeding the cubs odorous foods would eventually draw other bears. One night, after barbecuing salmon heads, I was awakened by a sound at the window near my head. Through bleary eyes, I looked out to see a bear looking in, his bright honey-brown eyes just two feet from my own.

"What is it?" Alatanna questioned me drowsily.

"Just one of the cubs," I answered, half asleep.

"I thought they were all inside," she said, confused.

They were. Glancing over behind the stove, I saw three thick furry rugs, each breathing heavily. Turning back toward the bear whose nose was now pressed against the plexiglass window a foot from my face, I realized it was more than twice as big as the cubs. Trouble.

Grabbing my rifle and chambering a round, I leapt up and slipped out the door, prepared in case the intruder was aggressive. Just the opposite.

The bear was as afraid of me as I was of him, running for his life, seldom allowing me more than a glimpse until well out of rifle range.

Before I could decide what to do, I was joined by all three cubs and Alatanna. Seeing that the intruder was probably just a yearling and no danger, I put the rifle away. The yearling had likely been driven away from his mother at the beginning of mating season, somewhere near late May or early June. He could be lonesome. Well, we already had three cubs; why not four? The more, the merrier. Even though winning his trust might be a lot of work, I was hopeful that association with the yearling would help the cubs learn a lot of ursid survival skills beyond what I could teach them. I had no idea whether the yearling would attempt to teach them anything, or whether these smart little tykes could learn much by imitation. These were aspects of bear behavior which had received almost no study then, and not much more now. But there was every chance that by simply following the yearling, the cubs would learn of new food sources; and they would be exposed to new challenges that would enable them to educate themselves. (According to my Native friend QuisQuiNee, that was one of the main ways his people educated their kids – by exposing them to challenges, and letting them sink or swim without *too* much advice and assistance.) Faced with the unknown, we proceeded cautiously.

To give the yearling courage, Alatanna and I hid inside the cabin. Within an hour the yearling was back. To my surprise, the cubs were frightened. Just outside the cabin window was a tall cottonwood. As the yearling approached, Chrislee and Ontak raced up the tree, while Jonjoanak briefly remained at the base. Body poised for quick ascent, her head turned toward the yearling, upper lip puckered, cheeks distending then flattening as she woofed and huffed at him, alternating with clacking her teeth. Suddenly pounding the tree with both forepaws several times, she leapt up the trunk and raced toward its crown.

Curiosity at a safe distance. *(Judy McClure Photo)*

Looking up, I could see all three cubs resting on branches. Jonjoanak stood on one branch, leaning forward, with her "arms" resting on a higher branch. Ontak lay prone, draped over a thick horizontal branch like a miniature bear rug. Chrislee sat behind Ontak, with one arm and leg on each side of that same limb, her back resting against the trunk. Any of those positions would have been so uncomfortable for me that I would have fidgeted constantly. Yet the cubs rested quietly, seldom shifting position. Their faces were alight with excitement, eyes glinting, ears forward and mouths slightly open as they looked ground-ward.

Reaching the base of the tree, the yearling stood upright looking at the cubs. His lips were relaxed and his ears forward, without visible signs of aggression. Clearly, he wasn't trying to intimidate the cubs. So why were they frightened?

Yearlings tend to be lankier than cubs *(Dianne Owen photo)*

Their fear, combined with his lack of threatening behavior, made me wonder whether he trying to prey on them. Predators don't threaten prey, which are easiest to ambush while calm and oblivious to the predator's intention, so that they can be approached closely before the fatal charge and attack.

Not knowing whether the yearling was just lonesome or predatory, I trusted the cubs' instincts and shouted to drive him away. Although he had to be chased off repeatedly over the next few days, he eventually disappeared, much to the relief of my little family.

Chapter 6
AFFECTION AND PLAY

Late June

Initially, I had no intention of actually "taming" the cubs. I would have been satisfied to have them trust us enough to stick around so that we could protect them, teach them to fend for themselves, and study their behavior. However, I came to question whether that would be enough. Not only might emotional bonding be important for controlling their aggression over food, but it might also be necessary for their psychological well-being.

I raised these cubs at about the same point in history when animal psychologists began testing how primates and other young animals respond to social deprivation. Without at least a fuzzy "toy" companion for company, infant primates become psychotic. Live companions are better, and mothers best of all. In many ways, bears are similar to primates and might be just as vulnerable to psychosis. A psychotic bear is the last thing anyone wants to handle. I had no way of knowing whether cubs provide each other with enough companionship to assure psychological health and socialization. But the "bearenthood" experiences of James Capen Adams, Peter Krott, and Bob Leslie indicated that a human could play the role of surrogate parent, and I intended to do my best.

The cubs' fear of us outdoors faded gradually. As the days wore on and we continued cooking salmon for them, they became so accustomed to being near us that they eventually ignored us as they played, fought, and explored. This was just a small step forward, but an important one – as was the next.

As the lowest–ranking cub, Chrislee was bullied by the others even in play. Also, she was the least successful at initiating play with her siblings. Her invitations to Ontak or Jonjoanak were often ignored or even rebuffed with mild threat. When that happened, Chrislee played with objects or reluctantly came to us for companionship – something which none of the other cubs had done so early in our relationship. Chrislee was also the first to occasionally allow Alatanna and me to stroke her head. Unlike her siblings, we were always ready to play and consistently gentle.

Soon, Chrislee became the tamest of the three youngsters, and there were days when she was almost slavishly hungry for attention. This seemed to be a dramatic change of temperament, for when first adopted, the little demon's disposition had been as sour as that of a proverbial grizzly – which is why I had given her the rhyming name of *Chrislee*. Weeks passed before I realized that the change was not so much in her personality as in her mood. The behavior which I had initially seen as offensively aggressive was, in fact, primarily defensive. She may have been more frightened than her siblings and thus more ready to do battle.

Chrislee, Jonjoanak, and Ontak were still little *beasts* in all senses of the word. But their beauty was finally beginning to emerge.

Although the cubs fared well on everything we fed them or for which they foraged themselves, they became ill when I neglected to boil their milk and sterilize their food pans after each meal. It was not enough to wash the pans with dish soap. To kill bacteria, these items had to be rinsed in water that was boiling or laced with bleach.

As a consequence of my negligence, the cubs developed *scours* – watery diarrhea that quickly dehydrated and weakened them. For several anxious days, none of the cubs could walk more than a few paces before sitting down to rest, or rolling onto its side where it lay panting. When we dribbled cool water on a cub's muzzle, this was lapped up gratefully. Afterwards, Ontak or Chrislee licked our hands with surprising gentleness. Gordon Burghardt likewise reported that when Kit and Kate were ill, "they became remarkably more gentle and, in fact, would often explore and lick the human face with no attempts to nibble, suck, or bite."[1] A conventional ethological interpretation might be that, because of their heightened vulnerability, sick cubs are especially careful to appease more dominant individuals. However, from an emotional perspective, I suspect that this is a manifestation of affection, like one finds in similar situations with dogs or people.

We couldn't even consider leaving the sick cubs outside in the hot sun and bright light where they would feel insecure and be in danger from predators. But that didn't make sharing the cabin with the youngsters any more pleasant. As soon as the diarrhea started, the cabin reeked like a zoo. Alatanna claimed that the odor was detectable a hundred feet away. Or was it a thousand? She eventually complained it could be smelled from the village, a dozen miles away.

We immediately began sterilizing the cubs' feeding bowls and bottle; yet the youngsters continued to scour. A local vet suggested that drinking milk from a bowl did not mix in enough saliva for proper digestion. On his advice, I tried bottle-feeding again, and provided the cubs with large bowls of rice laced with Karo syrup — much to their delight. They quickly recovered.

Even after their stools began to solidify, we always knew when a cub was about to let loose, for she began looking for a corner – not with her nose, but with her tail. Alatanna called this "bumble–butting." The cub would waddle backward, hiney swaying from side to side as the tyke maneuvered toward a corner – either a corner of the cabin or a corner where the bed joined the cabin wall. The cub would tuck her hind legs slightly under her hips, squat, then both defecate and urinate.

I could only speculate about the function of voiding in corners. Performed only inside the dark cabin, never outdoors, it may have been an adaptation to life in a hibernation den. During the first weeks after birth, a cub's urine and feces are lapped up by the mother. The same thing happens in other carnivores; urination and defecation may not even occur until stimulated by the mother's tongue lapping against the infant's groin.

In canids and felids, the mother is fully awake and functional throughout her infants' development. In bears, there may be times when the hibernating mother is too drowsy to perform sanitation duties. Do cubs wait to void until she awakens? If not, do cubs avoid fouling themselves? How? I'm not sure that would be possible when cubs are still so young that they can only crawl. But once they can stand and walk four-footed, they could back to the edge of the den, preferably into a corner, to deposit their wastes. Given the delayed development of a cub's ability to walk, backing into a corner to void might not begin until the last month or so of denning.

Only years later did I see adolescent and adult grizzly bears backing up, then leaning backwards just prior to defecation. In all cases, the bear had loose stool from eating salmon. This stance helps keep the fur from being soiled.

Adult black and grizzly bears may also back up while scent–marking their domains. They sometimes back up toward an elevated object, to deposit urine or dung. As a bear steps backwards, its hindquarters may sway and twist sideways in a manner at least superficially like bumble–butting, suggesting that the behavior my cubs performed in our cabin was a developmental antecedent to such scent–marking. Panda bears mark by actually going into a handstand while it rubs its anal area on a tree trunk, as though a bear's prestige is determined by how high it marks.

I have read of people house-training bears. For example, Gordon Burghardt placed his cubs in an indoor pen immediately after feeding them, whereupon both Kit and Kate would void within five to ten minutes. On one occasion, a cub even insisted on coming inside the house and going to her pen before voiding. Eventually, they learned to void outdoors. We were never that lucky; the only way to keep our cubs from voiding in the cabin was to shoo them outside as soon as one started bumble-butting.

*   *   *

Given that Jonjoanak and her siblings always fought over the single bottle we could afford to buy, I had to work out a way of keeping them calm while suckling. The only trick I could think of was to give them milk only after they already were full of cereal or rice. In this way, Ontak and then Chrislee began to accept warm milk that I squirted from a bottle onto my fingers, which they licked eagerly while purring vigorously. Ontak even allowed me to rub his belly while he sucked lustily from the baby bottle, without chewing up the nipple or having either of his sisters trying to steal the bottle. Chrislee did the same.

After they had eaten, I lay down between them and napped with the cubs, one arm loosely encircling each. Although I had initiated the contact, Ontak soon wiggled close, then kept his back or flank pressed tightly against me, head resting on my shoulder or across my upper arm. The cubs loved snuggling as much as puppies. Like sunlight breaking through dark thunderhead clouds, their affection was beginning to warm our lives.

Although the cubs were now much less rowdy while bottle–feeding than they had been a week earlier, there were still moments when their tempers flared and Alatanna broke into tears. The saving grace in these situations was that the cubs seemed to empathize with her discomfort, much as a mother bear might with her cubs, or as a dog might with a person. Chrislee or Ontak would approach gently, lay her or his chin on Alatanna's knee, and nuzzle or lick my bride's hand or face.

The most touching example of such empathetic behavior I have seen was in the movie *Send Word Mother Bear*. A grizzly belonging to Doug Seus had been trained to crawl up to actress Helen Stoltzfus as she "pretended" to cry in misery. The bear not only did as it was trained, but spontaneously nuzzled and licked Helen much as my cubs had done to Alatanna. What made this event so touching was not that the bear responded appropriately to Helen's "acting," but that she was not entirely acting. The film was based on a real trauma in Helen's life and on her vision of being comforted by a spiritual mother bear. This grizzly's affection reached past Helen's acting into her real emotions, providing the very comfort which had until that moment been only a dream: *Beauty within the beast.*

Curious that the only times my cubs were consistently gentle in licking a human face were when we or they were hurting.

Ontak and Chrislee's growing empathy and affection hadn't yet rubbed off on Jonjoanak. She continued glaring at us balefully, blowing, pulse-bellowing or bawling in a voice that sounded vaguely like a dog's growl, then slapping the ground or my leg with her paws and claws. Occasionally, she snapped too. But even for her, there was hope.

*   *   *

While Gordon Burghardt's foundlings sucked from bottles, their eyes were usually closed as they purred with utter contentment. When the milk in a cub's bottle ran out, however, she began growling and attacked her sister, perhaps in hopes of stealing her sibling's milk or out of frustration.

One consequence of not being able to suckle – to obtain the satisfaction of sucking at a teat – was that the cubs sucked on one another's ears, appearing quite content and purring loudly. Gordon Burghardt, and before him Peter and Gertraud Krott, also observed ear-sucking by orphans. As the smallest and weakest of my three cubs, Chrislee was at the bottom of the "sucking order." She rarely had opportunity to suck on the other cubs' ears; but her own were sucked on frequently, until they were nearly bald and ragged. We could well understand Chrislee's dislike of this treatment, since all three cubs sucked on the skin of our shoulders, elbows, hands, or fingers. Our skin suffered no damage from their lips, but it was sometimes scraped raw by the rasping of their incisors as they tried to induce milk flow. Alatanna was not amused at having to explain the source of her large red hickies.

I had also seen such non-nutritive sucking by moose calves that I raised and by hand-reared cattle calves. And, of course, children suck their thumbs or pacifiers. Baby mammals apparently have a need to suck which is separate from their need for food.

Although Jonjoanak did not want us petting or hugging her, she sucked on my skin as readily as the other cubs. When she heard one of them sucking, whether on the bottle or on us, she would hurry over with lowered head and gaping mouth to drive her rival away so that she could take his place. This was as close as Jon ever came to showing jealousy; but such behavior became increasingly common with her siblings. The more they sought our affection, the more they competed for it.

Like infant canids and felids, bear cubs "tread" while sucking; they put their forefeet up against the mother's teat and push alternately with their right and left forefeet. Moose and other hoofstock, by contrast, stimulate milk flow by butting the muzzle against the mother's udder. This is sometimes so forceful that I have seen a mother moose's hindquarters lifted a few inches, as though she were rising up onto the tips of her hooves. Treading and bunting both "massage" the mother's breast or udder to stimulate milk flow, by eliciting release of the hormone oxytocin from her brain. Oxytocin promotes contraction of smooth muscle in the breast, and is also involved in stimulating uterine contractions during labor. It reinforces the mother-infant bond.

Normally, our cubs kept their claws elevated while treading so that their claw tips did not dig into our skin. But when the rasp of a cub's incisors became painful and we tried to pull free, the cub sometimes gripped with her claws.

*   *   *

Initially, the only time a cub allowed us to pet her was while she was sucking on our skin or when her belly was so swollen that the youngster was pain. Then, light caresses on the tummy evoked contented purring. The vibrating *un-un-un-un-un-un* sound was almost identical to the purring of some raccoon kits, but very different from that of a cat.

*   *   *

All three cubs shared a number of peculiarities that I never could explain. Whenever I scratched a mosquito bite, rubbed on bug dope, or rubbed waterproofing mink oil into my leather pants, this seemed to spook the cubs, all of whom adopted defensive postures.

Much the same thing happened when they touched noses with me. Although they touched readily, each then spooked and withdrew defensively. Did I have *dragon–breath?* That was Alatanna's suggestion when she handed me a tube of Crest and a bottle of Listerine. But all that my use of these products accomplished was to intrigue the cubs with new odors. (If you don't want to be chewed on by bears, don't smell like food – for instance, by wearing citronella insect repellent that smells like ants, or fruity odors in perfume, laundry rinses, or shampoos.)

When I navigated around the cabin, the cubs sometimes ignored me, not even moving aside when I approached them, forcing me to step over them to pass. At other times, they did move, either languidly or suddenly, perhaps backing into a corner defensively. Occasionally, one would rear up, paws widespread as though prepared to fight; but her ears were not back against her skull and she did not blow or growl. However, she was clearly agitated, not inviting play. To my surprise, merely extending a hand toward the cub and allowing her to sniff my fingers would suffice to reassure her. The cub usually licked or mouthed my fingers gingerly – in contrast to the none-too-gentle bites that the cubs had delivered even a week earlier. Attempts to pet them were still rebuffed firmly, but more gently, one or both forepaws pushing my hand away *without* claw contact.

*   *   *

One night, after the cubs' play had awakened us repeatedly, we coaxed them outdoors with food, then blocked the door so that they could not return. This altered our relationship in ways I would never have anticipated.

The following morning, Jonjoanak and Chrislee were nearby, frustrated and irritated about being kept outside. Ontak was nowhere to be seen. Nor did he reappear all day. He had never been gone so long. By evening, we were frantic with worry. Alatanna and I began looking for him, calling frequently. His sisters followed warily at a distance.

After hours of searching, we finally heard distress-bawling in the distance. Following his cries, we fought our way over a steep ridge where the only passageway was an alder-choked ravine. Cresting the ridge, we pushed downhill through dense birch and spruce. With so much vegetation to mute his cries, it was a wonder that we heard Ontak at all from a quarter-mile away.

When we finally spotted him, he was on the ground, standing upright, watching us. Instead of approaching, he raced away to the base of a cottonwood, threatening with explosive woofs and pant-huffs as he pounded the base of the tree with his paws, one paw on each side of the trunk, much as a person might clap both hands against a tree.

Suddenly, Ontak raced up the tree, coming to rest amid a dense cluster of leafy branches. Afraid that we had frightened him, Alatanna and I retreated until we were out of sight. Trying to be patient, despite the clouds of mosquitoes and other insects flying into our eyes and crawling up our nostrils and ears, we waited for Ontak to descend. He clung to the tree, however, bawling forlornly. When spooked by us, he had never remained treed for more than ten or fifteen minutes. After half an hour, I began to suspect that something besides us was frightening the cub. But what?

A flash of gray gave the answer when a large hawk dive-bombed Ontak, as though trying to panic him into deserting his shelter. Was the hawk defending a nest or territory? Or was it planning to dine on our furry friend? Golden eagles sometimes dive-bomb a coyote, hitting it with such force that the canid's spine breaks. Did eagles or hawks use that or another tactic for killing a bear cub? I wasn't going to wait around to find out. When the hawk perched five yards from Ontak, watching the cub intently, I lifted my rifle and sighted in on the thick branch under the raptor. The heavy .338 slug hit the branch two yards from the bird, snapping the wood off completely. Concussion from the bullet must have shocked the raptor, which did not turn loose from the falling limb until it hit the ground. The hawk hopped away, regaining the ability to fly only several seconds later.

Even after the hawk was gone, Ontak remained cowed. Knowing how wary he was of us outdoors, we dared not approach. Instead, Alatanna and I retreated through the brush, and returned home – followed at a good distance by Jonjoanak and Chrislee. After we reached the cabin, both females remained agitated until Ontak raced over to join us, half an hour later – once again bold, brassy, and ravenous.

The greeting vocalization of bears has no obvious relationship to the greeting sounds of a canid. Yet both bears and canids greet by gently licking one-another's face or biting one-another's cheek or muzzle. Perhaps these greetings were   displayed by their common carnivore ancestor millions of years ago, whereas greeting vocalizations evolved after ursids split from canids.

When Ontak came to me, I imitated the greeting bite by gripping his muzzle or cheek hair in my hand and slowly shaking his head back and forth a few inches. He responded by gently biting my hand as though it were a muzzle. He then returned to his sisters and within a few minutes, all three cubs were racing around and sparring.

While waiting for Ontak, Alatanna cooked up a batch of oatmeal. That was usually my chore. We generally waited until the water was boiling before adding oats. This time, however, she added oats to the water while it was cold. More starch dissolved and the resulting cereal was a sticky paste. That was a mistake, since none of the cubs liked the oatmeal this way. They pawed at it and pulled it out of their bowls onto the floor, where they fought and rolled in it until they were coated with the stuff. I scraped what I could back into the bowls, then laced it with molasses, whereupon it disappeared under a blur of grumbling dark fur.

As the evening progressed, the cubs were noticeably less apprehensive and calmer than ever before. At their own initiative, they occasionally slept touching us. While awake, they allowed us to touch them and occasionally to pet them without threatening us, and sometimes without pushing our hands away. When Ontak and Chrislee did push, they were careful to avoid touching us with their claws. The only strong threat – a blow and swat – came after I let Jonjoanak touch noses with me. *Her* attitude, it seemed, had not changed.

She had the nasty habit of sneaking up on me and swatting or nipping me hard enough to bruise my skin and sometimes to draw blood. She seldom *assaulted* me while I was standing. When I was sitting, though – often with my chair placed so as to block the cubs from entering the kitchen – she sometimes approached with her ears back, lip puckered, and head low, tongue tip flicking in-out, and eyes *shifty*. Hissing and bawling, she would lunge forward and swat me. At other times, she seemed to invite me for rough play. When I responded playfully, she would accept, but bite much harder than the other cubs.

Over time, we became ever more adept at coping with mood changes by Ontak and Chrislee so as to maintain their trust and affection. When Jonjoanak got huffy, however, she often turned the other cubs against us, nullifying hours or days of effort to build trust and affection.

Clearly, their bond to us did not grow steadily as I had hoped, but through an up-and-down, two-steps-forward-and-one-back process which was wonderful one moment and terribly frustrating the next. Great patience was essential to achieve a lasting bond.

Eventually, though, our efforts paid off.

Chapter 7

TREATS, TOYS, AND TOOLS

TREATS

If cooked salmon was the cubs' favorite meat, watermelon was far and away their favorite fruit. Even the odor made them frantic with excitement. Their first experience with this succulent delight was scraps from our Fourth of July bash at Tony Zak's cabin.

It was nearly 2 A.M. before Alatanna and I got back to our own cabin. The Blue Mustang's bed was loaded with leftovers from the party which we thought the cubs might enjoy. That late at night, I had no intention of carrying in very much. But I did bring a plastic bag of watermelon scraps with plenty of sweet juicy red meat still attached to the green rinds.

Greatly underestimating how much this treat would be appreciated, I was stunned as one cub after the other grasped a couple of scraps in his mouth and dashed off into the bushes to eat. Moments later, the cub was back again for more. Twenty pounds of scraps disappeared in five minutes.

After this load of melon scraps was consumed, I haunted Safeway for more discarded fruit. One day I was given a perfectly ripe melon, around twenty-five pounds, which had been culled because it was cracked.

Hauling it home, I taped the crack and set the melon in the chill creek to cool. That evening, while the air temperature hovered in the 80s, and sweat dripped off us like summer rain, it was time for dessert. Because the melon was cracked only near one end, little of its succulent red meat was contaminated. I split off the bad section with a slash of a heavy knife. After saving a five-inch slab of luscious sweet heart meat for Alatanna and myself, I divided the rest of the melon among the cubs, much to their ecstatic delight.

Soon, only the greenest part of the rind was left by the cubs to rot – which it did within a couple of days, producing an odor that Alatanna said might have sickened a vulture. The cubs rolled vigorously in this, impregnating the foul stench into their fur so thoroughly that we refused to allow them into the cabin until they had been soaped in the creek while we all cooled off and romped.

For the next couple of days, piles of well-fertilized melon seeds were scattered around the cabin for hundreds of yards in all directions. If any of those seeds took root, the old homestead may still be a mecca for melon-loving bears.

When a cub ate watermelon, only the greenest part of the rind was left to rot.

TOYS

If Alaska gardens are known for any vegetable, it is cabbage. This is one of the few crops that truly thrives in the Land of the Midnight Sun. Forty-pound heads are common, and some cabbages exceed sixty pounds. The world record in 2009 was 127 pounds.

The first time that we brought a few small heads of cabbage home for our own cooking, the cubs were allowed to examine one of them. The cabbage apparently smelled good and leaves were pulled off and chewed. But there was no gusto in this response to compare with their greeting of watermelon. The little tykes could not decide whether to eat the cabbage or play with it. Soon, they did both.

This cabbage was the first "toy" we had ever given them that would roll. It was gentle Chrislee who figured out how to play soccer, dribbling the "ball" with both hands. Her initial swats were tentative, and the cabbage rolled only a few feet. Eventually she began swatting it harder and harder. Our yard of flattened grasses and herbs had long since been trampled into dust, allowing the head to roll freely.

In theory, the cabbage could have traveled up to fifty feet before being trapped in vegetation. But theory did not take into account two "intervening variables" in the form of Ontak and Jonjoanak. Both stood bipedally with head high, ears forward, and chin tucked in slightly, interested but cautious. Then, as curiosity won out, Jonjoanak took temporary control of the game.

Approaching with apprehensive aggression, marked by her stiff gait and slightly lowered head, Jonjoanak displaced Chrislee and tentatively patted the cabbage, then jumped back and pant-huffed nervously when the head rolled several feet. Stalking toward it again, with her face nearly vertical and her nose close to the ground, Jonjoanak made a short *hop-charge*, ending as her hands caught the cabbage from both sides with powerful slaps. Instantly, she leapt back, as though to gauge the effects of her sally on her vegetable opponent, before attacking again.

Jon's aggression toward the cabbage made the other two cubs more wary, and now all three approached it cautiously. It was Chrislee who next reached out tentatively and gave the head a pat, causing it to roll a few inches. Ontak abandoned all caution, barged forward, and pounced, knocking the cabbage a dozen feet back toward Alatanna – an occasional rugby player. Laughing gaily, she stepped forward and kicked the cabbage back toward the cubs, who scattered like ninepins in the path of a bowling ball. As the cabbage passed them, all three cubs leapt in pursuit, and exploded into a free-for-all that had less to do with playing "soccer" than with battling for who would play.

As usual in contests of this sort, Jonjoanak dominated. Yet she quickly lost interest, as did Ontak. This was normal. Although the black bear cubs raised by Bob Leslie had favorite toys with which they played day after day over weeks or months,[1] our cubs did not. They played intensively with new toys – usually sticks they had found themselves – but were soon bored and on the lookout for something novel – all too often selecting one of our belongings, such as a piece of clothing or my backpack.

They loved sticking their heads into things, even paper bags and clothing. It was incredibly entertaining to watch Ontak push his head into a leg of my jeans or into an arm of a shirt, then walk or charge around blindly, running into walls or furniture or trees, tripping and shaking his head so that the clothing leg or arm whipped around like a flaccid elephant's trunk. Although he was usually able to get free of the clothing easily enough, now and then his head got stuck. Frustration would soon turn into anger as he battled for freedom, and it was all I could do to quit laughing and hold onto the clothing to pull him free without getting clawed in the process. Yet despite the apparent trauma, he got stuck so often that it may have been a weird kind of game that he was determined to "win."

Each of the cubs also enjoyed rolling around on our clothing and wrapping themselves up in the item, then suddenly seeming to panic and ripping free. Time and again, they tried to reach and tear apart our sleeping bags and mosquito netting. Had we ever forgotten to hang these in the rafters out of reach, they would have been trashed within a minute. Gordon Burghardt's cubs Kit and Kate were just as hard on his household – not an old and crude trapper's line cabin, but a fine suburban home.

That Chrislee paid more attention than her siblings to the cabbage is perhaps not surprising, since she usually spent more time in object play. This seems typical for any bear that lacks a willing playmate, whether the bear is a social subordinate like Chrislee whose invitations are rebuffed, a singlet cub without siblings, or an older bear no longer associated with her family or friends.

Gordon Burghardt's subordinate cub Kit likewise played with "toys" more than her dominant sister Kate. Gordon states that "a favorite pastime was to lie flat on their backs, stretch out their legs, and pull down branches, twigs, or leaves from low-growing shrubs with their paws and bring these into their mouth. These they would alternately chew, rub, or even 'tickle' themselves with."[2] Our cubs did all of these things and many more, including holding a stick with both paws and rubbing or scratching it against their head, neck and various parts of the torso.

Leaving the cabbage to Chrislee, her siblings wandered off, first to check whether we had any better treats to offer, and then to other pursuits. Chrislee's approach to the cabbage was interesting. It seemed to fascinate her. She hopped toward it, lifting her upper body slightly, then slapping toward the cabbage without quite touching it, as her head tilted sideways and bobbed toward the ground momentarily. I had seen the cubs "phantom–fighting" with one another in just this fashion, before playful contact was actually made. I couldn't be sure, however, whether she was treating the cabbage as though it were another cub or like prey.

This was perhaps fundamentally similar to the way that the play of a kitten is patterned after either fighting with other cats or capturing prey. I well recall meeting the great felid ethologist Paul Leyhausen, and watching his films of cats hunting birds and of kittens using similar movements to capture toys dangled on the end of a string. Movements used by adults to catch mice or rabbits were employed by kittens to capture toys that rolled across the ground or were pulled by a string.[3]

As best I could tell, predation behavior plays a much smaller role in play by black and grizzly bear cubs, which is perhaps appropriate since they are much less predaceous than felids. Although polar bears eat mostly mammalian prey, the only hint I have seen that polar bears play more predaceously than grizzly or black bears is that polar cubs *may* be more inclined to throw large objects, just as they appear more inclined to swim and dive underwater. This greater preference for water sport seems to be instinctive, even though polar bears began evolving from grizzly bears less than 500,000 years ago – just yesterday on an evolutionary time scale.

Chrislee's play now took a new turn. She sat down and lifted the cabbage between both hands and began to chew on it. After pulling a few leaves loose with her incisors, she dropped the head, which rolled downhill away from her. For a few moments, she sat there watching the cabbage, ears cocked forward, mouth open, with the most marvelous expression of excitement. Even the cabbage leaves hanging from one canine tooth did nothing to dispel my impression that she was concentrating intensely. Using her right hand to pull the stray leaves from her mouth, without losing sight of the cabbage, Chrislee walked over to the vegetable. Again she sat. But she did not bite; she simply dropped the head and watched it roll. On her third try, she did not just drop the cabbage, but threw it down. Then a fourth time, and the cabbage flew several feet before it hit and rolled much farther than before. Again and again, Chrislee lifted the cabbage, eventually standing on her hind feet and lofting the head more than ten feet.

TOOLS

At the time, I did not see any particular significance to the way Chrislee threw the cabbage, aside from my strong impression that she had studied the effects of her actions quite carefully and refined them deliberately to be more effective. Nor was I especially impressed years later when I saw captive black bear cubs throwing bowling balls and zoo polar bears throwing aluminum beer kegs.

It was anthropologist/naturalist Richard Nelson who first awakened me to the hidden wonder of this behavior.[3] Eskimo companions from the Arctic coast of Alaska had shown him wild polar bears hunting walrus pups by pelting them with large chunks of ice. Pups were attacked this way when they were surrounded by a protective wall of adults whose powerful bodies and massive tusks were too formidable even for a polar bear. Once the adults moved on, abandoning a wounded pup, it was easy prey.

The only time I have ever personally witnessed "tool" use is when Ontak pounded our porch roof to amplify his threats, or when a bear lifted a stick or pulled down a tree branch and used it to scratch her head, back, or neck. A rock will sometimes be picked up and used the same way. I have never seen or heard of a bear manufacturing a tool, by contrast to chimpanzees who strip leaves off twigs to shape the twigs for catching termites. Chimps also chew leaves so that the leaves can serve as a sponge to extract water from holes that the chimp could not otherwise reach. For many years, these were the only examples of tool use by bears of which I was aware. Indeed, throwing objects is the only confirmed kind that ethologist Ben Beck reported in his book on animal tool use.[5] But those examples are far less impressive than one related to me by wildlife trainer Doug Seus.

For many years, the world's most famous bear was Doug's Kodiak bear Bart, star of numerous movies, including *Clan of the Cave Bear, The Bear,* and *The Edge.* Recognizing the animal's long and successful career, one might think that Bart was especially bright by bear standards. Not so. According to Doug, Bart was considerably less intelligent than some of his other bears; Bart seemed to him to be as bright as a chimpanzee or a gorilla. Not only did Bart learn many movie stunts in a single trial, but he seemed to think things out now and then.

Doug told me of walking with Bart along a ravine on his Utah property. A flash–flood had recently roared down the arroyo, depositing there a large hawthorn tree. Among the tree's thorny branches was a Coke can that attracted Bart's interest. He tried to reach the can, but desisted after being pricked by the long, sharp thorns. Bart sat and stared at the can; then he looked around. Again, he stared at the can, then looked around. After a few repeats, Bart focused on a 2×12 plank lying a short distance downstream. Bart's gaze shifted back and forth between can and plank a few times before the 1,500–pound Kodiak brown bear walked over to the plank. Flipping it end over end a few times, he moved the plank into position so that it fell across the hawthorn branches. Bart walked out on the plank, captured the Coke can in his teeth, then backed off the plank and walked away with his prize. Doug swears that this is a true story, and I have no reason to doubt its accuracy.

PART II

PREPARING FOR INDEPENDENCE

July–September

Chapter 8

EXPLORATION & SOCIALIZATION

One of my first tasks after adopting the cubs was to explore the land surrounding our cabin to discover its sources of prime bear foods and its hazards. While Alatanna earned our living at the café, I hiked for several hours each day – an extremely welcome break from the endless tedium of paperwork at the office.

Initially, when I was just beginning to win the cubs' trust, they fled whenever they saw me outdoors. Although they would not hike with me, I caught glimpses of them so often over the course of a day that they clearly were making an effort to stay in distant contact; not what I had hoped for, but a step in the right direction.

I began by exploring the area systematically. I penciled a grid across my none-too-accurate U.S. Geological Survey topographic map so that I could explore it section by section and document what I found in each section. Identifying locations of major food sources even roughly required following precise compass bearings and counting my steps rigorously to measure distance.

Although it was still too early in the season for fruit to ripen, many berry-producing plants were already revealed by their blossoms. Elderberry bushes up to fifteen feet tall were easily spotted from afar by their fist-sized clusters of yellowish-white blossoms. Mountain ash trees could be identified the same way. Far rarer, and found only in sunny areas with disturbed soils, were thimbleberry and salmonberry, both of which have purple blossoms a few inches wide. Every such source of fruit was mapped diligently, as were sources of forbs (herbs) like skunk cabbage.

Every such source of fruit was mapped diligently, as were sources of forbs (herbs) like skunk cabbage.

Skunk cabbage is one of the most abundant and obvious of all Alaskan forbs, if only because so much of the country provides the kinds of wetland habitat in which it thrives. Like a commercial cabbage, its leaves grow directly out of the root with no obvious stem. Initially, the leaves are bright yellow. Soon, though, all but one small leaf turns dark green as they grow to three feet or more in length and a foot in width. The plant's only stalk, about one inch thick and up to one foot long, does not support leaves, just a conical seedhead–which is commonly preyed on by tiny black narrow-bodied beetles.

I had read turn-of-the-century writings by Wm.. H. Wright and Enos Mills which described heavy foraging by bears on skunk cabbage; but it was not entirely clear what parts of the plant bears consumed. I found several references to bears consuming the seedhead or digging and eating the root, but no unambiguous reference to bears eating the leaves, whether in the yellow or green stage.[1] Although I glanced over thousands of these plants in the course of many days, and occasionally found signs of moose browsing on them, I initially found no evidence of bears doing so.

The beauty of yellow and dark–green skunk cabbage growing in wetlands was often offset by the growth of young fireweed with its scarlet stalks and bright green leaves. Soon, these plants would sport columns of lavender or pink blossoms cloaking entire mountain slopes.

As the cubs gradually gained enough trust to join my hikes, I was so delighted that I let them lead wherever they wanted. After a few days, however, when the cubs kept traveling through the same general areas repeatedly, I realized that we could easily end up concentrating on areas close to the cabin and missing out on other areas with vital resources. I therefore tried to lead them across the landscape systematically, to introduce them to many other potential food sources which I had discovered during my recent surveys.

This proved impossible. I had expected the cubs to follow me as they would have followed their mother, wherever she led. But except when anxiety kept them glued to me, what the cubs usually followed was their own interests. As much as the orphans and I came to enjoy one another's company, they were far less dependent on me for security than they would have been on their mother. That is, they were almost as independent as typical yearlings, perhaps because they had spent so much time foraging on their own during the first weeks after Doddy's death. I intended to keep fostering this independence in case the Fish & Game Department denied me a permit to move them to a more remote and safer area. The cubs had to achieve self-sufficiency as quickly as possible.

All such considerations aside, their precocious independence was a nuisance when I was trying to help them learn vital information. They were no more attentive than human children. They were either dashing off in the "wrong" directions or spending hours at favored feeding sites, unwilling to move on to accommodate my agenda.

Finally, it occurred to me that the way the cubs were getting to know their domain now might also be how they would relate to it in the future. Instead of trying to learn it "scientifically," I needed to learn it through the "eyes" of a bear. This is exactly what my Native friend QuisQuiNee had been trying to drum into me through his instructions in *walking as a bear*. I had made progress in that and other Native ways of *knowing* nature. But I had never been able to really abandon my Western cultural background. Indeed, I didn't really want to; there were already enough people who excelled at seeing nature from just one of those perspectives. (My goal was to see nature from both perspectives, *biculturally* – a story best left for my book *Becoming Bear*.)

TRAVEL ROUTES AND CONCEALMENT

The cubs usually preferred traveling on game trails or along waterways; and they tended to choose the route of least effort, avoiding steep slopes and rock slides. The cubs also traveled ridgelines, possibly because this enabled them to view broad vistas while remaining in cover.

Although they avoided brush so dense that they had to force their way through, they had no hesitation about weaving among shrubs and saplings the trunks of which were separated by a foot or so – routes where I had great difficulty following them. The worst trees, by far, were the slide alder with trunks that curved along the ground before bending skywards. It was sheer hell to spend a day following the cubs among interwoven trunks of alder, willow, and devil's–club as they foraged on devil's–club berries, lowbush cranberry, and succulent forbs.

In many cases, these and other small deciduous trees and shrubs were not only almost impenetrable along each side of a trail, but their canopies closed over the trail, turning it into a dark tunnel. Since these tunnels had been created by the passage of bears and other four-footed animals, they were seldom higher than three or four feet. In some, I could walk hunched over; but in many, I had to crawl on my hands and knees. Without knee pads, crawling over sharp-edged rocks and rough roots was simply too painful, and the tendon sheath on each kneecap quickly became inflamed. Thereafter, even with kneepads, my ability to crawl after the cubs was badly curtailed.

Even at the best of times, my ability to follow the cubs through brush was so limited that they became frustrated by my slow progress. Eventually, they seemed to grasp the situation and joined me in reaching a workable compromise. When they wanted to forage or explore in areas where I could not or would not follow, they either stayed within hearing distance most of the time, or one or more of the cubs joined me every half-hour or so for at least a brief hug and scratch. A cub typically greeted me by nuzzling my hand, lightly biting it, or using its incisors to nibble on my hand or thigh.

Dense cover served the cubs in two ways. First, it provided visual and auditory concealment from potential enemies. Second, darkness seemed to make them feel more secure – here, just as in the cabin. One sign of their greater security was that they fed more single-mindedly, without peering around as often or for as long.

Their preference for cover was accentuated when they were nervous; for instance, after they detected another person in the area. The first few times this happened, I had no idea what was bothering the cubs. Then I spotted boot prints on a trail they had suddenly abandoned, and began to understand. Although Fish & Game had predicted that the cubs would approach anyone they encountered to get food, in fact the only people the cubs approached were Alatanna and me.

I did my best to accentuate the cubs' wariness of strangers. On one hand, I didn't want them so afraid that they would lash out and swat or bite a stranger who surprised them at close range. On the other hand, I didn't want them to ever approach anyone else, even to beg for affection, much less to demand food.

Our only frequent visitor was Zak, and the cubs seldom let him approach within fifty yards. On only a few occasions did they approach him closely – occasions when he brought Limburger cheese that smelled to me like rotting meat. Tony was not only determined to keep that cheese for himself and Alatanna, but he understood the need to never feed the cubs.

As soon as they started pestering him, he chased them off. Naturally enough, they ran up the nearest large tree, which wasn't good enough. At my urging, Tony kept throwing rocks at the cubs every now and then in an effort to convince them that tree refuges aren't completely safe from a person, in hopes that they would learn to flee along the ground until far from any potential hunter.

Likewise, whenever we knew a visitor was coming, I led the cubs at least a few hundred yards away from the cabin and treed them – then chased them back aloft if they crept down before the visitor left.

The Salvation Army gave me old shoes which had been donated in too poor a condition to sell. Occasionally, I dragged a few shoes at the end of a long rope, to leave a scent trail, then let the cubs happen across the trail on our next foraging hike to expose them to the odors of strangers. These scents invariably alarmed them, which I reinforced by woofing, pant-huffing, and imitating jaw pops with hand-claps – whereupon I raced away, huffing, gulping, and calling their names to get the cubs to flee with me. This seemed to markedly increase their skittishness toward any people but ourselves.

When we were among climbable trees, it was to these that they usually fled if disturbed. Otherwise, they disappeared into the brush and occasionally would not come out for an hour or more.

The cause of their skittishness was often obscure – probably an odor I could not detect. But on occasions that I could discern causality, different sources seemed to determine whether they sought refuge by diving into brush, climbing a tree, or clustering around me. They were always excited when we happened upon fresh carnivore scat or a tree (usually spruce) on which another bear had recently urinated and rubbed its head and back – as evidenced both by odor and hairs snagged on the bark. Some of these sites were also scent-marked by my cubs through rubbing their head and body on the tree or urinating on it or nearby.

Signs from another bear often caused Ontak and his sisters to cluster at my feet until they were sure the other bear was gone; then they typically stalked around investigating with heads held low and legs stiffened. The actual presence of another bear either sent them racing up a tree or gathering at my feet.

The first time that we ran headlong into another bear family, the sow – whom I called JeenTo – stood upright, watching me nervously as she seemed to search for the mother of Ontak and his sisters. Perhaps I was anthropomorphizing, but she seemed confused by the cubs grouping around me, rather than around a mother bear. Given that this sow's home range presumably overlapped Doddy's, JeenTo had probably known Doddy and may have even been close kin. That she would have recognized Doddy's cubs as such was more iffy. Yet she showed no aggression against them when they hesitantly mingled with her own triplets – whereupon I couldn't tell by sight which cubs were hers and which were mine.

JeenTo's tolerance was in marked contrast to grizzly sows I've watched that had little tolerance for litters mixing together. In one extreme case, observed by Adolph Murie in Mt. McKinley (Denali) National Park, one grizzly sow killed the cubs of another sow. [2]

My cub's obvious attachment for me may also explain why JeenTo didn't flee with her offspring, despite her nervousness. Although she finally dropped to all fours and tried to lead her youngsters away, they were too engrossed in playing with my cubs to pay heed. So JeenTo remained, feeding intermittently as she kept close watch on all six cubs and on me. It finally occurred to me to sit down, and then to lay on my belly facing her – ways in which a fellow bear would signal peaceful intent – JeenTo soon relaxed and eventually paid me little obvious heed. She was a beautiful animal with short sleek fur from which all of the previous year's coat had already been shed. Her muzzle was covered with platinum–blonde fur maybe an eighth of an inch long, and her chest sported a small white patch that looked something like a four-pointed star.

As happens so often among cubs, the play bout ended when one of the youngsters got too rough, which made its partners angry. Again, JeenTo grunted and gulped to call her cubs away, and this time they followed – with my cubs in tow. When I tried to tag along, JeenTo and her cubs fled in alarm, which spooked Ontak and his sisters into following them. At that point, my feelings were mixed. On the one hand, it would have been wonderful for Ontak and his sisters to be adopted, ending all worry that Fish & Game would demand that they be killed. On the other hand, Alatanna and I would miss them deeply. I dreaded arriving home and having to explain that our youngsters were gone.

For better or worse, my worries were for naught. Jonjoanak and her siblings tracked me down within the hour, still keenly excited by what may have been their first encounter with other cubs.

Our next encounter was less benign. The cubs backtracked another bear to an abandoned homestead with several crabapple trees that were heavy with fruit. Chrislee and Ontak climbed into the branches to feed after Jonjoanak usurped all fruit that had already fallen to the ground. Sometime later, Ontak woofed. Following the line of his gaze, I spotted a lone yearling – whom I called KeeSaw – in another tree perhaps fifty yards away. This was a birch which the animal had apparently climbed to look us over. Although nervous about our presence, the lure of crabapples dominated, and KeeSaw finally approached slowly and apprehensively, puckering her upper lip but without any hint of threat. I remained still to keep from further frightening the youngster. Since there was no evidence of another bear with KeeSaw, I could only surmise that the little sow had been weaned a month or so earlier when her mother came into heat and bred again. Although my cubs had readily played with JeenTo's lilttle ones, they converged on KeeSaw with more than a hint of aggression. Suddenly all four youngsters were embroiled in a fight. Even though KeeSaw was twice the size of my cubs, three of them were too much for her, and she bounded away with them in hot pursuit. My attempts to recall my cubs were futile as they disappeared from sight, not returning for more than thirty minutes. That evening, KeeSaw reappeared and gradually approached the crabapple tree. This time, Ontak and his sisters did nothing more than bristle at her and stalk around stiffly for awhile, without intense threats, much less combat. Whether the initial fight with KeeSaw had settled her subordinance to my trio, or whether my cubs were now too satiated to defend this food source, I never knew. Soon, KeeSaw was play-fighting with Chrislee, who was always eager for a friendly tussle.

Whenever Chrislee was hurt or frightened by KeeSaw, her anger drew support from her siblings. This consisted only of group threats, without attack. By the time my cubs were satiated and ready to accompany me back to the cabin, KeeSaw was still eating her fill.

We had gone no more than a hundred yards when I heard jaw-popping behind us and looked back to see an adolescent boar, whom I called QuiLog, approaching the crab apple tree. He must have been there for awhile, waiting until my cubs and I left before daring to share in the feast. Perhaps KeeSaw had not seen QuiLog until he was near the tree; or perhaps she was just too stubborn to leave. In any event, by the time KeeSaw did jump down to flee, QuiLog charged after her and swatted her on the hindquarters, bowling her over, then began biting toward her throat. KeeSaw fended off his claws and jaws by batting them away with her own hands, whereupon QuiLog bit her right hand. This mode of defense probably explains why I have seen combat produce more hand injuries than any other kind.

Finally breaking loose, KeeSaw sprinted away to the nearest large cottonwood, then raced toward the top. This escape tactic would have worked fine against moose, wolves, or even grizzly bears. But it was little use against QuiLog, who raced after her. KeeSaw momentarily stopped on a thick, nearly horizontal branch and sat down, straddling the branch with both hindfeet dangling over the sides. Before she could escape, QuiLog caught up with her, snagged one foot with his claws, then bit into her heel. Only then, with loud angry vocalizations by both bears did QuiLog retreat down the tree, leaving a very chastened yearling in his wake.

Although I have seen a few "wild" bears with bloody wounds from similar bites to the hand, hindfoot, ankle, or calf, none of my cubs ever bit each other hard enough to draw blood.

Ben Kilham reports that heel bites are common among black bears in New Hampshire. These "message bites" serve primarily to drive home the message of dominance. That certainly fits what I have seen, whether the "victim" is a bear or a person, and the "aggressor" is a black or a grizzly bear, for the amount of damage done is minor compared to what could be done. That most people survive being mauled by a bear suggests that their wounds derive from "message" bites rather from failed attempts to kill them.

A few times when another bear actually approached and threatened us, the cubs seemed to panic and actually climbed *me*–something cubs occasionally do to a mother bear. As painful as it was to be climbed when the cubs were but twenty-five pounds apiece, it was overwhelming by the time they reached forty pounds. Their claws were not sharp enough to penetrate my heavy leather clothing, but where their claw tips reached skin, they did occasionally draw blood. Much as I would have liked to simply push them away, their fear was so intense that they would not have understood being rebuffed. Maintaining their trust depended, I was sure, on providing whatever security they sought, however painful that was for me.

When I was alone, being faced with an "angry" bear at close range initially scared me so much that I dared not respond aggressively. All that changed when I was with Alatanna or the cubs. Being responsible for their safety – much as if they had been human children – gave me great courage, and I faced the aggressor with absolute self-assurance. Walking toward the animal, with my eyes locked onto him, usually sufficed to drive him away. When that failed, I escalated my threats by sometimes clapping my hands together and yelling explosively in the deep tones of a growl or roar. As a last resort, I charged.

Only twice since that time have I encountered a black bear which I did not dare intimidate this way. One was a giant boar whom I called Mallic. I happened upon him as he was eating another bear, less than a hundred feet from me. When the cannibal turned his attention toward me and approached, I jumped back into my pickup and fled. The second boar, whom I called Malgor, was equally heavy (about 500 pounds), but smaller in stature. Yet he too carried a palpable sense of menace that chilled me. I never saw him attack, much less kill, another bear. But he was highly domineering. He seemed to relish forcing other bears to signal submissiveness, usually by fleeing.

There were no bears with the temperament of either Mallic or Malgor in the area where I raised the cubs. Even QuiLog lost his nerve whenever the cubs and I stalked toward him. So the biggest challenge I faced was not intimidating resident bears but limiting my intimidation enough to keep these neighbors from avoiding us entirely. Although I recognized a need to establish the cubs' "right" to their home range, and to limit competition by other bears for scarce foods, I also knew that socializing my cubs would be essential to their eventual ability to survive independently. Whenever possible, therefore, I brought them into contact with JeenTo and her youngsters, KeeSaw, and other bears, in hopes that my cubs would learn to live with these fellows with some degree of harmony, while also learning how to win struggles for social rank, and to recognize which opponents were too large to challenge.

*   *   *

Helping Jonjoanak and her siblings establish themselves socially was only one of the challenges I faced as their "bearent. I also had to guide their learning about foraging for plants, catching fish, and hunting for terrestrial prey.

Chapter 9
FORAGING

BLUEBERRY BANQUET

I began by introducing the cubs to major plant food sources, starting with the largest berry patch in the region. This was on a recently cleared homestead belonging to Harry, one of Zak's longtime drinking buddies. More than twenty acres of his property were covered with highly productive blueberry bushes.

The mild spring that year, followed by plenty of rain interspersed with abundant sunlight, had combined to produce an enormous crop of blueberries, many of them as large and as succulent as green grapes. I harvested almost a gallon per hour by hand, while Alatanna harvested at several times that rate using a "picker" – a metal scoop with one lip lined by three-inch teeth at quarter-inch intervals. As we picked gallon after gallon of berries to fill the plastic bags in our backpacks, the cubs filled their tummies.

Once our packs were full of berries, Alatanna and I were anxious to get back to the cabin. Mosquitos and other biting insects were especially prevalent among the blueberry bushes, where the underlying duff was thick and spongy wet. We were desperate for relief from the bugs and eager to get home to clean the berries so they could be hauled to Zak's cabin and stored in his freezer. Although Alatanna promised to bake a pie that weekend, we would wait until the cool weather of fall to make jams and jellies.

There are few animals more single-minded than a hungry bear at a feast. Even when they were so full that their tummies were drum-taut, the cubs refused to leave. When they could eat no more, they played, slept, then played again, wrestling and racing around for an hour, as joyful and fun-loving as puppies and small children.

I found a squirrel-gnawed moose antler spike about a foot long and an inch in diameter. I tossed it out in front of Ontak, much as I often tossed sticks. He was the only one of the cubs who ever retrieved something back to me to be thrown again. Ontak gripped the antler in his teeth and raced around for a few minutes, pursued by his sisters. When they veered off to tussle with each other, Ontak lay down with the antler and chewed on it, rubbed it over his head, neck and torso, or lay on his back and juggled it on the soles of all four feet. Awhile later, Chrislee wandered over, sniffed the antler, then gingerly reached forward with one paw and pulled it to herself. Ontak watched with more interest or curiosity than defensiveness. Meeting no resistance, Chrislee grasped the antler in her jaws and wandered off with the toy. Several minutes later, Ontak stole it back. Chrislee reciprocated. Then Jonjoanak took a turn. These exchanges of the antler were so low key that it was hard to think of this as a form of play. Yet but for pace, it was not fundamentally different than the keep-away in which dogs engage. Otherwise, why keep stealing this toy back and forth rather than each cub finding one for himself? The only thing special about the antler was its novelty. When the cubs resumed the game a few hours later, a stick was chosen.

I rarely saw the same object used regularly as a favored toy – except in the case of our clothing and some personal items. When one of my

Lowe hiking boots was taken by Jonjoanak and I chased after her to retrieve it, she fled into the surrounding forest and a week passed before I found it again, and then only after the tongue had been badly damaged by a salt-hungry red squirrel or vole. Eventually, I learned the hard way to play according to bear rules. For instance, when Ontak took Alatanna's favorite hairbrush, I waited several minutes before approaching gently, whereupon he allowed me to recover the brush virtually undamaged. When he later tried to retrieve the hairbrush, Alatanna distracted him with a handful of raisins, and he was content.

On that first day in the blueberry patch, play was followed by eating more blueberries for another couple of hours, followed by another nap – a cycle they repeated twice more before finally calling it a day around 7 p.m. By that time, Alatanna and I were both covered with insect bites and as cranky as Jonjoanak.

Back at the cabin that evening, we faced the chore of separating berries from leaves. Although berries come off of branches more easily than leaves do, neither we nor the cubs could avoid accumulating a large number of leaves with our berries. Whereas the cubs swallowed the leaves, from which they may have extracted nutrition, we were more finicky.

With the mischievous cubs so full of berries that they could barely waddle, we were for once able to work on food outdoors without being harassed for tidbits and play.

To separate the berries from the leaves, Alatanna laid a three-foot square of dampened polyethylene plastic on the table, scattered berries across its top edge, then lifted that edge slowly. The berries rolled down into the bucket which I held, while the leaves tended to stick to the plastic. Drawing from a bucket of precious water hauled from the creek, I washed the plastic free of leaves. The process was repeated twice more, until there were so few leaves among the berries that it was easiest to pick the rest out by hand. Then on to the next batch of berries; and the next, for hours.

As we worked, we were entranced by the night sky. So far north and so close to the summer solstice, the sun set only briefly. It did not cross the sky directly from east to west, as at lower latitudes. Instead, it circled the sky, like a ball circles your head if it is held by a string and whirled by your hand – rising from the east, high to its zenith in the south, then sinking to the northwest and beyond. Each evening, as the sun dipped out of sight below the northwestern horizon, it produced a celestial firestorm that blazed for an hour.

When we had started separating berries and leaves around 9 P.M., thin layers of cirrus cloud had spread across the sky, like Alatanna's long tresses blowing in the wind. The bottoms of the clouds had been as golden as her hair, while the upper strands of cloud were more platinum. Later, they had shifted slowly into honey and then peach, which deepened into orange while I was sorting berries. Now, shortly before midnight, we stood enthralled as the heavens transformed around us. Just above the hills north of us, the clouds turned blood–orange. They became glowing embers that gradually darkened into cinders and charcoal.

So far, the sunset had been much like those seen elsewhere in the world, just prolonged several-fold. The real difference only now became apparent. So close to the Arctic Circle, sunset merges into sunrise during late June. Instead of burning out, the ember clouds burst into flame again, burning ever hotter from red back into burnt orange, peach, gold, and finally platinum. The sun did not die each night, to be reborn each dawn like the proverbial phoenix. Rather, it was a firebird that glided down to the horizon like an osprey swooping to the surface of the sea to snatch a herring; then it rose again into the heavens, blazing in glory.

*   *   *

At first, I was delighted that Harry's land provided such a rich food source for the cubs. But over the days that followed, when the cubs refused to forage any place but the blueberry patch, I began to worry. Their dung, stained green from berry juice, was filled with unbroken berries, and I was unaware then that a bear's digestive system can extract sugar and other nutrients through a berry's skin. I was afraid that they were getting little benefit from eating berries and pondered how to teach them to chew their food. (In my imagination, I could almost hear my mother in the background, decades before, telling *me* to chew my own supper thoroughly.)

More important, Harry would soon be planting commercial crops on his land, destroying this berry patch. Although the cubs would eventually find other good patches, no major berry crop lasted more than a month or two, and there would be many years when the crop would fail. To thrive, a bear must learn about many sources of each food and many different kinds of food.

Although I had no luck trying to lure the cubs away from Harry's blueberry fields, Ontak and his sisters eventually lost interest of their own accord; this happened after three days of heavy rain and wind knocked most of the berries off the bushes. Although there were still millions of berries available to the cubs, these were distributed so sparsely that the cubs' rate of harvest had plummeted. Just as it now took me almost two hours to pick a quart, an eightfold decline, the cubs' intake was so slow that they finally lost interest and joined me in looking for richer pickings.

HABITAT CARRYING CAPACITY

This incident taught me two important lessons in ecology. First, a given food may be little utilized unless its abundance exceeds some minimum threshold. Second, the conventional concept of "carrying capacity," which I had learned about in college, was greatly oversimplified. The "carrying capacity" of land for a species – the number of individuals of the species it can support per 1,000 acres – was supposedly governed solely by the amount of food present. In reality, other factors also play a major role. In my first scientific publication on bear ecology, I thus distinguished the conventional concept as *potential* carrying capacity. By contrast, *realized* carrying capacity depends not just on the total amount of food available, but also on how efficiently it can be harvested, which in turn depends on how concentrated the food is in time and space. Moreover, just because food is present does not mean that it is *accessible*. As salmon swim up a stream, there are typically areas where the fish are readily caught and areas where they are safe. Even if two streams have equal numbers of salmon, the fish might be easily caught in a slow stream with water under six inches deep but not in a fast stream with water over two feet deep. Bears at the former stream might be much better fed than those in the latter.

Knowledge is also a big factor. Unless bears know where and when each food is available, and how to harvest it efficiently, it adds little to the *realized* carrying capacity of their habitat. This is obvious to anyone who has watched young bears trying and failing to catch salmon, missing a hundred times for every success, whereas some adults succeed every few attempts.

Bears also differ in the methods they use to eat salmon. In some habitats, bears first strip off the salmon's fat-rich skin, consume that, then begin eating the meat. A salmon is most readily skinned by holding its head with one hand, then gripping skin with the other hand and pulling backwards. In other habitats, where the head is eaten first, there is no part of the body that a bear can hook with its claws to anchor the salmon in place so that the skin can be pulled off. So the salmon's head may be the only part of the prey eaten, vastly reducing the amount of food and nutrients consumed per salmon caught.

Consequently, even if potential carrying capacity were solely a property of the total amount of food present, the amount of food actually eaten by bears would also depend on accessibility, efficiency, knowledge, and other factors inherent to the animals. The same logic applies to any other limiting resource such as water or space.

Accessibility problems might limit realized carrying capacity for any species, but the gap between potential vs. realized carrying capacity may be especially great for animals like bears, whose foraging efficiency depends heavily on learning.

Suppose that during droughts, or after late spring freezes, the only food-rich habitats available to bears are ones which are utilized by few bears during normal years. Suppose too that ten or fifteen years have passed since the last famine. Which bears would be likely to know where to forage under each set of conditions? Mainly those old enough to have coped with the last famine? That would be my guess.

When people kill off the older adults, they might also be eliminating a significant portion of the population's knowledge about how to cope with unusual conditions, and thus impairing the ability of many bears to thrive even during famine. Granted, even bears ignorant of these refuge food sources might eventually discover them; but probably not as quickly as if they could simply follow the trails of more experienced bears. Meanwhile, the ignorant bears could end up raiding garbage cans or even homes.

There is little doubt but that harvesting bears, and reducing mean ages of survivors could thus decrease realized carrying capacity and thereby increase the incidence of marauding. But, there is no way yet to predict how severe this effect would be in any given circumstance. That is something only research can reveal. Unfortunately, asking politically incorrect questions generates backlash than research grants or permits.

DIETARY VARIETY AND BALANCE

We found countless small patches of blueberries, lingonberries, and other more scattered fruit such as watermelon-berries and raspberries. I was particularly happy to find many patches of wild roses, since their sweet "hips" would be one of the last foods to remain available when snow covered the land – a final source of nourishment before the cubs entered hibernation a few months hence.

Mountain ash and red elderberry trees, which likewise retain fruit through early winter, were also common, though scattered. When Jonjoanak first spotted a tree loaded with bright–orange mountain ash (rowan) berries, she gripped the tree's five-inch trunk with her hands and was up among its branches within seconds, gingerly walking out along a horizontal limb. Reaching up with one hand, she gripped a high branch, the ends of which supported several clusters of berries. Using the upper branch for balance, she rose to stand on her hind feet, then walked out further from the trunk until she could reach a cluster of berries. Jonjoanak pulled it down to her mouth and tasted the fruit, whereupon she spit it out while shaking her head violently a few times. Yuck! Releasing the branch, she jumped to the ground. Sampling one berry myself, I found it terribly bitter. Elderberries were no better at that time of year. But both species supposedly become more palatable after they have been frost-bitten in early winter.

Mountain ash

Adult male black bear and red elderberry

It is these thorns that give Devil's club its name. Although this plant is a relative of gensing and its root is used for medicinal purposes by humans, I don't know of bears eating anything but its new leaves (left) and its fruit. Mature leaves are more than 1 foot in diameter.

In some areas where I have worked, bears have fed heavily from one or both of these species during autumn; in other areas, one or both species was entirely ignored. I have never seen mountain ash berries eaten during summer. The only place where I have ever seen evidence of heavy feeding on red elderberry at that time of year was the central Alaska Peninsula. Although I could taste no difference between those elderberries and others I have sampled, perhaps the bears did.

In all of our searching, Ontak and his sisters found only one large copse of serviceberry, with fruit the color and size of blueberries, but so sweet that sugar crystals crusted their powdery blue skin. This species grows naturally only at lower latitudes (e.g., southeast Alaska), but these have apparently been planted by someone on the homestead where we found them. All three cubs quickly went to work harvesting this treat. Jonjoanak and Ontak boldly climbed out on branches, from which they frequently fell without apparent harm. Once, Ontak slipped while gripping a berry-rich branch in his mouth. Rather than letting go with his teeth, he held on, and the springy branch absorbed much of the shock of his fall before the branch itself broke. Down on the ground, Ontak finished stripping the berries off this branch before climbing back into the tree.

I never saw Ontak repeat this technique for bringing fruit down to ground level; nor did either of his siblings employ it. But I later saw Montana black and grizzly bears use essentially this same technique to harvest apples and aspen catkins. On a large tree, they would climb the trunk and bite down on a branch, then jump off to break the branch free. On a medium-size tree they would bite down high on the trunk itself before jumping, thereby bending the whole tree over. Small trees were not climbed, but just pulled over. I think it was in the Swiftcurrent Valley of Glacier National Park that I found hundreds of aspen which had been battered and broken this way. Biologist Lynn Rogers sees this commonly in Minnesota.

Chrislee, less bold than her siblings, used a different technique to harvest the serviceberries. Too timid to walk out along limbs far from the trunk, she instead reached out and pulled the flexible branches back toward the trunk. This allowed her to sit at the base of the branch and pull berries from its tip.

At this young age, Chrislee's technique was crude. But I later watched the sow JeenTo use this tactic very efficiently, despite interference from her cubs. As the end of each branch was pulled in toward the trunk, the sow gripped it firmly by hand while using her teeth to strip fruit off the twigs. Eventually, as she bent the branch farther and farther to get more fruit, the wood's flexibility declined and it resisted JeenTo's efforts more strongly. At this point, she tucked the branch tip under her hindleg or rump and sat down, using her body weight to keep the branch from springing away as she resumed feeding. To completely strip a branch of its fruit, she kept pulling the branch inward, by gripping with both her paws and teeth, until the branch broke in the middle. Some trees had dozens of branches folded back and broken this way. As each new branch was tucked under her legs or rump, the network of branches on which the sow sat became ever larger and more solid until it formed something which very closely resembled a chimpanzee's nest.

Although I have occasionally seen bears nap in these nests during the daytime, I have never known of one spending the night this way – unlike the chimpanzees studied by Jane Goodall, which spent every night in very similar nests.

Why the difference? Perhaps chimps fall more readily than bears and thus need nests for security. I don't know how commonly bears spend the night in a tree, but I personally have seen this numerous times, mainly among cubs. Sometimes their mother was in the tree with them. More often, she slept at or near the base of the tree. In all cases, the treed bear slept while sitting or lying on a branch where it joined the trunk. Sometimes the bear sat with his arms wrapped around the trunk or with his back against the trunk. More often, the bear draped himself like a rug over the base of one or more branches, arms and legs hanging down. Only once did I see one of my cubs slip off a branch while apparently asleep, and she caught herself easily.

A BROADER DIET

Our discovery of additional berry sources added to the cubs' security, but it was only a beginning. To make sure that Jonjoanak and her siblings would be able to keep themselves *fat and sassy* during all seasons and all years, without turning into marauders like their mother, I had to make sure they knew of a much wider range of foods.

Shortly after adopting the cubs, therefore, I began consulting scientific and popular works for information on bear diets. Hunters and naturalists tended to say bears could eat nearly anything. But biologists such as Drs. Al Erickson, Chuck Jonkel, Lynn Rogers, and the Craighead brothers, who actually studied diets, reported that although bears could digest a wide range of plants, they could thrive only on a much more select bill of fare. Back then, in 1972, the list of plants that bears were known to eat in quantity was surprisingly short. Surprising, at least, until I realized how difficult it must be to document what bears eat unless you can watch them from very close range, which was seldom possible with fully wild individuals. Raising cubs was a distinct advantage.

Nearly all of the plant foods of known importance fell into four groups: fruit, nuts, succulent greens, or starchy tubers, corms, bulbs or roots – just about the same wild foods that humans prefer. In a leap of "divine" intuition, I suspected that bears could safely eat anything that we can, without risk of toxicity – an hypothesis supported by the fact that bears eat our garbage without apparent harm. For further insights into what my cubs could eat, I therefore turned to lists of human-edible plants, at the time, a much richer literature than that on bear diets. Approaching the problem from both these angles yielded a long list of plants which the cubs could probably eat, virtually all of which have since been confirmed (see the list in the Appendix).

Terrestrial plants had never interested me in their own right; but as bear foods, they now became fascinating. I borrowed plant field guides and began learning how to identify species eaten by bears or people. With no money to purchase these books, I photocopied selected drawings and photographs, then used watercolors to paint over the black-and-white images.

Identification was easy enough for plants with berries or distinctive flowers at this time of year, but difficult for those which had to be distinguished by subtle differences in leaf shape and arrangement, how leaves were joined to stems, and other esoteric criteria. These were all aspects of plant anatomy which I had once learned in my college course on general botany, then forgotten during my years as a marine ecologist. Marine plants are so different from terrestrial species that knowing oceanic plants provided negligible help in learning land plants.

Each day as I walked with the cubs, I kept an eye out for plants known to be edible by bears or people, then collected several specimens of each. Multiple specimens allowed me to document the range of variation in appearance according to each plant's maturity and habitat. Specimens were preserved in a plant-press. Once dry, I laminated each specimen in plastic; punched holes on the left edge of the plastic sheet; attached notes, photos and drawings; then inserted the packet into a loose-leaf binder that I carried in the field for quick reference. I likewise sampled, identified, and preserved anything that the cubs ate in abundance. Some sparsely growing plants disappeared down their throats so quickly that damage to the remnant stems was the only way I could be sure that the plants I sampled were the same ones the bears had been eating. Only continued observation would resolve ambiguities.

Many known bear and human foods are present in Alaska, and I encountered scores of species on each hike with the cubs. Blueberries abounded on some well-drained gravelly soils where the forest was dominated by large mature conifers. But on more silty soils, covered with sphagnum moss and spindly black spruce, the only common berries were the dull red lingonberry (lowbush cranberry) with its small dark leaves, and the tiny, brighter red bunchberry (dwarf dogwood). We occasionally came upon concentrations of highbush cranberry. But other berries tended to be much more scattered; for instance, highbush cranberry. Although each of these species could be succulent and sweet, full of energy-rich sugar, they tended to be so sparsely distributed that they could be consumed only as the cubs happened on them, rather than sought out in the way blueberry patches were. To fill their tummies, the cubs had to forage for up to ten hours a day, being schooled by me with frequent recesses for play and naps.

Although none of the sparser berries were consumed in large quantities individually, together they actually constituted a much greater volume of food than did blueberries. But did that make these sparser berries more important? Identifying the foods bears ate or could eat was only the first step in assessing importance. I also wanted to find out which contributed most to their nutritional needs, both during typical years and during famines.

Little was known then about the relative amounts of each kind of plant or animal eaten by bears, or the kinds and amounts of nutrition extracted from each food. Individual plants of many species had been analyzed for contents of protein, carbohydrate, fat, vitamins, and minerals; but how much of these nutrients were actually utilized or needed by bears? (For example, later studies by Steve Mealey showed that whereas soluble protein and storage fat are used almost completely, structural protein and structural lipid have little nutritional value to bears.)[1] Even less study had been done on variation in nutrient content according to season (for example spring versus fall) or to the parts of each plant eaten (such as roots, stems, or leaves). I thus had no way of knowing what role each of these factors played in explaining food selection by bears, including my own cubs.

Historically, Native Americans learned much about which wild plants could be eaten by observing what grizzly/brown and black bears ate. However, this required considerable caution, due both to difficulties of distinguishing among plants similar in appearance (e.g., between the extremely toxic water hemlock *Cicuta mackenziana* vs. edible wild celery *Angelica lucida*), and to differences between bears vs. humans in tolerance for some toxins. For example, whereas both Alaskan species of wild celery (*Angelica* and *Heracleum*) contain furocoumarin toxins that that make human skin hypersensitive to sunlight, brown bears feed heavily on the young leaves and seeds without showing ill effects.

Bears relish three species so-called Eskimo potatoes, the tubers of (*Hedysarum hedysaroides, H. alpinum, H. mackenziei.* According to folklore humans can eat only the first two; *mackenzi* is toxic to humans. However, review of medical literature and chemical analysis reveals no evidence for toxicity. Either the plant is not actually toxic, or toxicity varies perhaps with season or soil type. [2]

I was especially worried about water hemlock because of its similarity (from a human standpoint) to wild celery, one of the cubs' favorite greens. Other dangerous plants include baneberry, various lupines and vetches, false hellebore, and death camas.

Many plants eaten by bears, such as Devil's club, yarrow, and both Alaskan species of wild celery are known to have medicinal properties for humans. But whether they do for bears is yet unknown. Claims by Alaska's indigenous people that bears eat a certain plant (e.g., wild celery) when ill or wounded [3] must be tempered with knowledge of whether they also eat it when healthy. Indeed, both species of wild celery are commonly eaten by Alaskan bears.

Cow Parsnip

Those questions would eventually be analyzed by chemists. Meanwhile, I sought to better understand the separate roles of instinct and learning in food selection, and the extent to which learning is based on personal experience as opposed to cultural inheritance from other bears.

Chapter 10
INSTINCT, LEARNING, AND CULTURAL KNOWLEDGE

I suspected that a bear cub's food selections are governed by a combination of instinct and learning. Contrary to popular conception, "instincts" are not necessarily rigid. They can be modified by maturational changes or as information which an animal inherits genetically is augmented by information gained from experience.

Maturational changes can alter either an animal's neural "software" or its neurosensory "hardware" – such as the senses that allow it to discriminate between toxic vs. nontoxic plants on the basis of flavors or odors. D. W. Cooper (the father of one of my closest college friends, renowned photographer Thomas J. Cooper) was an expert on dietary selection by livestock. He told me that a mammal's tongue has its highest concentration of bitter (alkaline) and sour (acidic) taste buds when the animal is very young, making it extremely sensitive to these flavors and likely to avoid foods in which they are concentrated. As the mammal matures, sensitivity to sour and bitter flavors declines, reducing its aversion to them. Desensitization occurs over the same period that the youngster is observing which plants its mother and her peers eat, sampling those plants in small amounts, and perhaps noting whether this is followed by sensations of illness, such as nausea -- thereby learning which flavors and plants to avoid. This decline in sensitivity to sourness and bitterness with age is supposedly one reason why vegetables and some other foods which taste noxious to human children are highly palatable to adults.

Depending on the experience of illness to identify toxicity could be fatal with plants such as water hemlock and certain fungi. The spoors of such fungi are so toxic that even sniffing them is dangerous. With other plants, though, taste and scent serve quite well for identifying which are no more than mildly toxic.

A good example of instinctual avoidance was provided on one of our hikes when we entered a vast area from which the forest had burned a year or two earlier. Although grass was beginning to sprout heavily in many spots, there were enough bare areas for us to find morel mushrooms. I had never eaten them personally, but they had been described to me as one of the tastiest of fungi, and one that is virtually impossible to mistake for anything poisonous. I pointed them out to the cubs, who investigated them only briefly before moving on. Nothing I did could induce them to eat what should have been a first-class food. Disappointed, but unwilling to give up, I filled my pack with the fungi and carried them all day until we got back to the cabin, and then later on to Zak's place where I planned on frying up a nice batch and freezing or canning the rest. Zak took one look at my prizes and started cursing me for having nearly poisoned all of us by mistaking false morels for the real thing.

Morel (left) and false morel (right). These specimens are clearly different, but some false morels are much more similar to the true morel.

Tony was a superb cook and a deft hand with olive oil.

From then on, I rarely tried any fungus without carefully checking a reference book, and even then I sometimes found differing opinions about which species are mildly toxic and which are not. (Strangely enough, I made the same mistake of picking false morels again recently and once more was lucky enough to have someone warn me of the error before I ate them–a harsh reminder of the fallibility of memory.)

Over time, the cubs came to relish several fungi which people also enjoy, such as true morels and various kinds of boletus.

After my mistake with the false morels, I gave first priority to learning the identifying characteristics of each of the plants known to be poisonous to people and to finding specimens of each. When we encountered one, I drew attention to it by offering the cubs a few peanuts while holding my hand near the plant. Then, when their noses came close to the plant itself, I warned them away by woofing and pant-huffing, imitating jaw pops with hand – claps and then commanding them, "NO."

In a few cases, I was able to provide specimens of both the poisonous and nutritious plants (for instance, certain berries, gilled fungi, true versus false morel mushrooms, or hemlock versus wild celery) simultaneously, so that I could warn each cub away when she approached the poisonous plant, but reward her with a treat for approaching the nutritious plant. With a single cub, this would have been easy. But with a whole litter, one cub could be investigating the poisonous plant while another was investigating the nutritious one, forcing me to concentrate on the cub in potential danger.

Bunchberry and the moderately toxic *Amanita muscaria* (which Robert Leslie's cubs ate) – cousin to the lethal white death angel *A. virosa*.

Bunchberry (dwarf dogwood) & lowbush cranberry (lingonberry) These common Alaskan plants have berries that survive winter snows and are thus available for animals to harvest during spring. Bears eat both, but people have been sickened by bunch berries.

Water hemlock (above) and Angelica wild celery (below)

Whether my efforts really helped them avoid eating poisonous plants, above and beyond the protections provided by instinct, I never knew. But I had to try and I may even have succeeded. Robert Leslie reported one of his cubs eating a death angel *Amanita* mushroom. But I never saw my own cubs eat any of the toxic fungi or vascular plants about which I had warned them.

As time passed, I became ever more convinced that bears typically learn a great deal about when, where, and how to forage by paying close attention to one another, perhaps by direct observation and certainly by examining spoor left by their fellows. In at least the rudimentary sense of adaptive information being passed from one individual to the next, bears do have cultures.

One of the most revealing stories I have ever heard on this point came to me second– or third–hand, allegedly from biologist Dick Russell. Supposedly, two Canadian grizzly cubs were orphaned when only about six months old, at a time when the main food available to their mother was the starchy tuber of Indian potato *Hedysarum alpinum*, a nontoxic member of the pea family. Even after berries and other rich foods became available in their home range, these two cubs continued on a nearly steady diet of this one plant, not exploring far enough to find a variety of other foods, and not recognizing the value of some they did find.

By contrast, there are numerous cases where orphaned black bear cubs – some temporarily reared by humans, then released into the wild, others entirely on their own – have ended up eating a variety of wild bear foods to which they were probably not introduced by their mother. Whether they learned these foods on their own or from other bears vs. recognizing these foods by instinct is still unknown. Nor do we know whether orphaned cubs learn as wide a variety of food types or locations for obtaining those foods, as do mother-reared cubs.

Indeed, even among mother-reared bears, not all individuals or populations eat the same selection of available foods, even of normally popular foods. When I compared information on bear diets from across North America versus distribution of bear foods, it was apparent that some foods which were heavily utilized in one region were apparently ignored in other regions – a discrepancy that has been confirmed by continuing research.

I suspect that most geographic differences in diet arise from learning. But I cannot yet preclude the possibility that the palatability of some plants varies geographically, due to differences in their contents of nutrients or toxins, which can be related to the amounts of certain minerals (such as selenium or arsenic) that they absorb from soil.

Whereas my cubs ate a variety of mushrooms, Ben Kilham has seen no evidence of this among bears in New Hampshire. When I lived in Montana, raspberries grew abundantly on recently logged areas, yet I saw little evidence of their consumption by either grizzly or black bears.

In the Adirondacks and Vermont, by contrast, raspberry patches in areas clear–cut by loggers were bear havens.

Such local differences in food usage have been pointed out at least since the early 1900s when naturalist Wm. H. Wright observed grizzlies both in Idaho and Canada. Wright noted that grizzlies in the Bitterroot mountains of southern Idaho ate the leaves of the shooting star, but ignored the bulbs of spring beauty and dogtooth violet. Farther north, in

Purple shooting star, white spring beauty and yellow dogtooth violet

the Selkirks, bears had just the opposite preferences. Yet all three plants were abundant in both locations. Equally puzzling, grizzlies preyed on game and ate carrion in areas where game was abundant, but ignored meat in an area where game was scarce; when Wright set out the shoulder from a dead horse as bait in the latter area, it was ignored. Perhaps the likelihood of bears preying on livestock or people also varies geographically, possibly due to different cultural traditions.[1]

Although my cubs discovered many foods through their own spontaneous sampling or with my guidance, some were found by tracking other bears.

I could usually tell when they found the scent trail of another bear because of their intense excitement. Whether or not they were nervous, they seemed to shift to a heightened level of awareness, as though "they had just been switched to high–octane fuel," in Alatanna's words. They moved around like bloodhounds, sniffing audibly, following the scent trail in various directions before finally choosing one direction to follow.

Then, for as long as the next few hours they carefully examined where the other bear had fed and sampled some of the things it had been eating. I too collected samples and took detailed notes.

Upon encountering a tree which another bear had marked, they occasionally marked it too by rubbing against it with their backs and/or by urinating on it. I could only speculate that the choice of whether or not to mark depended on the identity of the other bear(s). The cubs may have instinctually avoided antagonizing certain individuals, such as adult males. Whether mother-reared cubs also mark, or whether they leave that chore to her, I haven't yet discovered. I was surprised to see marking at such a young age in bears, if only because marking does not develop among dogs until the animal is much more mature.

The ground over which we traveled seldom revealed visible footprints. It was mostly either bare rock or thick with grass, moss, and other vegetation, along with dead leaves. The only places I could count on finding distinct tracks were muddy or sandy spots. We were often far along a trail before I could even roughly estimate the size of the bear(s) we were tracking, much less determine whether we were following on the heels of the animal or backtracking it. Sometimes I never knew. But on those occasions where I could identify size and direction, the cubs *never* chose to follow on the heels of a large boar, but backtracked it instead, unless the spoor was at least a day old – judging from rebound by vegetation which had been stepped on, fall of leaves onto the tracks, drying of scat, or insect activity on scat. Even when spoor was no more than a few hours old, the cubs sometimes tracked adolescent males or lone sows (I could seldom tell which were which without seeing the animal). The only bears which my cubs consistently followed were fellow cubs with their mother or independent preadolescents.

Over time, I realized how little most people really understand about bear sociality. Bears are typically described as being "solitary," except for mother/cub families, recently weaned sibling groups, and courting pairs. In fact, however, black and grizzly bears are intensely social. This is easiest to see where they live in open habitats such as the coastal wetlands and tidal flats where I now study them, but it also occurs in forests. People think bears are solitary because they are seldom seen interacting, and because they tend to be separated by distances ranging from dozens of yards to miles. But that is no more a measure of true isolation in bears than it is in teenage girls. While bears don't have telephones, they have odors – what Alatanna called *smellophone* – through which they are in frequent communication. Odor reveals not only which bear is which, but where each bear has been, what it was doing, what it was eating, and where these foods can be found.

The cubs learned what other bears ate by examining the actual plants from which leaves or berries had been stripped, buds nipped, or roots torn out. They learned from the scat (dung) which other bears left behind. Whereas some scats were virtually ignored, others seemed to supercharge the cubs, and they would quickly start backtracking the bear in an unusually determined manner that wasted little time to "enjoy the roses" as they seemed to race toward some distant goal, not stopping until they reached a favored but scarce food. This was how we discovered rare fruit trees (e.g., serviceberry, apple and crabapple) near the decaying remnants of long-abandoned cabins.

In this same way, my cubs learned to avoid certain hazards. I well recall once when we tracked a sow and her cub. Although my cubs were quite calm for the first hour or so, they suddenly became agitated and changed direction – just as the sow and cub had done. Although initially mystified, the explanation became obvious when I caught sight of a cabin which the sow and cub had circled. Whenever we ventured near that cabin again, Ontak and his sisters avoided it spontaneously, suggesting that they had learned to do so from the spoor of their mentors, possibly scent left by the sow's feet, much as caribou and certain other ungulates mark trails with glands between their hoofs. This sort of thing happened often enough that I became convinced that bears that know how to coexist with people fortuitously "teach" other bears how to do so too. Some of them heed the lesson; others don't.

My orphans certainly weren't unique in learning extensively from other bears. One of my oldest mentors, Margaret Altmann, spent many years studying the behavior of moose in the Yellowstone and Teton regions. She also enjoyed watching grizzlies and was once intrigued to notice an orphaned cub persistently following a large adult boar. Contrary to popular ideas, the boar made no attempt to kill and eat the cub. Nor did it actively protect the youngster. But allowing the cub to follow it closely may have provided passive protection, since large boars tend to be avoided by other bears. And the cub probably learned a great deal simply by observing what the boar did and noting what and where he fed.* Even mother-reared cubs probably learn a lot from other bears besides their mother. All this is evidence that bears develop local cultures.

*   Likewise, zoo keepers sometimes find that adult males make wonderful companions for cubs, even play-fighting with the little bruins. This has been reported both by Else Poulsen (author of *Smiling Bears*) and by Donna Anderson (former Director of the North American Bear Center in Ely, Minnesota).

*   *   *

I noticed that my cubs at least sampled a lot of plants which did not show up on the "official" lists of either bear or human foods. This reminded me yet again that few biologists had ever had the opportunity to watch bears foraging from close range, day in and day out.

Back then, in the early 1970s, most scientific analyses of bear diets had been made by examining stomach or scat contents. Few stomachs were available except from hunter-killed bears, which were usually taken in the fall or spring; those samples overlooked plants eaten primarily during the summer. Even for spring and fall, chewed–up plant fragments provide little clue to which species had been consumed. Scat provided samples from all seasons, but scat contents were even harder to recognize, with a few exceptions, such as the bones of fish or the hard carapace, legs, or wings of an insect.

Both seeds and pieces of berry may still be whole when excreted in dung, so they can often be identified as to species. This is a skill I have never mastered, and years later I was happy to pawn the chore off on tracker Susan Morse, founder of *Keeping Track* in Vermont.** Her knack for seed identification is but one of many skills which make her an extraordinary naturalist and educator. Although Sue has no formal science degree – her graduate work was in literature – she is actually much more knowledgeable about certain aspects of wildlife behavior (e.g., bear scent marking) and ecology than I and many other Ph.D. scientists. *There are many routes to Rome.*

** For assistance, talks or courses by Ms. Morse, contact her at the *Keeping Track* foundation, Wolf Run, 55a Bently Lane, Jericho, VT 05465.

Extracting berries and seeds from bear scat isn't pleasant. Not that all bear scat stinks. Dung full of sedge grass smells like a newly mown hay field. Dung full of apples or berries smells like those fruits. It is mainly dung from eating meat or fish that would "gag a maggot," as Zak so delicately phrased it. But the very idea of smelling *any* dung and picking it apart was nauseating. The trick, therefore, was to let a machine do the work – a washing machine, to be precise.

With some amusement, Alatanna honored my request to collect worn-out nylons and pantyhose from her girlfriends. A colleague had advised me to fill a stocking with several piles of scat, each separated from the next by tying a loop of string around the stocking, so that the finished product resembled a chain of link sausages. When all available stockings had been filled, they could be tossed into a washing machine. The "crap" would be washed out, leaving fish bones, insect body parts, plant seeds, and whole berries behind for identification and counting.

The method was simplicity itself – to biologists who owned their own washing machines. But *we* did not even have electricity in our tiny shack, much less appliances. My only option was a Laundromat. Even without Alatanna's pained expression, I would have been cautious about letting anyone see what I was doing. Fortunately, the local facility was open around the clock, allowing me to use it unobserved well after midnight. I got a few loads through without anyone coming in and catching on. But while preparing my third load, one of the stockings burst open. While I was cleaning up the mess, a local drunk looking for a bathroom came in and caught me *red*–handed. Needless to say, I did not dare return to that Laundromat, and was supremely grateful that, although the drunk's story was widely retold, no one quite believed it.

Then Lady Luck really smiled. On a visit to the local landfill, Alatanna and I found an ancient wringer-washer that was not too rusted for the gears to turn when I pulled the drivebelt by hand. Now I had to figure out how to make the agitator drive spin without an electric motor. My lovely lady came up with the idea of a potter's wheel. If I could attach such a wheel beneath the washer, and turn it with my feet, the washer could clean the scat samples.

Now, where could I latch onto a potter's wheel? Continued search through the landfill turned up a gear wheel about the same diameter as the washer, weighing maybe 200 pounds. We wrestled the washing machine and gear wheel up a ramp into the back of Blue Mustang. A friend welded the wheel to the shaft of the washing machine agitator. Finally, I was set to go back into production – or was it *reduction?*

That weekend, with Zak's help, we reloaded the washer into Blue Mustang. Then we headed off to the creek that would provide my water supply.

As we drove, Tony sat by the opposite window, with Alatanna between us. To keep his long white beard from blowing around, Tony folded the tip over a few times and tied it up with a rubber band. Sweat beaded his high cheekbones and bald forehead. Between sips of ice-cold beer, he and Alatanna sang folk songs. There was no room in the cab for her to play her guitar, but her fine alto and Tony's gravelly bass rumble sounded nice just the same.

Turning off the pavement, I steered down the dirt road leading to the landfill. Actually, it was not really a road so much as a track, a swath of land from which trees and brush had been bulldozed so that trucks could drive in to get gravel for constructing roads. Little gravel had been laid down on the track itself. It had washboard corrugations as thick as my forearm where the soil stayed dry, interspersed with ruts and potholes more than a foot deep where the ground was sometimes soft and moist. Anyone trying to drive more than 5 miles an hour risked breaking an

An old wringer washer found at the dump was converted for analyzing bear diets.

axle or leaf-spring. The old Blue Mustang had good axles, but some of her springs were already broken and her shocks completely worn out. Even creeping along in low gear, the truck's frame bent and twisted as one wheel dropped down into a hole and another wheel lifted out of a rut, making the pickup groan, screech, bump, and clang like a tribe of demented blacksmiths pounding away at the devil's forge.

Dust billowed up under the tires and formed a cloud more than twenty feet high in our wake. It quickly coated the inside of the pickup and found its way into our eyes, throat, and nostrils. Zak coughed and Alatanna sneezed, but we kept the windows open. Once more, the Blue Mustang felt hot enough to bake bread.

The gravel had come from a hillside of glacial moraine containing material ranging from silt to boulders several feet in diameter. Some of the boulders had been scarred with parallel grooves where they had been scraped against other rocks by moving glacial ice, over 10,000 thousand years ago.

After the road construction had been completed, no more gravel was needed. The "borrow pits" had been abandoned. The deepest pit penetrated more than twenty feet into the water table. It eventually filled, providing a wonderfully cool dip even when the surrounding rocks sizzled. I shivered in anticipation.

The cliff face behind the pit was also glacial moraine and too crumbly to be trusted completely. But on days this hot, who cared about safety? Many a time, I had climbed it myself, then dived back into the pit. There was one ledge, about thirty feet up, from which I loved doing double flips. (Like father, like son; I was a second-generation acrobatic diver and gymnast.)

Several cars, pickups, and bicycles lined the edge of the pit. Bathers waved as we drove past, but no diving for us until the "washing" was done.

A shallower pit several hundred yards away had been appropriated by local residents as a landfill. Then, another few hundred yards back through a grove of spruce and poplar, a creek tumbled over a waterfall more than fifteen feet high. If we could get the washer close enough, I would be able to run a hose to it from the top of the falls. Even ten feet of head would give enough pressure for washing.

The trees turned out to be so thick near the falls that the truck could not get within a hundred feet of it over dry land. The creek bed itself provided an unobstructed alternate route. It was at least ten feet wide with a bed of heavy cobbles, and the water was no more than a foot deep in most spots. Tony offered to walk ahead of the truck to check for holes and boulders.

Creaking, groaning, and sometimes screeching, the Blue Mustang bent, twisted, and bounced upstream, in its lowest possible gear. All went well until one rear wheel hit a slick, mossy spot. Without traction, it spun uselessly, throwing spray twenty feet back down the creek. The other wheel did not even spin.

It was then that I learned that so-called two-wheel drive vehicles are really one-wheel drive unless both have traction. Our next hour was spent jacking up each side of the truck so that we could pile flat stones under each rear tire.

Tony convinced me that easing forward off the rough stones would just drop me back onto the slick rocks, where I would get stuck again. He told me to pop the clutch so that the Blue Mustang would leap ahead as fast and far as possible, hopefully onto better traction – which is exactly what I tried. The truck lurched forward so powerfully that spray exploded up over the hood, windshield, and roof, as well as into the engine, drowning it. The bumps we hit threw me into the air, cracking my head against the truck's roof and straining my neck. My head was locked to one side by muscle spasms for the next few days. Worse, the sudden spurt forward was more than the top-heavy washer could take. It tumbled out of the back of the pickup and into the river with such force that the agitator shaft bent, rendering the whole machine useless.

Overcome with anger and frustration, I cursed, pounded the truck's hood, kicked the washer, then lay down in the creek to cool off. For awhile, neither Tony nor Alatanna said anything about what had happened. They just sat in the shade, smoking, sipping beer, chatting, and letting me stew in my own juices.

Finally, though, they began to laugh. Thinking they were mocking me, my temper boiled. As I got up to stalk away, I saw Tony pointing. Following the direction of his finger, I looked down into the creek bed. When the washer had fallen out of the pickup, the tub of dung-filled stockings had gone too. They had been scattered across the creek bottom. Some had already floated away and the rest were starting to do so. Meanwhile, the creek had begun washing the "crap" out of the stockings, just as the washing machine was supposed to have done. Now I laughed too, so hard that I just flopped backwards into the water again. All that work for naught. Anytime I wanted to wash bear scat, all I had to do was tie the stockings to a tree with a long cord and toss the stockings into the creek. Nature would do the rest.

Although I examined hundreds of scats and kept detailed records of my findings, these and all of my other scientific records from my first two years of bear research were soon destroyed by fire. You can, however, read the results of dozens of more recent scat studies by my colleagues. Especially revealing are observations on bear diets by the few biologists who employed the same approach I did of observing black bears at close range – most notably Lynn Rogers, Sue Mansfield, Greg

Wilker, Terry Debryun and Ben Kilham.[2] These individuals have lived with black bears in the field night and day for years. Rogers, Mansfield, Wilker, and Debryun worked solely with fully wild bears; Kilham has worked mostly with hand-reared orphans – just as Charles Russell and Maureen Enns have done with brown bears on the Kamchatka Peninsula.

Biologists consistently find that bears focus on foods rich in readily digestible protein, lipid, and carbohydrate. Bears digest liquid protein from inside plant body cells more readily than they digest structural protein (for example, in hair). Non-structural lipid is obtained from a variety of plant and animal sources. At lower latitudes, nuts are a major source of lipid, and at least a moderate source of protein and starch. At higher latitudes, such as Alaska, the only nuts are from conifers, which may be too strong in turpines and other toxins; and they can be harvested efficiently only from rodent caches. So these nuts are unlikely to be a major part of any Alaska bear's diet.

When lipid is first eaten, it may taste and smell like its source. For example, when bears feast on salmon, the fish oil is incorporated into the bear's own fat, making it oily and fishy. Left to go rancid, the fat of a fish-eating bear can smell like rotten fish. However, the fat of bears killed in the spring tends to be more solid in texture and more palatable – judging from my own experiences and that of several Native friends who have depended on bears as their main source of "grease." Although it is possible that the spring-killed bears were not fish-eaters, two alternative hypotheses are that (a) oily fat gets burned up first during hibernation; or (b) it is converted to a more solid form of lipid that does not produce the same byproducts when decaying. I have often hoped that some enterprising grad student would investigate this for a master's thesis.

There is also great uncertainty about how much cubs learn about diets by noting exactly what their mothers eats or avoids. Important clues have sometimes been gleaned from information on other species; for instance, turkeys. Observing that turkey chicks are much harder to raise than chicken chicks, pioneering ethologist Val Geist noted that chicken chicks learn what to eat with little or no maternal guidance; but turkey chicks seem to need several days of guidance, pecking right beside the mother's beak. Likewise, bear cubs may learn about some foods by biting right beside the mother's mouth.

Alatanna's next day off was a beautiful sunny day that was pleasantly warm, rather than hot. After a week of hearing stories of my latest outings with the cubs, she was eager to join us for a hike. Long blond hair hanging in twin braids, and eyes shining with excitement, she packed our lunch. I usually traveled with just a sack full of nuts and raisins – fruit which the cubs enjoyed, but not enough to make them aggressive. Not that aggression was still much of a problem; even Jonjoanak was learning that whatever we brought along would eventually be shared with them, and that our lunch was seldom as tasty as what they could find for themselves. Also, the cubs were becoming increasingly gentle with us, due perhaps as much to their increasing maturity as to their growing affection. Trusting in this restraint, Alatanna decided to add cheese and crackers to our usual hiking menu.

Restraint or not, when it came time to eat, the cubs were terrible pests. Not only did we have to keep shoving them away to keep them from stealing our cheese, but even after we had eaten, they insisted on shoving their noses against our faces, especially near our mouths.

Had they been canids, I might have understood this, for pups typically beg by nosing the corner of an adult's mouth. In wolves, this makes the adult regurgitate food – usually meat that the adult has carried in its stomach from the site of a kill back to the den. Although an adult can carry some food in its mouth, this can impair breathing and travel through dense brush; its odor may attract thieves, and the food must be dropped when the wolf defends itself. The stomach is a far more convenient and secure means of transport, with greater capacity, as well as a method of getting digestion underway quickly.

Bears use other means to provide for their young. Whereas grizzly cubs usually accompany their mother, and eat alongside her, black bear cubs are commonly left in a tree while mom feeds in a potentially hazardous location, such as on carrion. Although bears will commonly carry attractive foods off to hide it from competitors while they eat, and sows may carry food by mouth to cubs, I know of no evidence that mother bears ever carry food in the stomach, then regurgitate for cubs. So why would bear cubs nose the mouth of their mother or foster parent?

Our cubs, like dogs, frequently made sniffing sounds when they nosed or licked our faces, suggesting that they were trying to get the scent of what we were eating. But, I just wrote that off as an evolutionary throwback to a canidlike ancestor or to obnoxious curiosity – how wrong I was.

It took the recent intuition of Ben Killam to reveal that one way that cubs learn what to eat is by sniffing their mother's breath. Ben has reared orphaned cubs from a number of litters, developing this into a real art and science. He had the simple genius to exploit this sniffing trait to teach orphans what to eat. New foods which they would not even test when offered by hand were sampled readily after the cubs smelled them on his breath or beside his mouth. I wish I had been as insightful while rearing Ontak and his sisters.

Enjoy life, take time to smell the flowers. Eat the good ones.

Chapter 11
FISHING

As important as plants are in the diet of an Alaskan bear, salmon are its best source of energy-rich lipid. My cubs' prospects for long-term survival and reproductive success would be greatly enhanced if they could learn to fish. It was essential that they learn where salmon could be found and have the opportunity to learn how to fish efficiently, while I was still available to provide supplemental food if necessary and protect them from rivals.

For the cubs, competition was a fact of life which I never dared to forget. Their mother and JeenTo were not the only adults that used this area. Within a mile of the cabin, I had seen the adolescent boar QuiLog and at least two fully adult boars, at least one sow who struck me as being fairly old, JeenTo with her triplets, and one pair of preadolescents who had probably been weaned that spring. This latter pair included KeeSaw, who was sometimes with her pal or sibling and sometimes alone, as on the occasion when she met my cubs and was chased by them. That was a total of least six adults, two juveniles, and three infants who spent at least part of their time in the center of my cubs' domain, with a lot more bears living further away. So far, we had had few direct confrontations with other bears because I avoided salmon streams, and most bears fled immediately upon sensing my presence. But the time had come when avoidance would no longer suffice.

The brook that ran past our cabin eventually joined Catlin Creek, which in turn flowed into a river where red salmon were running in modest numbers – as evidenced by bleached salmon skeletons and jaws all along the creek's gravel bars. For now, salmon numbers were so low that competition from other bears would be fierce. I could only hope that once Catlin Creek was filled with reds, other bears would be too busy catching fish or digesting them to rebuff the cubs; and the cubs would have more success in catching their own salmon.

Meanwhile, Jonjoanak and her siblings needed to be fed. Not only had they consumed the supply of fish heads and offal collected by Zak and Alatanna, but we were out of steaks and fillets for ourselves. I would have to catch more.

In preparation, I practiced casting with the heavy pole and reel which I had recently bought at a garage sale. The line on the reel wasn't wound properly and failed to unwind smoothly. The cubs were still inside the cabin with Alatanna, so I took the opportunity to rewind the reel. Tying the tip of the line around a springy willow stem, I backed down the trail for a few hundred yards, then began winding it in slowly and carefully.

Man proposes; Murphy disposes. Less than half the line was back onto the reel before all three cubs appeared nearby. The willow stem wiggling at the end of my line proved irresistible. They attacked. Within moments, Jonjoanak was entangled in the monofilament fishing line. Her angry bawling did nothing to dissuade the other cubs. They were soon entangled too, quickly stripping line back off the reel as fast as a 200–pound halibut heading for the depths of the Pacific Ocean. As I released the pole with one hand to pull a knife and cut the line, the pole was jerked out of my hand and pulled into the maelstrom of panicked cubs. The fiberglass rod was snapped within seconds as I stood by helplessly, wondering how in Hades I could cut the cubs free without being shredded by their claws and teeth. The main thing keeping them safe from each other was the fact that they were bound together too tightly to reach one another.

In a moment of rare wisdom, I simply sat down and waited for the inevitable. The more the cubs entangled themselves, the less they could move, and the more exhausted they became with the effort and heat. Finally, all three were panting heavily and had nearly given up trying to break free. They seemed to have reached a stage of perceived helplessness which instinct told them demanded surrender, as though to a mother bear. As I cut the fishing line, I watched them carefully, lest Jonjoanak or one of the others "blame" me for this mishap and retaliate. But even the normally aggressive little female seemed to be watching me expectantly, as though knowing she depended on me for rescue. When I cut the line binding her mouth, she licked my hand gently, something she had rarely done before. Strangely, this incident was the turning point in our relationship with Jonjoanak. She was never as friendly and trusting as her siblings, but her previous antagonism gave way to something warmer than neutrality. More than ever, the cubs looked toward us for protection and security.

The next morning, I dropped Alatanna off for work, then headed to Zak's. He had borrowed a riverboat for my fishing trip, to be towed behind the Blue Mustang. Tony himself would have to spend the day at work, but he was looking forward to king salmon steaks every bit as much as the rest of us.

Tony was in high spirits when I arrived. He helped me switch the boat and trailer off of his green Jeep and onto the Blue Mustang. Then we sat down to heaping plates of fried potatoes and onions, eggs, and kielbasa.

When salmon crowd together passing through shallows, especially ascending a falls, they are such easy prey that even unskilled bears can just walk up and grab them. The strange pink humps are dorsal fins. *(Larry Travis photo)*

Grizzly with a male (cock) humpie salmon. *(Larry Travis photo)*

During my first hour on the river, I passed numerous schools of salmon fighting their way upstream toward the oxygen-rich gravel beds where they would spawn. Only where the turbid river was less than two feet deep could the fish be clearly seen. When they raced through shallows over gravel bars, humpy (pink) and chum (dog) salmon were readily identifiable by their shape and color. A cock (male) humpy has a high humped back, a long hooked jaw, and dark grey back and flanks with a slight greenish cast. A chums has a smaller hump, elongated jaw and greenish-silver body slashed with maroon-colored tiger stripes. A humpy reaches about ten pounds; a chum occasionally reaches thirty. Although both humpies and chums are fine if cooked right, they are disdained by most Alaskans. Nobody would object to me catching these species for the cubs, if I happened to hook one. They would probably be abundant within a week or two; but for now the current humpy and chum runs had barely begun.

Meanwhile, to fill Tony's freezer and the smokehouse with salmon for us, I was looking for more flavorful species. The few schools of chinooks (kings) that passed through the shallows were easily distinguishable by their bright–silver color and enormous size. Although some chinooks approach 100 pounds, I never saw one more than half that big. In the opinion of most Alaskans, this is the tastiest of all salmon. Personally, I like sockeyes (reds) and cohos (silvers) just as well. Cohos reach 25 pounds, and sockeyes only about half of that. Creeks filled with them were so red that they poetically reminded me of lava flows.

Such an abundance of salmon was a sportsman's dream come true. But with three hungry cubs to feed, sport was the last thing on my mind.

When I started fishing that day, I had no premonition that filling Tony's freezer and smokehouse would have to wait until I had fed an overly friendly grizzly bear. It took an hour to land two kings. After hauling the first ashore, I threaded a line through its gills, and lowered the fish back into the chill water of a nearby creek to stay fresh.

It was only when I had my second king in hand and walked over to add it to my rope stringer that I realized that I had a guest. Approaching the little creek with that second salmon dangling from one hand, I discovered that my first fish had been vandalized. Little remained of it but the mangled corpse, which had been skinned and gutted of any roe. The brain had been bitten out. Obviously, the culprit was a bear; the tracks suggested grizzly.

There he was, not twenty feet away, eyes locked onto the king in my hand, following each swing of its body. As quickly as it takes to tell this, I tossed my fish into the creek to distract the bear. Then, with a leap that would have done credit to a kangaroo, I was off the riverbank and inside the boat. An instant later, I was yanking furiously on the boat's starter rope, but the engine wouldn't fire.

I was dripping with sweat and shaking with fatigue when the curious grizzly wandered over and sat down on the bank, just beyond the bow of the skiff, as though bemused by my antics. Fortunately, he didn't climb into the boat with me, or I would have taken my chances in the river with the salmon.

Light brown in color, weighing at least 300 pounds, this bear had the long-legged gangly appearance of a teenage boy. His head was far longer than it was high, as seen in profile, and somewhat narrower than high when seen frontally. By contrast, the head of a mature bear is usually thicker and wider relative to its length. This was a juvenile, probably around four years old.

Bears are still juveniles – sexually immature – when they become independent of their mother so that she can breed again and rear a new litter. Having gotten used to sharing the mother's status while intimidating rivals, some juveniles remain aggressive through their first few months of independence, until they learn the hard way that they are at the bottom of the pecking order. Then they tend to become the meekest of bears. Only gradually, as they reach sexual maturity –

adolescence – does their aggression rise again as they begin competing vigorously to climb the social ladder. Years may pass before a bear reaches full adulthood, not merely able to reproduce, but fully developed

physically and behaviorally.

Lean and lanky preadolescent blackie. *Dianne Own photo)*

Although this juvenile was hungry enough to risk coming out in the open to steal my salmon, he was still too diffident to barge his way onto the skiff. He sat with his head hung below shoulder height, ears forward, mouth relaxed with lips hanging slackly. Sitting down is one way bears may signal peaceful intent -- as shown in this *Kent Fredriksson photo.*

I quit tugging at the starter cord, wiped the sweat from my forehead, and sat down to rest, half convinced that I was safe for the moment. Only then, in my growing calm, did it dawn on me that I had forgotten to reset the motor's kill switch and activate the ignition. I took care of that, but the motor was already flooded. I had two choices: wait there until the carburetor cleared of excess gas, which could take half an hour, or untie the boat and drift downstream until the boat would start. I looked around for oars; there were none. The idea of floating down the river out of control had little appeal; too easy to get into serious trouble.

So we waited – both of us, the bear and I. Having eaten close to twenty pounds of salmon may have taken the edge off his appetite, but it hadn't satisfied him.

What the heck; if necessary, I could catch a few more fish for his dessert, and then start all over to lay in my own supply. I considered that approach, but I had a hunch that this fellow could keep packing them away until he was too full to waddle. I have heard that bears can eat up to a hundred pounds of salmon a day, but suspect that no bear could eat more than 15 percent of his own body weight – or about 45 pounds for this individual. In any event, waiting the bear out was as good an excuse as any for doing nothing. I just leaned back and waited for the carburetor to clear or the bear to leave, whichever came first.

Eventually becoming rather bored, my mind drifted to Alatanna. Her way of combating ennui was to play card games, usually Hearts, Old Maid, or Fish. Come to think of it, "playing fish" is exactly how this bear and I had spent our morning, except that he'd gotten to take all of my fish without giving me any in return.

Finally losing patience with me, he rose and stretched, arching his back, bowing it up, then down, and yawning, sticking his tongue out so far it curled under his chin. Taking a few steps backwards, he tucked his hind legs a bit under his body, swatted slightly, and deposited the semi-liquid residue of his meal on the gravel bar.

Showing no further interest in me, the young grizzly turned and lumbered down the river bank. Wading along a gravel bar to the eddy at its base, he watched intently for several minutes, leapt out into the river, and slapped his hands down on something. Dipping his head underwater, he then lifted it again, moments later, jaws filled with a fiercely flopping king of roughly forty pounds. Only as he climbed the bank did he chance to look in my direction, as though to say, "*This* is how it's done!"

(Larry Travis photo)

By the time the boat would start, there was no need to leave. The grizzly was content. He had caught two more salmon. He had taken the fat-rich portions of these fish too – the bright reddish-orange roe, the skin, and the brain. The protein-rich flesh was abandoned, and the bear wandered off, leaving the carcasses on the sand for any passing eagle, gull, or fisherman.

Well, fair's fair. Time to turn the tables; he'd stolen the "choicest" parts of my fish. so I stole the remains of his. Combined with what was left of my two salmon, this gave me nearly fifty pounds of mangled flesh for the cubs and nearly that much rich, reddish-orange flesh from which to cut thick juicy steaks. Tony, Alatanna, and I dined well for the next few weeks.

*   *   *

It was in the third week of July, on Alatanna's next day off, that we finally enrolled the cubs in *fish school,* where they majored in salmon. The cubs would find eating them delightful; and catching them was incredible sport.

The day before, I'd made a solo hike down to Catlin Creek and found only a few dozen reds left in the pools, where the water came up to my knees. As shallow as that was, it would thwart every effort the cubs made to catch salmon – unless the cubs could drive the salmon up– or downstream over gravel bars were the water was sometimes only inches deep, a trick I could teach them. Judging from the lack of fresh fish carcasses and scat on the shore, other bears had apparently moved on to richer pickings, so the cubs weren't likely to run into trouble that I couldn't handle.

Leaving the cabin early Sunday morning, Alatanna and I were filled with light–hearted joy, and all three cubs were bursting with playfulness. Half an hour of hiking brought us to the slope above Catlin Creek. Soon, we were deep within the shady gorge, refreshing ourselves in the clear, cold, spring water.

The only hint of the salmon were occasional splashes and ripples where their fins and backs momentarily broke the surface. These were initially ignored by the cubs. My attempts to entice them into the water were futile.

But nature takes its own course. After thirty minutes of climbing trees and racing around on the ground, our furry charges were panting with exhaustion and heat. One by one, they waded out into the stream, where they stretched out, neck deep, and lapped water. Only by chance did one cub notice an exhausted salmon and follow it halfheartedly until the fish found itself in a shallows and panicked, spurting forward suddenly in an attempt to reach deeper water. The violence of its movement caught the attention of all three cubs, and the race was on.

Quickly, the pool became a maelstrom of surging fish and splashing cubs, running this way and that, having the time of their lives.

Unfortunately, enthusiasm is no substitute for skill. The only salmon the cubs got to eat that night was one that I caught on a hook and line. I could only hope that the cubs' dismal success trying to catch reds was not a harbinger of things to come.

On the last weekend of July, we again descended into the valley toward Catlin Creek. The cubs raced around, chasing and wrestling, so full of fun and joy that they made our hearts sing. Alatanna bounced lightly down the slope after them, carrying a few sandwiches and apples in her pack, along with her guitar. I plodded along last, with nearly 100 pounds of video equipment, 35mm camera, and tape recorder. Traveling last made it easiest to keep track of what everyone was doing and make sure no one got left behind. It also increased my chance of spotting any bear approaching our small family. Before I could detect other bears upwind or ahead of us, the cubs often scented their wild kin or spotted their movement, but the cubs rarely noticed any bear approaching from downwind or behind us until he was within fifty yards. Ontak and his sisters were extremely sensitive to movement up to about three hundred yards away, so long as something was moving crossways to them. But they were poor at spotting anything standing still or walking straight toward us – keeping its appearance nearly constant – while more than 50 yards away. Adult bears often detected movement at much longer distances.

We were still a quarter mile from Catlin Creek when Alatanna pointed out several eagles riding the thermal air currents along the creek. The birds were silhouetted against scattered cumulus clouds that were like giant snowdrifted icebergs floating in an azure sea.

Descending the steep trail toward the creek, the white heads and dark bodies of more eagles became visible on the tops of majestic jade-green spruce trees lining the shore.

So many eagles meant that another run of salmon had arrived; other bears might already be fishing in the creek. Alatanna and I tried in vain to call the cubs back and keep them close to us. "Ontak," "Chrislee," we yelled repeatedly, not wasting any effort on Jonjoanak, who was in the lead, as usual, and who never complied anyway. This was not one of the few times the cubs decided to cooperate.

These youngsters had learned their names within a week of being adopted. Even when Alatanna cooed one of their names softly, that cub's ears would usually prick up and his head swivel toward her. Ontak and his sisters paid closest attention to us when we had food to offer, or when they had caught the scent of another bear and become agitated, blowing and jaw-popping in fear. But rarely did they come when called, much less desist from any activity we wanted to halt, or stay away from something that we feared might endanger them. I had observed mother black bears grunting, huffing, tongue-clucking, and gulping to summon their cubs or to warn them. I tried repeatedly to imitate those sounds closely enough for my cubs to respond as though I were their parent. But it did not work then, and it has never worked since. Perhaps I would have better luck with high quality tape recordings, but the opportunity to try has never arisen.

In any event, Chrislee and her siblings showed no sign of agitation as we neared Catlin Creek. They raced pell-mell out onto the gravel bar at the creek's edge, apparently heedless of who or what might lay ahead. Either they had become reckless because of the overpowering scent of fish, as I have seen numerous other bear cubs do, even with their mothers calling loudly with concern; or their sensitive noses had already assured them that we were alone. As much as I was tempted to trust their instinctual alertness, wariness, and powers of perception, Alatanna frequently reminded me that they were just babies and almost as dependent on learning how to survive as a young ape. She was right; it was imperative that I keep constant watch. Before the day was out, we could be sharing this section of stream with another black bear or two and maybe a grizzly.

My worries about the cubs running headlong into trouble proved groundless. Although the creek was swarming with fish, neither the cubs nor I detected any fresh sign of another bear. All scat and fish carcasses were at least a week old, from the last run of red salmon, not from the current run of humpies. Perhaps the salmon had arrived only within the past few hours. And most local bears might have gathered a mile or more downstream at Otter Creek, or farther away at the river, both of which supported much heavier runs of fish. While we couldn't count on having Catlin Creek to ourselves for long, at least we had it now.

The air throbbed with the cry of the gulls. Some of these white birds were resting on gravel bars; others were riding the current downstream. A few were paddling slowly upstream, occasionally lifting their snowy wings and surging forward several inches as their black beaks stabbed through the shimmering surface, apparently catching some prey too small for us to see.

As soon as the cubs raced into the creek, the harsh cries of gulls and ravens more than doubled in volume, like a crowd of eager fans watching a football team take the field. With a touch of wry humor, I wondered whether the birds really were enthusiastic over the arrival of my cubs. The gulls were unable to catch any of the hundreds of pink salmon which I now saw swimming here. For access to that feast, the birds depended on scraps left by bears.

Peering into the creek, it would have been easy to see the salmon if they still had the bright-silver bellies and flanks they had sported during their years of growth and maturation in the ocean. But no sooner had they gathered in the brackish water at a river mouth than their bodies had begun to darken – camouflage that would increase their chances of surviving their upriver fight through the gauntlet of hungry bears and eagles.

Over much of the creek's length, its canyon walls were cliffs of bluish-black shale, sprinkled with patches of gray, green, and orange lichens. Hundred–foot spruce and fifty–foot cottonwood overhung the creek, casting deep shadows and dark reflections on its gently roiling water. In this water danced the images of those shadowed walls, splashed here and there with blue sky. The water itself had been slightly stained to the color of coffee where it had percolated through muskeg swamps, a few miles upstream.

Yet, whatever protection was provided by those reflections and stains, and the fish's own camouflage, was undone by the high visibility of the salmon's whitish or pale pink wounds. Some had lost patches of skin and scales up to two inches across from by being battered against rocks as they fought upstream through rapids. Others, wounded in combat with rival males, looked like they had lost strips of skin, especially along the spine, which could run the entire length of a salmon; or rivals had nipped off the tips of their fins and tails, or chunks of flesh, leaving them with roughly hemispherical wounds up to an inch in diameter and a quarter-inch deep. The hooked jaws and enlarged teeth of the cocks weren't just for show! Injuries were often covered with a white layer of fungus.

While Ontak and his sisters were on the gravel bar nearby, exploring eagerly, I continued to study these fish. At first, I thought they were just resting in the shallows, gathering strength for the next phase of their tough upstream journey to mate, then die. Some were holding stationary positions in the river by swimming just hard enough to counteract the current. Then, two to five fish would converge, swirl around, and shoot off together – soon to be replaced by others.

Or so it seemed, until I realized that the replacement fish at each site had a similar pattern of discolorations to the one which had left seconds earlier. No, not just similar; identical. Watching closely, I finally realized what I was seeing. In the pool before me, each of several individual fish was defending a particular area of the riverbed, presumably where it and its mate had buried their fertilized eggs. They were protecting those eggs from being eaten and/or evicted by rival fish that wanted to incubate their own offspring on the spot. When an intruder tried to crowd in, the resident would drive the intruder away, perhaps violently, then return to guard its nest. I wondered whether a male and female remained paired after mating to guard their nest jointly. But I never saw any pair of fish that I could be sure remained consistently together, if only because the hens tended to be less heavily discolored than the males, making them harder to see and to identify individually.

As clusters of fish competed for mates or nest sites (redds), they sometimes whipped their bodies back and forth in the foot-deep water, making splashes that my cubs could not long ignore. The sounds of splashing made the bears pay attention. Their eyes were drawn to the shining white wakes thrown up by the fish. Perhaps reluctant to face failure again with these pinks, as they had previously with the sockeyes, all three cubs held back for several minutes, standing poised on the creek bank, heads high and ears cocked forward, as though ready to dive in, yet never doing so. Finally, in frustration, I jumped into the nearest pool, scattering fish in every direction. Several pinks raced upstream into a riffle mere inches deep, where their bodies threw roostertail wakes a handspan above their backs. The cubs burst into pursuit.

Pounce, miss, pounce, bite, catch salmon, lift to carry ashore, lose grip, lose fish, stand in confusion, then race off again, pounce, miss, pounce, and SUCCESS!

Jonjoanak caught the first salmon and carried it ashore with her head held as high as possible. Even then, the five-pound fish was so long compared to her short legs that its tail and head dragged in the water. Once she reached the gravel beach, the usual squabble erupted, with all three cubs bawling loudly as Ontak and Chrislee sought a share, and Jonjoanak tried to keep the fish entirely to herself. She stood over her prize, ears back, nose down and face elongated, making sudden short lunges at her siblings to drive them away.

Hoping to prevent a serious fight, I pulled a fishing line from my backpack and quickly caught a salmon. There were so many fish that it took only minutes.

Normally, when the cubs were competing for some goody, they ignored my attempts to distract them. Lately, though, they had begun to realize that when I called, I often had more treats to offer; so it was now. Ontak saw the salmon and hurried over. Before he could claim it, I lifted the fish above his head and walked toward a shallow riffle to release it again. Ontak followed, protesting loudly and trying repeatedly to reach up and take the prize away from me. When I dropped the fish into the riffle, it struggled momentarily, then began to swim away. Ontak pounced. Minutes later, I repeated this process with Chrislee. Soon, all three cubs were munching lustily – after I had taken a knife and opened each salmon for them, since the cubs did not know how, and had difficulty biting through the skin of these fish.

Even as small as the cubs were, still under forty pounds, none was satisfied with a single fish. Each abandoned her fish while only partly eaten and returned to the creek, leaving a flock of squabbling gulls and ravens in her wake. Now that each of the cubs had caught a fish, this success overcame whatever discouragement they had learned from failing in attempts to catch the more vigorous sockeye salmon. They quickly tried again. Although each spent at least another half-hour before succeeding a second time, none quit trying. During the interim, there were many near successes as they chased fish and caught them momentarily in their claws, or sometimes even in their teeth, before losing them again. Although the flopping of a captured fish sometimes intimidated a cub into releasing it or physically tore the fish free from the cub's jaws, the cubs were not discouraged. Literally, the "taste" of success and the sport of it were enough to keep them trying. Because these fish were physically exhausted from swimming upstream, and had to swim through shallow riffles where they were highly vulnerable, my cubs enjoyed far greater success in catching them than most wild cubs I have observed. It often takes years to master the art of catching salmon. My cubs just happened to be in the right place at the right time.

While my cubs explored along the creek, Alatanna and I took advantage of the brief respite to enjoy the lunch she had packed, savoring ham sandwiches and apples without having to fend off three voracious youngsters. I chewed contentedly, enjoying the cubs' excitement and the affectionate company of my wife..

After cleaning up from lunch, Alatanna picked up her guitar and softly sang folk tunes. Much as I would have liked to join her, the sound of my own voice would have blended well only with a chorus of frogs.

By the time Ontak and his sisters had their fill of salmon, all they wanted to do was sleep. Alatanna and I were sitting side-by-side against the cool creek bank. Ontak and Chrislee shuffled over and plopped down on either side of us, rolling onto their backs, with their taut tummies bulging upwards like balloons swollen almost to the bursting point. As had become our custom, Alatanna and I stroked their tight bellies, scratched under their chins, and lightly massaged their limbs. They purred briefly, then were asleep, breathing heavily, sometimes snoring. Twitching of their legs, occasional whines, and rapid movements of their eyelids made me wonder whether they were now chasing salmon in their dreams.

Jonjoanak, as usual, kept her distance. She had buried her last salmon in sand and gravel, then bedded down atop her cache. As David Henry showed with red fox in Canada, caching is a good way to hide prey from aerial scavengers, such as gulls and ravens. But, at least in Jonjoanak's case, it was a lousy way to get any sleep. Her eyes were rarely shut for even a minute before an overly bold bird provoked her into leaping up and lunging at it. The gulls and ravens, and even a magpie, were well aware of what the cache held, and seemed determined to steal a share.

Generally, these birds are far too fast to be caught by a bear. But the evolution of superfast reflexes came with a price: the death of "retarded" birds. To my surprise, Jonjoanak contributed to the genetic fitness of ravens in general by eliminating one of their culls. As she lunged forward, the bird leapt into the air a bit too slowly. She batted it down with one paw, pinned it to the gravel, bit down, and shook her head violently. Rather than eat the bird, she dropped it and walked back to her salmon cache, with her tongue repeatedly extended several inches, then withdrawn, getting rid of clinging bits of feather.

After waking up, Ontak pulled my hand to his mouth and bit it gently, inviting me to play. Lulled by a belly full of lunch and the warm afternoon sun in which we basked, I had no interest in anything so energetic. To distract Ontak, I fished out a handful of peanuts and raisins, then dropped a few onto his tummy. Pulling his chin to his chest, he could barely see the treats; but that was enough for him to recover them one at a time, gripping each peanut or raisin between the tips of two middle finger claws as if they were chopsticks – in much the same manner as another black bear had her claw tips to pluck willow catkins that she could not reach with her lips.

Although we commonly refer to a bear as having four "feet" because it walks on all of them, I refer to its forefeet as "hands," since that is essentially what are formed by its metacarpal bones and phalanges. Its fingers are joined by webbing and don't move as independently of each other as ours do. Yet they still have far more dexterity than the digits of a canid or felid. Small objects can be gripped between any two adjacent "finger claws" (analogous to our fingernails). Even without an opposable thumb such as we and pandas have, other kinds of bears can exert a powerful grip on larger objects. For example, an adult black bear once jerked a walking stick away from me by gripping the stick with two middle claws over the stick and the outside claws under the stick (you can use your fingers to firmly grip a pencil the same way).

As delighted as I had been at slowly winning the cubs' trust and affection, and helping them learn to forage, I was even happier at the great strides made this day in advancing their self-sufficiency. Catching salmon wouldn't always be this easy, as their defeat by the sockeyes had shown. But their next attempt with those challenging fish would be facilitated by whatever skills they had learned with today's easier prey.

Bears employ many methods to catch salmon. Some differences among bears may be just idiosyncratic variations; but others are clearly tailored to different circumstances.

When I have watched bears along a stretch of river where the water was no more than about one foot deep, each bear typically sat or stood on the shore, or in the water itself, listening and watching for a fish or for the V-wake above its back. Then the bear would lunge forward and try to pin the fish to the bottom with his claws. Once a salmon had been pinned, the bear's head would dip underwater and he'd grasp the fish in his jaws.

Sometimes the bear's claws were driven like spear prongs into the fish; at other times, the fish was apparently held mainly by the pressure of the bear's hands. Bears occasionally bring a salmon to shore, then discard it – which gives me an opportunity to later examine the fish closely. Some of these victims have indentations of claw and tooth tips on their skin, but little or no wound at all.

I have seen this pounce-and-pin technique thousands of times with bears fishing for salmon and a few times with bears fishing for trout. I once watched a black bear in California miss while using this technique and accidentally swat the trout ashore. It may have been such accidents which led turn-of-the-century writers to describe Rocky Mountain black and grizzly bears purposefully swatting salmon ashore. Personally, I have never seen that, and don't know anyone who has. You could speculate that fish-swatting was a local tradition confined to bears in the Rockies, and that the tradition died out due to over-hunting of knowledgeable bears, or to elimination of salmon through over-fishing and downstream dam construction in those watersheds. But any bear attempting to swat a fish out of the water would be likely to fail most of the time. The fish would get away, or its carcass would be stolen by another animal.

Where the water is a few feet deep, a bear using the pounce–and–pin technique is rarely successful on more than one in 25 attempts. Although water turbidity (murkiness) and glare off its surface seem to affect both the ease with which bears can spot salmon and probably vice versa, I have never been able to draw a clear correlation between visibility and fishing success. Water depth, salmon abundance, and salmon vigor seem to play at least as great a role. Indeed, some bears are very successful at night, when fishing may be guided more by hearing than by sight.

Fishing techniques differ where salmon are climbing a waterfall. In Katmai National Park, I have watched salmon struggle upstream over slopes of twenty degrees or more, weaving among boulders as they fight their way through just inches of water, moving from one pool to the next. They rest in these pools, mouths opening and closing like sprinters gasping for air at the end of a race. Just as we gasp air, fish gasp water to increase oxygen uptake.

The pools and shallow passageways between boulders became so crowded with salmon that the bears could walk up, dip their heads, and pluck salmon out of the water almost as easily and calmly as if they were plucking mushrooms off the ground. Most of the bears walked out to catch a fish, then returned ashore to eat it, often going out of sight to avoid having the fish stolen by a rival. More dominant bears ate their fish where they killed it.

The fish might be steadied by using the right paw to hold the fish on the back of the left paw, or against a rock. Then the fish was bitten, usually on the back, just behind the head, and the fat-rich skin pulled off. Any roe were eaten, and then the brain was bitten off with a crunch so loud that I could clearly hear it fifty feet away.

Even after listening to that crunch several thousand times, it still makes me shudder, with a kind of premonition of the noise that would be made if a bear were chewing on me. Bears fascinate me and evoke my affection. Generally, I trust them, sometimes so much that I have fallen asleep briefly while making observations of bears within fifty yards of me. Then, little things like that "crunch" jerk me back to the reality that these are extraordinarily powerful predators, with no more hesitation about killing mammals than they have about killing fish. Rarely, a bear preys on other bears or even people. Serial killers and cannibals are not confined to the human race.

One boar I watched on another creek had broken his lower jaw, either while fighting another boar, or by being shot. He could not bite down to catch salmon or to chew them; to compensate, he had developed an alternative and nearly effortless method of fishing. He sat at the base of a falls facing upstream. Boiling white water hid him from the fish, which came to rest in the pool between his legs and belly – a living larder for the bear, who speared the fish with his claws, tore the fish apart, then used his finger claws to stuff flesh into his throat.

Another bear, at Katmai's Brooks River, sat facing downstream in chest-deep water so that her body formed an eddy where salmon rested, likewise providing her with nearly effortless meals. The same thing has been seen at McNeil Falls, just north of Katmai.

Brooks Falls at Katmai presents an unusual challenge to both fish and bears. These falls are at least five feet high, and salmon try to leap this distance. I have watched sockeye salmon race upstream toward the falls, explode out of the water like blood-red titan rockets, flying high and far until they landed on the lip of the falls, then give another tremendous burst of speed to move upstream before the river flow and gravity could sweep them back down again. Some fish try again and again before they succeed. Others never do make it over the falls, either because they lack the strength, or because they fly into the jaws of a waiting bear.

At any given time, I have seen up to three bears stand at the crest of Brooks Falls, ready to snap up salmon. Footing is precarious, and bears don't generally take more than one step to either side to catch a fish, lest the bear stumble and be swept over the falls. Although the range of motion for a bear is thus limited to several feet to either side of where he stands, the bears are so quick that salmon sometimes seem to literally fly into their jaws, as though the fish had been caught in some kind of *Star Trek* tractor beam emanating from the bear's mouth.

The most dominant bears fished either at the falls or where the river was shallow. I saw several grizzlies attempt to chase down salmon in water over three feet deep, but the fish easily outswam most of them. Only subordinates, like the two-year-old female I called Nitsi, were forced to fish in deep water near the end of Brooks River where it emptied into Naknek Lake. This area of the river was over ten feet deep that summer – the year before I became foster father to Chrislee and her siblings. I suspect that Nitsi caught salmon by swimming up underneath them as they rested beside the riverbank, often in a shadowed area where the bank had been undercut by erosion.

*   *   *

Although salmon are what most people normally think of when anyone mentions bears fishing, in fact, bears also catch other species. I have watched both grizzly and black bears prey on suckers and cutthroat trout, which leave Rocky Mountain lakes to spawn in streams. Both grizzly and black bears likewise catch trout which have become stranded in pools as a river dries up. My fellow grad student Tommy Smith saw catfish taken this same way by black bears in the White River area of Arkansas. Grizzly and black bears on the seacoasts of Alaska scavenge dead or dying halibut, crabs, and other animals washed ashore; they flip over rocks for tiny sculpins and blenny eels.

*   *   *

I write this paragraph just hours after returning from a stream filled with hundreds of salmon that were being preyed on by two adolescent black bear boars. Although the water was murky, the fish and bears were readily visible to one another.

Where the water was more than a foot deep, a healthy fish could easily evade a bear. But with so many fish, in small pools, they often

escaped by accident into shallow riffles where they were easily caught. Moreover, most of the fish were exhausted from their upstream migration, and from combat for mates. Many of them, especially the "cocks," had ulcers more than half an inch wide, and were missing chunks of the fins or tail. Visible wounds, compounded by injuries, made these fish easy prey. Nevertheless, the two bears I was watching scavenged old carcasses as often as they caught live fish. These carcasses had already been high-graded by the bear which had caught them. The fattiest portions of their bodies had been taken – brain, skin and roe, if it was a "hen."

Look carefully at the following photos. The upper one shows the dorsal fin of one salmon. The second shows dozens of salmon milling around. Unfortunately, they are uncatchable in such deep water, forcing bears to scavenge dead ones floating on the surface.

Or bears pick up salmon which have accidentally stranded themselves while leaping from pool to pool in a shallow, rocky steam.

I started educating my cubs in fishing techniques where the water was shallow and fish were relatively helpless, hoping that this would give the youngsters a head start for graduating to areas where the water was deeper and rougher, requiring much more skill.

I wanted them to learn as many fishing techniques as possible in hopes that they would never be at a loss for a successful method, no matter what the water conditions or species of fish. I didn't dare take them where they could spend several hours a day watching other bears fish, but I tried to guide them to situations where they could learn for themselves.

On occasions when I tried to demonstrate new methods personally, however, I could rarely get the cubs to pay attention. Either they took these as invitations to play with the fish and with me; or they were too busy using their own fishing techniques, however unsuccessful. I sometimes felt like a father trying in vain to get his kids to stop playing football long enough to learn a few pointers. The excitement of chasing fish left little room for distractions such as my attempts at education.

Mother bears don't face quite the same problem with their youngsters. Although cubs commonly play while their mother grazes, they spend a lot less time playing while she fishes. One reason for the difference is that most play occurs only after the cubs have dined well, whether on milk, plants, or meat. Cubs are free to eat their fill of plants, and then to roughhouse. But meat-fed cubs have to wait for mama to provide salmon or other prey, so the youngsters are hungry most of the time.

Perhaps there is a second reason. Almost no skill is required to graze, whereas catching salmon can be extremely difficult. Even some adults succeed no more than once in every 10 to 100 tries to catch a fish. Given the wide variety of fishing challenges, and the need to employ somewhat different techniques in different situations, you might expect these highly intelligent animals to pay rapt attention to those of their fellows which are most successful. In particular, you might expect cubs to pay close attention to their mothers. In fact, however, cubs seem no more attentive than human children. Much of their time is spent looking around, napping, or playing in a rather distracted manner. Even when cubs watch their mothers, they remind me of myself as a kid while my own mom cooked supper; I was far less interested in the *how* of preparation than in the *when*.

At the same time that I was rearing and studying black bear cubs, Mike Luque investigated development of fishing skills among fully wild grizzly bears at McNeil Falls.[1] There, cubs did not seem to learn much about fishing by watching their mother. Even trial and error attempts on their own were infrequent until they were several years old. The water at McNeil is so deep, swift and turbulent, and the number of aggressive adults so high, that fishing is both difficult and dangerous. Although most learning seemed to be by trial-and-error, Tom Bledsoe did observe a few cases of clear imitation at McNeil.[2]

I suspect that imitation has occurred anytime I find a stream where several bears exhibit a fishing style which is seldom seen elsewhere – like leaping forward so powerfully that salmon are splashed up on shore, where they can be captured. While I can't preclude the possibility that each bear independently invented this technique and discovered that was especially effective in this situation, I could detect no features of any fishing site so unique that they could have shaped learning so uniformly or selected for one particular technique over so many alternatives.

My own observations indicate that fishing skills develop much faster at locations where fishing is easier and competition less intense. On occasions where I have seen unweaned cubs trying or succeeding in catching fish, their techniques did not necessarily correspond to their mother's – further suggesting that imitation plays little role for most cubs. However, I do not believe that we have adequately assessed the extent of imitation. Given the keen intelligence of bears, I would have expected them to depend heavily on imitation – as heavily as chimpanzees do for culturally transmitting knowledge from individual to individual and generation to generation. As research continues, we may indeed find many examples of imitation among bears, although it may play a larger role in relatively simple skills than in something as complex as fishing. After all, how many of us could watch someone fly fishing or playing a musical instrument or using a computer, then imitate their expertise without months or years of practice?

* * *

Once Chrislee and her siblings were full of salmon, they played for awhile, then settled down for a midday siesta. Later, they played again.

Like many bears, the cubs loved walking on logs, both those lying on the ground and those which bridged a creek. Here and there, the bedrock of the cliff behind us was draped with a thick layer of organic soil as rich and brown as cocoa which had eroded from the slope above. From these deposits of soil sprang spruce and birch trees, as well as shrubs, forming a dense canopy that was all but impenetrable to a person, but perfect cover for a bear.

At the top of the cliff were large spruce and cottonwoods. Where the soil had eroded, exposing their roots, some trees had fallen prey to wind and gravity. As though they were walkers who had stubbed their toes and tripped, these trees had pivoted on their roots and fallen headlong across the valley. The taller ones struck the far rim with such force that their crowns snapped off as neatly as if Madame La Guillotine had done the job. Their headless trunks dropped farther down the slope and lodged there. In time, some of the root–masses broke loose too, and the whole tree slid down into the gorge. This produced a maze of trees cris-crossing the narrow canyon from the cliff rim down to the creek bed. As though this maze had been constructed for their enjoyment, Jonjoanak and her siblings raced up a trunk, leapt to the bank, jumped onto a higher or lower tree, then sped off in pursuit of one another.

The cubs were able to romp back and forth across the creek, for few of the "beheaded" trees had more than a few branches on the surviving portions of their trunks. One cottonwood, the trunk of which exceeded three feet in thickness at its base, had a foot-thick branch thrusting out and up more than twenty feet. Up this climbed Chrislee, followed closely by Jonjoanak. Chrislee climbed until the branches became too small to support her weight. There, she performed a pirouette that might have delighted gymnast Michelle Kwan and turned to face her pursuer. Gently, they chewed at one another's cheeks, and batted each other's head and shoulders. Jonjoanak rose up on her hindquarters and pressed forward against her sister. The branch under them cracked. Their support fell away, and they were plunged forty feet into the creek. Unlike cats, they were not able to twist in midair to land on their feet. Chrislee hit the water on her back, and Jonjoanak landed on her flank. Their splash rose up and outwards a good twenty feet, nearly drenching us. By the time Alatanna and I could get to our feet, to race over and rescue the tykes in case they had been wounded, both of their heads had popped to the surface and the little daredevils were swimming ashore, where they shook violently to rid their fur of water. Chrislee walked toward us as though to see what we were making such a fuss about, then turned back, sprinted forward, and leapt on her sister's back. Then they were off again onto the maze of fallen trees to catch their brother.

As a dead tree decays, moisture collects under its bark, which loosens the bark's grip on the wood beneath. If the bark becomes covered with moss, this accelerates the decay and the bark separates into pieces. Trunks that might appear to offer good footing thus become treacherous. When stepped on, the bark can break loose, sending the walker slipping, sliding, and perhaps tumbling. This has happened to me countless times, which is one reason I sometimes hike wearing hardened steel spikes on my boots and carrying a ski pole in one or both hands to provide added stability. You might expect this to be less likely to happen to bears. Although a bear's foot might slip on bark as easily as a person's, a bear has four paws for balance, a lower center of gravity, and twenty claws to pierce through bark to the solid wood beneath. Yet our cubs seldom dug their claws in deeply enough to penetrate through the bark, so they slipped frequently.

This is what happened to Ontak as his sisters chased him. One instant, he was racing along a trunk; then, too fast for my eye to see, he was dangling by a single paw, more than thirty feet above a pile of shattered rock which had been split from the cliff face by ice expansion during winters long past. His sisters had fallen farther without injury because they had landed in a couple of feet of water. Ontak would not be so lucky. Alatanna stifled a scream, lest she distract the cub and cause his death. I was already running forward, trying to find a place beneath Ontak where I might be able to catch him if he fell, hoping that he would not claw me too badly in his terror.

Even as I scrambled over the rock slide under him, he took his rescue into his own hands. Hanging by his left hand, he reached upwards with the right one and sank his finger claws into the wood. Then he strained to lift his hindquarters to get a grip with his toe claws. Failing in that twice, he swung his body back and forth several times until one of his feet, then the other, gained solid purchase.

Now what? He was hanging upside down with his arms and legs extended as far as possible around the underside of the sloping trunk. Had the trunk been thinner, he could have reached completely around it and sunk his finger claws into its upper side, then slipped down its length toward the ground. But with a trunk more than two feet thick, he could not even reach its vertical sides. Moving one "hand" and foot at a time, he gingerly turned until his body was crossways under the tree so that he would be able to inch upwards, around the trunk. His hands were just coming up over the curve of the trunk when more bark slipped, and his toe claws tore loose. Again, he was dangling by just his hands, and then by a single hand.

Bawling more loudly than ever, he surveyed the ground and me beneath him, then tried again to climb to safety. Another fifteen minutes of heartrending gymnastics were required for success. Then, as though the whole thing had been part of their game, all three cubs were back at play.

On another occasion when Ontak ended up dangling by a single hand, he was on a birch limb just a few inches think, with bark too smooth to offer much grip. There was no way for him to climb back up; and again, he was too high, over rocks, to simply drop to the ground safely. He swung back and forth a few times from the single hand, then reached out and grasped the branch with the other hand . Letting go with the first hand, he repeated the process, moving hand over hand several times until he reached safety. That was my first clue that black bear cubs can brachiate almost as well as a gibbon or chimpanzee.

Brachiation is much less common as black bears mature and grow in body size (I have never seen it in grizzlies). However, biologist David Garshellis[3] recently told me that brachiation remains common even into adulthood for Asian sun bears, perhaps because those bears seldom exceed 100 pounds. Furthermore, sun bears have finger claws at least two to three times as long as those of a black bear; similar to those of a grizzly, but even more strongly curved. Long, heavily curved finger claws may facilitate brachiation because they can curl entirely around to the top side of a branch or vine so that the bear can hang by its claw tips – much as I have hung from a gymnastic "horizontal bar" by a wood dowling under my fingertips, supported by leather "grips" that covered my palm.

Sloth bears, which are of intermediate body size between black and sun bears, have finger claws similar to those of a sun bear, which a sloth bear commonly uses for ripping apart termite mounds to eat the insects. It would be interesting to know how commonly they brachiate, especially as adults. I once saw a spectacled bear grip an ice cream cone in one hand by folding its hand sideways, much as a person closes a baseball glove; like panda bears, they have an opposable pseudothumb, in addition to five fingers..

As evening drew upon us, the cubs regained interest in the salmon and resumed fishing. They chased many and caught several apiece, but ate little of each fish, as though they fished now mainly for sport. Had they still been with their mother at this stage, our three imps might have observed her eating only the fattiest parts of each fish – its roe, skin, and brain – and learned to follow suit. In Doddy's absence, Alatanna and I tried to mentor her cubs. A firm squeeze to the belly of each fish revealed whether it contained reddish-orange roe or white milt (semen). Most bears readily eat roe; but they have no liking for milt, despite its popularity with some people; for instance, when fried with onion, pepper, and eggs. When one of our cubs carried a fish ashore and discovered it was a cock, it was abandoned, whereupon we rushed the poor creature back into the water, even though it had no more than a few days to live. Or, if the fish was already dead, I cut into its head to expose the brain. Unlike fully wild bears, our cubs showed little interest in brains, which they just sniffed, pawed, and licked, but generally did not eat unless cooked. Nor were the cubs much interested in raw skin. At this stage, my youngsters were much more finicky than fully wild bears. I would have to try again when they were far hungrier.

They had mastered important new skills this day. Not all that we had tried to teach, much less all that they would need in the years to come, but, there would be many more chances to teach them – and to learn from them. Meanwhile, I would have to continue tutoring them about edible plants and sharpening their skills in hunting land animals.

Dining on salmon

Enormous adult male

Chapter 12

HUNTING

RODENTS
VOLES, LEMMINGS & SQUIRRELS

Ontak and his sisters could seldom resist dashing off in pursuit of any rodent that they heard rustling through leaves. I have never seen lemmings by the thousands during a population eruption, but they were sufficiently abundant during this summer that the cubs caught several each day, and sometimes a dozen or more apiece. Red–backed voles were almost as abundant.

I have watched red and Arctic foxes and wolves hunt these small rodents by listening for them, then leaping high into the air with arched backs and landing with their forefeet together on the rodent. This can be amazingly effective, with few misses. The cubs' technique was far less refined, and for every small rodent or shrew that they caught, many others escaped. I don't know whether bears share the canid ability to hear supersonic vocalizations by rodents, or whether bears simply hear the tiny animals moving. But like a canid, a cub would begin the hunt by stopping and looking intently toward a bunch of grass, a pile of leaves, or a log. The cub's ears were typically cocked forward and her head might be tilted a bit to one side, then the other – probably to increase her ability to sonically locate the prey precisely in three dimensions. The cub would stand tensely, nose close to the ground, inhaling deeply and exhaling explosively through her nostrils, as though clearing them of air so as to scent better. Then, suddenly the cub would spring forward, and slap down, usually with a single paw one or more times. Only rarely did this lead to an immediate capture of the rodent. More often, the incredibly rapid paw slaps missed and the rodent ran, dodging undercover with the cub in hot pursuit. Usually, the rodent escaped entirely, but sometimes it took refuge in a burrow, a log, or the root–mass of a fallen tree, whereupon one or more cubs would dig furiously to reach it, sometimes succeeding, sometimes not.

Hanging by its toes to feed on a donut dangling on a string.

Although they never managed to catch a red squirrel, I often found them spellbound for several minutes watching one of these little rodents scurry up a tree, then chatter down at them, often as not hanging upside down from a branch by its hind-feet with its big fluffy tail stretched out behind, or standing facing down with its tail arched over its back.

Such scolding seemed to taunt the cubs. Had the squirrels simply disappeared, Chrislee and her siblings would have quickly lost interest and moved on to the next thing to arouse their curiosity or hunger. But the prolonged scolding was too difficult for Chrislee and Ontak to ignore. Although Jonjoanak always remained on the ground, her siblings persisted in climbing after squirrels long after they should have learned that the hunt was futile. I think they and Jonjoanak were fully aware that each chase would end with the squirrel seeking refuge at the tip of a branch too small to support a cub; or the rodent would simply jump to another tree. But that did not stop these two cubs from trying again and again.

Is taunting predators some how adaptive for squirrels – for instance in the same way that mobbing is for birds; or is taunting just a kind of sport for a squirrel toward predators from which it feels safe? I certainly never saw a squirrel taunt a weasel, which could follow the rodent any place it went. In one case, both a squirrel and a pursuing short-tailed weasel (ermine) had four babies – one prey for each tiny predator, a grim symmetry that gave me the chills.

As exciting as it was to watch the cubs chasing voles and lemmings, nothing quite compared to watching them chase down ground squirrels which were several times larger than voles or lemmings, and thus much easier for me to see, at least while the rodent was running through a short–grass meadow, across a sphagnum tundra field, or under a grove of conifers–the acidic needles and shade of which had killed off all under-story plants. In these circumstances, the squirrel was visible and the bears were incredibly swift and agile, banking into turns like motorcycle riders and shifting directions with an ease that would have made an NFL quarterback jealous. I never watched such a chase without being amazed that an animal as relatively bulky and top–heavy as a bear could maneuver as well as an eight–inch rodent – at least so long as the rodent remained visible and didn't have cover to run through where the bear couldn't follow.

(Dianne Owen photo)

It is said that squirrels, foxes, and many other small animals owe much of their agility to their tails; for although the tail adds nothing to locomotion, *per se*, it allegedly serves as a counterbalance, despite its small weight. Even the tail of animals as large as a wolf or puma supposedly serves this important function. Personally, I am skeptical. Not only is the relative weight of the tail quite small, but large tails are lacking in cervid ungulates like deer and moose, as well as in bears, which can all be quite agile. Bears somehow compensate for the lack of a tail and contribute their share to preventing rodents from overrunning the world.

I don't think it too far off the mark to say that bears sometimes fish and hunt as much for sport as for meat. In fact, I have to wonder whether the amount of energy and other nutrients gained from eating a ground squirrel really make up for the cost of catching it. The benefit/cost ratio is probably even worse for digging ground squirrels and marmots out of stony ground.

BEAVER

Where there was a creek, even one just a few inches deep and wide, Jonjoanak and her siblings usually followed it, looking for food along the shore or flipping rocks in the water to look underneath for minnows, insects, or other small prey. In milder climates, salamanders could be found this way; Bob Leslie [1] reported that his three orphaned black bears ate salamanders in British Columbia, but I know of no other reports that bears do this; indeed, some salamanders are apparently quite noxious, if not poisonous.

When our path merely crossed a creek, the cubs rarely waded or swam across if there was an alternative. More often, if the creek was too wide to jump, they would hike along its bank until they found a log spanning the water, then tightrope-walk across the log. At least, it was like tightrope-walking for me. Their balance was superb, and they crossed a log with a width of four inches as easily as if it were four feet. I was not so skilled, and more than once slipped and nearly ruined my camera.

Jonjoanak and her siblings were also adept at crossing beaver dams, stopping now and then to peer into the water, perhaps looking for salmon or Dolly Varden trout, or at a curious beaver which had come to investigate us. Although the cubs swam after beaver a few times, the speed a bear can muster by dogpaddling with just its arms and hands, while its legs and feet serve primarily as rudders, was far too slow to threaten any of these aquatic rodents, who literally swam circles around the cubs, perhaps purposefully taunting the bears, much as red squirrels did.

Ontak and his sisters were also unsuccessful at their unskilled attempts to stalk a beaver which was on land gathering branches for its winter food supply. Although adult bears can become highly successful ambush predators, this skill apparently takes months or years to master, just as it does among wolves and African lions. But unlike those pack-living carnivores, each bear must learn to catch prey independently; bears rarely hunt cooperatively. Personally, I have seldom seen it. In narrow streams, especially those with shallow water, two bears approaching one another from opposite directions can corral and confuse salmon enough to greatly increase the bears' rate of salmon capture. In wider streams, when one bear drives salmon into a shallow riffle, a bear closer to the fish can sometimes race over and catch prey that might have otherwise escaped. Also, in rare cases, two bears working side-by-side can drive salmon into shallows more effectively than can single bears, whereupon both bears catch more fish. In most cases, however, the cooperation seemed as much accidental as intentional.

Years later, I saw rudimentary cooperation between pairs of bears while fishing for salmon. However, the only cooperative predation exhibited by my cubs was in catching a beaver. The beaver caught by Ontak and his sisters was a young animal, probably in the process of leaving its parent's pond and emigrating to find a home of its own. The creek it had been ascending had shallowed out over a gravel bar, and that is where the cubs found the twenty-pound rodent. Bold as usual, Jonjoanak charged in, batting the beaver's head aside as she tried to bite its neck. Somehow, the animal twisted around and sunk its three-inch incisors entirely through the cub's cheek. All attempts at predation ceased as Jonjoanak panicked in her desperation to get free. She thrashed around, but the beaver hung on and would probably have ripped the cub's cheek open in a long gash had Chrislee and Ontak not joined the fray.

Soon, all that remained of the beaver was its skull.

I knew all too well the violence of nature and the essential roles of predation. But knowing it intellectually and being so close that I was spattered with blood were radically different things. At moments like that, I hated the cruelty of nature. Indeed, I even hated this side of the cubs' nature. No matter how affectionate and trustworthy they had become with me, they remained wild predators, something I could never allow myself to forget. Life in the wild can be brutal; unavoidably so.

PORCUPINE

One afternoon, as we hiked along the rim of Catlin Creek's gorge, the cubs became excited by some odor. They moved with abrupt, quick steps as they sniffed loudly and sometimes explosively, clearing their nostrils of other scents. Their attention focused on a pile of aspen branches the leaves of which were still fresh and attached. The stub of each branch bore the gnaw marks of a porcupine. Porkies are beautiful creatures with black and gray wooly underfur, covered by long blond guard–hairs and quills. Beautiful or not, porkies are also potentially one of the most dangerous animals in the woods for curious and impetuous young bears.

Before I could stop the cubs, they followed the rodent's scent to the base of a nearby aspen and hauled themselves up its trunk. I yelled, trying to call the cubs back, to no avail. Desperate to warn them, I woofed explosively and imitated jaw-popping by clapping my hands rapidly.

That was just the wrong thing to do, for it scared the cubs into climbing higher, where they ran right into the porcupine. Switching tactics, I tried huffing, tongue-clucking, and gulping, like a sow to call the cubs back to me. They paid no heed, if only because the rodent had aroused an overwhelming curiosity or predatory instinct.

Only the fact that the porcupine and the cubs were all in the tree together saved each cub from getting her face and hands filled with needle-sharp barbed quills, for the cubs came at the rodent from the sides, and the porky couldn't attack well in any direction but up toward its own back. Yet even one tentative swat by Chrislee drove a single four-inch quill through the webbing between two of her fingers, making her bawl loudly.

Jonjoanak was not only more aggressive by temperament, but also defensive of her sister. Her swat came from near the porky's head down toward its back, in the direction that the quills normally flattened out. Although the force of her blow knocked the rodent off the tree, Jonjoanak escaped with only a few quills puncturing her paw – which must have been agonizing.

As his two bawling sisters gingerly held onto the tree, unable to find a way of climbing down with just one usable hand apiece, Ontak slid rapidly down the trunk in pursuit of the rodent, which had by now regained its feet and was waddling off.

Rescuing the two females would have to wait until I saved Ontak from a potentially fatal clash. One good tail swat into his face could blind him. Or, at the very least, he could get a mouth full of quills that would make foraging extremely difficult for weeks to come. To a fully wild cub, this could be fatal.

I tried to grab Ontak as he slid to the ground, but in his fervor, he batted my hand aside. Reaching the porky, he headed it off, then rose to his hind feet, with arms widespread as though prepared to swat. Reaching him just in time, as the porky switched ends to confront him with its back and tail, I swept my foot under the chest of the spiny rodent and kicked it aside. It rolled several times, then came back to its feet, stunned. Before Ontak could attack, I reached down and used a stick to pin the porky's tail to the ground. Quickly grabbing it by the tail and pulling backwards, I hoisted its tail high enough to lift the porcupine's hind feet off the ground, while its forefeet dragged. In this position, it was powerless to assault me.

As I dragged the porcupine away, Ontak kept trying to attack. Although I could fend him off with a stick, this just seemed to infuriate Ontak – an all-too-common reaction by bears to frustration.

About that time, the porcupine thrashed around, jabbing several quills right through my glove and into the palm of my hand. As though my hand had caught fire, I dropped the rodent instantly. Ontak tried to dodge around me to catch the porcupine, but the rodent evaded him by scrambling over the lip of the cliff above Catlin Creek, no doubt seeking refuge. In its panicky haste, however, the porcupine slipped over the brink and plunged onto the rocks sixty feet below. Within seconds, Ontak found a way down and slid after his prey. I followed as quickly as possible. Even dead, the rodent was still dangerous.

The porcupine's immobilization calmed Ontak, but he approached with stiff forelegs and puckered upper lip – still ignoring my attempts to dissuade him by yelling "NO!" and by trying to simulate woofs and jaw-pops. One sniff was enough to jam his tender nose painfully against several quills, but not enough to drive the barbs into his skin. Instantly, he swatted the porcupine and jumped back, again painfully contacting quills without being deeply pierced by them. Despite his frustration, Ontak was smart enough – much smarter than any dog I have known – to desist. Somehow, he seemed to grasp that swatting the porcupine was a no-win situation, and that this is what I had been warning him away from. Prior to that day, the cubs had paid little heed to any of my attempts to stop them from doing something dangerous or inappropriate. After this incident, however, they began to listen more carefully.

One of the most intriguing and daunting things about bears is the speed with which they sometimes learn; a single experience can suffice to produce the critical spark of insight. There are times I wonder whether I could do as well without the aid of language.

While Ontak was distracted with the pain in his paw, I stole the porcupine's carcass and dropped it into a four-foot cleft of rock and tumbled a couple of heavy boulders on top.

Rescuing the two females would be a real challenge. Each had tried repeatedly to descend from the tree, but found the experience too painful. Now that each had only one hand with which to hug the tree against her chest, there was no way for the cub to come down hand over hand as she normally would. And neither cub was rash enough to try sliding down while hugging the slick-barked aspen trunk while holding on with just the one hand. They were stuck until I could climb up to help them descend. For that, I needed climbing gear, which meant running to the cabin and back.

When I was finally able to reach Chrislee, over an hour later, I positioned myself behind her, with my boot spurs driven deeply into the trunk below us and held there by my weight as I leaned back against the climbing belt. As I petted her muzzle gently, Chrislee licked my hand and looked over her shoulder in a mute plea for help. Despite her fear, she was finally persuaded to let go of the tree and turn to face me, with her "arms" around my neck and her face beside mine, with her belly against my chest. Much as I might have wished her to relax, she gripped me as tightly as she had gripped the tree, digging her claws in for security. But for my heavy leather clothing, her claws would have penetrated deeply into my flesh. Thank God her claws weren't as sharp as a cat's!

As painful as it had been to rescue Chrislee, I was amply rewarded by her obvious joy when we reached the ground. Temporarily ignoring Jonjoanak's pained bawls far overhead, I sat down and rolled Chrislee onto her back, head across my left thigh. This gave me free access to her right paw, which she held up as though asking for help. Unclipping a pair of fisherman's needle-nose pliers from my belt, I grasped the barbed end of the quill where it protruded a half-inch beyond the web between Chrislee's first and second fingers. The quill came free with a sudden jerk, with no protest from Chrislee. In fact, she seemed unaware that the quill was gone, as though her paw may have still hurt as much as when the quill was in place. Well, time and bit of antibiotic ointment back at the cabin would work their cure.

I climbed back up to rescue Jonjoanak. Although I positioned myself behind her, with my chest against her back, Jonjoanak was unwilling to release her grip on the poplar and hold onto me instead, as her sister had. But she was clearly happy that I had come to help. She licked the hand I held near her muzzle and rubbed the back of her head against my chest as I straddled her. Finally, leaning her back against me, much as I leaned back against the climbing belt, she seemed to understand that this would keep her from falling. Almost more quickly than I could see, she released the grip of her left hand above her head, then reached down past her shoulders and dug her finger-claws in again. Then she stepped down with her feet, one at a time, and repeated the entire cycle again and again until we reached the ground.

Like her sister, Jonjoanak rolled over onto her back with her quill-festooned paw extended toward me. Helping Chrislee had been easy, for the single quill had fully penetrated just through skin and could be pulled straight out in the direction of the barbs. But several quills had been driven at least a quarter–inch into Jonjoanak's paw. Left in place, the barbs would catch on connective tissue and muscle fibers and be drawn or pushed ever deeper into her flesh, each quill working its way through the entire hand to eventually emerge from the top. By that time, nerves or tendons might be damaged by the quills; and the whole hand could be infected. I could see no alternative to pulling the quills out backwards. But I also knew Jonjoanak would rebel the first time I tugged on any of them, and heaven help me when I tried for a second tug.

Finally, in a moment of inspiration, I pulled the porcupine corpse from its hiding place and brought it over to the cubs. While keeping them at bay, I pretended to smash my right hand against the animal, yelped and began bawling – bear fashion – as I raised the hand with several quills held between paired fingers, as though they had penetrated my hand. As usual, the cubs were very interested in what I did with my hands and watched closely as I took the pliers in my free hand and pretended to pull the quills loose from the "injured" hand, with loud yelps to indicate pain, then gradually louder sighs of relief. Bears can be acutely sensitive to human body language, and although my acting would have won no Oscars, it seemed to get the message across – if not the first time I did this, then at least by the third time. To my surprise, all three cubs crowded around me as dogs might, as though to comfort me. Poor ailing Jonjoanak even reached up with her left paw, pulled my "injured" hand close to her nose, and licked it gently.

Taking a cue from her behavior, I raised her pin-cushioned right hand to my own face, then gently nuzzled and licked it – taste and sanitation be damned. She watched with more trust and affection than I would have ever dreamed possible even a few weeks earlier. Now was the time I would have to put her improved temperament to the test.

I have removed quills from the mouths and faces of dogs on several occasions and each trusted me only until the first quill was pulled – a trust that was seriously compromised by the sudden stab of pain which followed. Pulling the rest of the quills required wrestling the dog down and muzzling it, or tranquilizing the animal.

I expected an even more violent response from Jonjoanak. She was powerful enough to have ripped me apart with her twenty inch-long black claws. Indeed, had the quills been imbedded more deeply, she might have defended herself. But the quills had penetrated only about a quarter-inch, and she did nothing more than jerk away, pop her lips, and huff before sitting down and licking the injured hand. After twice more mimicking painful removal of quills from my own hand, I was able to approach her once more, and with surprising stoicism, she allowed me to lick her paw once more, and then to remove the last few quills.

I now had a final set of lessons to teach. Over the course of their lives, the cubs would undoubtedly encounter numerous porcupines. Dogs which have been injured by a porky sometimes develop a chronic hatred for them and will attack again and again, despite the futility and agony of doing so. In case the cubs might be so inclined, I wanted to teach them how to deal with a porky. First, I let them examine the carcass at their own initiative. Each would approach cautiously and tensely, nose the animal, then jump back, with or without swatting it. Because the porcupine was dead and its quills were flat, those quills which stabbed into sensitive cub noses and hands were easily pulled free without my help. Finally, when they tired of this sport, I again mimed injuring myself by handling the porky with its belly against the ground and its well-defended back bowed upwards. I was especially demonstrative about being hurt by its tail. Last, I flipped the porky upside down and made a show of handling it in that position without being hurt.

Fishers (a kind of weasel about the size of a house cat) specialize in hunting porcupines, and no doubt bear cubs can learn to do the same. Mine might need every source of meat they could find. Reluctantly, therefore, over the next few weeks, I did this twice more with road–killed porcupines, trying to make sure that my cubs knew enough to bite only into a porcupine's belly. Learning how to flip a live porky over and kill it safely would take longer and be much riskier.

Some cubs are not so lucky, such as the infant grizzly I encountered whose mouth was filled with quills. Over the period of an hour, I won his confidence enough that he allowed me to come within a yard and see exactly what was wrong. A few quills penetrated through his gums or cheeks, several in his palate, and at least one through his tongue. Even after quills have been softened by saliva, they can supposedly still work their way ever deeper into the flesh. Those in the lips or cheeks and palate would probably do no lasting harm, but those in the tongue could seriously interfere with eating. I was afraid the cub would starve, and tried to figure out a way of luring him close enough that I could grasp the most dangerous barbs with my Leatherman pliers and jerk them free. Although I finally induced the cub to sniff my left hand as I moved the pliers forward with my right, the cub was too wary and I finally had to give up. A year later, I found a cub skeleton in the river just yards from where I had last seen this cub, suggesting he soon died.

MOOSE

Although Alaska is home to a variety of hoofstock (ungulates), including deer, sheep, mountain goats, caribou, and moose, only moose lived in the immediate vicinity of where I raised the cubs. Other than porcupines, wolves, or other bears, moose were the animals which posed the greatest danger to my cubs. Having once watched a mother moose stomp a grizzly to death, I was constantly afraid for my tykes.

During the two years that I studied moose and lived with them night and day, their reactions to me changed from attempts to kill me to guarded tolerance. I would have liked to win the same kind of tolerance for my cubs, but that was just wishful thinking. Moose calves are just too tempting as prey, and moose mothers are too defensive.

I thus nearly panicked one afternoon when I saw the cubs slow down and stalk toward the shore of a deep pond about fifteen yards away. A moose calf of roughly 100 pounds stood up there. Why it didn't flee before the cubs got that close, I don't know. Although it may have been dozing, moose never doze deeply, and usually wake up when leaves or branches rustle within, say, fifty yards. (A few years earlier, while making close-range observations of moose, I found it almost impossible to remain still enough to avoid waking them repeatedly.) Instead of running away, this calf seemed curious – too curious for its own good. The little moose stepped toward Chrislee, lowering its nose towards hers. The cub reciprocated. As they gently got to know each other, Ontak and Jonjoanak approached and circled around their sister to one flank of the calf. Now the calf began to get nervous, and she laid her ears back while facing Ontak. The calf's head lifted and tilted a bit, revealing an eye with a crescent moon of white sclera visible, a sure sign of fright.

Suddenly, a thunderous roar came from the direction of the pond. The calf's mother must have been feeding underwater when we arrived, for she had appeared seemingly out of nowhere, with her head dripping water and her ears hanging upside down. Had the pond's bottom been solid gravel, she might have reached the cubs before they could flee. But the bottom was muddy and the shore rimmed with a quivering mat of floating vegetation through which the mamma moose had to fight. In the minute or so it took for the cow to join her calf, all three cubs escaped to the tops of trees, from which they pant–huffed and clacked their teeth in fright.

Although I had started looking for a tree as soon as I saw the calf, knowing its mother would be nearby, and was already climbing before the cow appeared, I was still not out of reach when she galloped over and stood beneath me, head low, neck and rump mane standing on end, growling, gnashing her teeth, and salivating heavily. I have seldom been so terrified. Once before when I was treed by a mother moose, the animal reared up and hit the tree with her chest with such force that she knocked the tree over. Had that tree not lodged against others, but fallen to the ground, I could have been stomped into hamburger by her hooves. Fortunately, this moose made no attempt to attack and soon trotted off with her calf. It was an experience I would not soon forget; nor, hopefully would the cubs.

Researchers have estimated that wolves and bears together kill up to 80 percent of the moose calves in some parts of Alaska. Although there are reasons to suspect that the typical loss is considerably lower, the fact remains that black bears take a substantial number of calves each year. No doubt my cubs would eventually give this a shot as well. If so, I could only hope that this day's experience would improve their chances of surviving the attempt.

WILD GOOSE CHASE

Several grouse lived within a mile of our cabin, and the cubs flushed them now and then. Each time this happened, and the birds escaped with a thunder of wing-beats into the nearby spruce trees, the cubs gave chase. Since this was hasty flight by the grouse, rather than a mother's broken-wing display down on the ground, these birds may not have been fleeing their nests and trying to draw the bears away from eggs, but I was always thankful that the cubs never found any grouse eggs while they were with me; I enjoyed having these birds for neighbors. The cubs did occasionally find bird's nests in trees and made short work of any eggs or hatchlings. Indeed, there were times when they seemed to deliberately search out nests. Fortunately, they found no more than one or two a week. Although I could reconcile their attempts to prey on game birds, I did my best to dissuade them from bothering song birds – those most pleasant, but all too uncommon neighbors.

The raven which Jonjoanak killed while guarding her salmon is the only one of its kind that ever fell prey to the cubs. But these winged nuisances followed us on many occasions, picking up bits of salmon and other scraps which the cubs left behind, or searching through soil exposed when the cubs overturned carpets of sphagnum moss looking for worms, beetles and other small prey. I hadn't really paid attention to these birds until I began hearing a yowl very much like that uttered by a Siamese cat in heat. The cubs were as intrigued as I, and we hunted for the source without success. Not yet even dreaming that the yowl could be coming from a raven, I was baffled by how the sound kept shifting from the ground to the trees in situations in which I saw no mammal moving around. Days passed before the sound was uttered from so close that I spotted the raven. Even then, a few repetitions were required before I could believe what was happening.

Less surprising, perhaps, was the raven's ability to imitate the gulps and tongue clicks of a bear –which weren't too terribly different than a raven's own natural gulps and clicks. My own success at mimicking these bear sounds had been limited at best. The cubs came when I made these calls only because they had learned to do so. But time and again they were drawn out by the raven. I couldn't quite believe that this was intentional; but perhaps I wasn't giving the bird enough credit for intelligence and playfulness. Indeed, I didn't really believe that ravens played until years later when I watched them sliding down a snowy rooftop, much as bears slide down avalanche chutes, again and again and again – except that whereas bears and telemark skiers have to climb back to the top, ravens hop or just fly back to their starting point.

Another raven in this flock uttered calls that sounded for all the world like a diesel engine. I could only guess that it had spent a critical period of its youth at the landfill a few miles from our cabin, and had "imprinted" on the sound of the dozer which buried trash each weekend.

Although ducks were a frequent temptation, the cubs never caught one.

The only adult birds the cubs ever caught and ate were a couple of geese. Now and then, a flock would settle down on a shallow pond about a mile from the cabin and either dip for food or come ashore to graze. Whenever the cubs saw geese ashore, they charged headlong. Generally, this simply forced the birds to fly off and find another feeding site. But on one occasion, perhaps during a period of molting, one goose failed to stay airborne. Although it got several feet into the air and flapped rapidly away, it wasn't able to maintain enough altitude. As it landed in the pond, Ontak plowed in after it. As the bird became airborne again, it did so too slowly, and Ontak leapt upwards, his short claws hooking the goose and dragging it down into the water. Meanwhile, Jonjoanak had caught another goose. Neither cub was willing to share the prize with Chrislee, who went back and forth between her siblings, alternately begging and fighting in vain for a share.

Although geese rarely fall prey to bears, undefended eggs are vulnerable

This was one of the few times I have ever seen a bear beg. Chrislee did so by crawling forward with her elbows touching the ground and her hindquarters low. Her head was also held low, with her chin or one cheek on the ground. Not until several years later did I see a young grizzly likewise beg for a chunk of salmon from his mother; this was a year after he had been weaned and dissociated from her. Although the mother griz didn't chase away her youngster, neither did she provide him with a meal.

While goose hunting provided two cubs with a meal this once, they weren't so lucky on subsequent attempts. When the cubs next rushed a flock of geese, the birds did not flee, but turned on the cubs and mobbed them, pecking furiously. Ontak and Jonjoanak escaped quickly, but Chrislee waited too long – perhaps determined this time to succeed where previously she had failed to catch a bird. Quickly surrounded by dozens of geese, she was attacked mercilessly from so many sides at once that she could not defend herself. Fearing for her safety, I rushed to the rescue. This is the only time wild geese have refused to flee from me.

They held their ground and several attacked my legs. Their beaks packed the wallop of a person's fist, and their pecks ended with nips as painful as a dog's, pinching my skin even through the heavy leather of my pants. This left my legs covered with bruises, and injuries to Chrislee's face suggested that she had been pecked near her eyes. Perhaps the birds were deliberately trying to blind her – an antipredator defense that was new to me, but eminently practical.

Predation can be a tough way to make a living.

INVERTEBRATES

The cubs constantly licked up beetles, grubs, and other invertebrates found hither and yon, but there were few that they could obtain in even moderate quantity. Earthworms were the first exception. Although the cubs had occasionally eaten earthworms, even on our earliest hikes together, they did not actively search them out until we chanced upon a concentration of the juicy invertebrates.

Much of the forest north of the cabin consisted of black spruce trees. Their trunks were seldom more than six inches in diameter at ground level. Bare gray branches up to an inch thick and festooned with hairy lichens started a few feet above the ground and continued to the crown. Only those branches above six feet or so were still alive, with inch-long, dark-green, needles. Branches lower down were dead, dry, and so interwoven from tree to tree that much of the forest was impenetrable to humans and possibly to moose. Although the dead branches could be cut with a heavy machete, advancing a hundred yards would have been an all-day job. Instead, I stuck to the trails wherever possible.

These thickets were, however, no impediment to the short-legged cubs, and it was usually through the forest, not on the trail, that the cubs traveled as they foraged, constantly on the move with a few bites here and a few there, interspersing feeding with exploration.

One afternoon, we came across an old tract which someone had once hacked out of the forest, despite the enormous labor required. It was too narrow, rough, and filled with ankle–high stumps to have ever been used by a jeep. Probably a dogsled route for someone's winter trapline, I speculated. Whatever its origins, it had received enough use by moose and other game that a foot-wide trail remained, flanked by a thick regrowth of young birch, and then by the spruce forest itself. Wondering where the winding trail led, we hiked along it for more than a mile before reaching an old line cabin, the roof of which had caved in under the weight of winter snows. Inside, I found a stained and faded *Life* magazine dated only five years earlier, suggesting that the cabin had been livable at least that recently.

Extending roughly eight feet by ten, the cabin walls had been knocked askew, probably when the roof collapsed. The walls were made of spruce logs that were now rotting – more from improper preparation than from age, for the sill logs were lying against the damp, mossy ground, instead of being elevated on rock pilings. Just as bad, the logs had never been peeled; they were havens for boring insects and for moisture, which in turn fostered the growth of mold, mildew, moss, and other agents of decay.

After the cubs wore themselves out exploring the shack and ferreting out red-backed voles that were consumed with an audible crunch, they moved on to a collapsed horse stall where they spent the next hour digging earthworms out of a pile of ancient manure. Apparently the cabin's owner had found a summertime alternative to dog-sledding – for one season, anyway. Although horses do fine in Alaska during our few months of summer, they can be prohibitively expensive to feed during the rest of the year, especially at a site this remote.

The manure had been exposed to the weather long enough that much of its nitrogen had been leached out, making it an ideal habitat for earthworms. These were consumed with gusto by all three cubs. I even managed to snag a few worms for fish bait.

Despite the cubs' intense rivalry when I fed them store-bought foods, they seldom fought over any natural foods except meat. Violent competition seemed to be triggered by the perception of scarcity and by frustration.

After this first heavy meal of worms, the cubs sought them avidly; for instance, by peeling back the layer of sphagnum moss that covered much of the ground where the soil was poorly drained, or by rolling over logs. The cubs also tore the bark off of logs, or tore the logs apart to find carpenter ants and a variety of other insects, including beetles, grubs and ants – eggs, pupae, and some adults. These invertebrates were a major source of food. (Beware that citronella insect repellent supposedly contains the scent of ants; when you wear it, you may smell like bear food.)

The decay pattern of birch trees is unique. The bark of other trees sloughs off soon after decay begins, exposing the wood to weathering and insects. Birch bark however remains strong enough to support the tree even after the wood has lost all structural strength – resisting buckling in the same way as does a soda straw filled with bits of styrofoam or cornmeal. But allow a straw's contents to leak out,, and the "straw" collapses under a little pressure. Countless times, I watched the cubs rear up against a dead birch and knock it over. Initially, I suspected that the cubs were drawn to these trees by the scent of insects inside the decayed wood, and that they were taking advantage of how easily this wood could be torn apart to find tiny prey. However, as best I can recall, they seldom found many insects in the wood; most of the decay seemed fungal. Why then knock over so many dead birch? Possibly for sport.

Although yellow–jacket hornets were fairly common in our area, I saw no indication that the cubs recognized them as potential food until we came across JeenTo digging out a nest of these insects one day. Since we had last seen this sow, two of her cubs had disappeared, which may explain why she and her remaining cub, PeeTee, immediately fled on detecting us. Whether PeeTee's siblings had been lost to a hunter[1], a boar, a porcupine or some other hazard, I had no way of knowing. More than two weeks passed before JeenTo regained her trust of us and allowed my cubs to join PeeTee in play.

After having been introduced to yellow-jackets this way, Ontak and his sisters hunted and dug up their nests avidly. They also learned to find the hanging nests of "paper wasps" and knock these down, consuming the pupae and sometimes a few adults. Although the cubs' fur presumably protected most of their bodies, they reacted so violently, if briefly, to stings to the nose that these must have been quite painful.

Considering the potentially crippling effect of a sting to the eye, I personally would have considered supping on such dangerous insects far too risky to be worth the small reward. Obviously, bears do not look at it this same way.

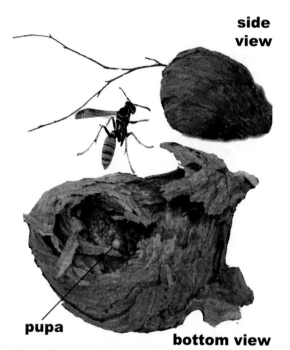

side view

pupa

bottom view

Yellowjacket "paper" wasp and nest (about 6" wide) whose bottom had been ripped open, exposing pupae inside, one of which is visible here

Over the period of a month, these and other invertebrates probably provided my cubs with more protein and lipid than did any other terrestrial prey except voles and lemmings.

Although salmon were a much better source of protein and lipid, the fish were available for shorter periods each summer, and competition from other bears and occasionally from wolves was much greater. Just as bad, bears feeding on salmon are easy prey for hunters. So being insectivorous might be vital to the survival of Ontak and his sisters.

Flying insects can be especially important as grizzly bear foods. In certain areas of the Sierra Mountains ladybug beetles gather in inch-deep swarms on widely scattered alpine boulders. At higher altitudes in the Rockies, army cutworm moths gather by the millions on boulder-strewn talus slopes. Such insects provide feasts of gargantuan proportions for grizzlies. In all reports that I have read, moths were found far above the timberline. I suspect, however, that moths may also gather in talus slopes well below timberline. When I lived on the Blackfeet Indian Reservation, just south of Glacier National Park, I collected hundreds of these moths from my firewood pile and from within boxes of books and clothing stored in my barn. So cutworm moths may be available to bears in far more locations than have yet been discovered, and may be an even more important food source – if not now, then potentially in the future.

Bears also feed heavily on ground dwel-ling colonial insects. One of the most obvious and common signs of bears in a forest is logs ripped apart to reach burrowing ants or termites. Indeed, termites are so abundant in Southeast Asia that the sloth bear is specially adapted to gather this food with extremely long, hooked claws that can rip a termite mound apart, despite the earthen mound's tough, hard exterior. When the termites boil out of their broken nest to defend and repair it, the bear blows loose dirt away from the ants, and then sucks them up through long flexible lips that form a tube, and then through a gap at the front of its mouth where the inner pair of incisors on each jaw has disappeared evolutionarily. Chimpanzees also feast on termites.

When winter ice thaws each spring in Russia's Lake Baikal, cadis flies hatch out in such enormous numbers that they are feasted on by brown bears. Whether North American bears enjoy a similar annual caddis fly banquet is unknown to me.

In this way, as in so many others, variety is not only the "spice of life," but the key to survival – at least in the face of strictly natural hazards.

HUNTED

Ontak and his sisters not only hunted a wide variety of prey; they were themselves in turn potential prey. Several large predators haunted the woods in the general vicinity of our cabin, any of which could have made short work of a single cub. Together, however, the three cubs were harder to surprise and overpower. On the few occasions that the cubs were confronted by the local family of coyotes, the canids were quickly routed without my help.

The greatest danger to Ontak and his sisters was people. Despite all my precautions to reinforce the cubs' inherent wariness toward humans, this nearly proved insufficient.

One of the unfortunate aspects of life in Alaska was that the hunting of black bears was legal virtually year-round. Indeed, black bears were the only large game available during summer and were avidly pursued by some hunters looking for meat or sport. One of these tried to kill Ontak, apparently thinking that even ten to thirty pounds of meat would be welcome, the equivalent of several rabbits, and much tastier.

While his sisters wrestled near Alatanna, Ontak and I had followed the trail of another bear that he had sniffed out. This quickly led us to another abandoned cabin with a nearby serviceberry tree. While Ontak began demolishing its crop of dusty blue berries. I ate several handfuls, then settled back to nap.

Some time later, I was shocked awake by an explosive woof from Ontak. Leaping to my feet, I looked around for the cub, who was still in the serviceberry, but standing upright and looking downhill while he chomped his jaws in agitation. Following his gaze, I saw a man with a rifle at his eye, taking aim at Ontak.

Clapping loudly and screaming to warn the cub to tree, I waved my arms and shouted at the hunter to stop. He shot anyway. Ontak's quick obedience to my command may have saved his life, for the bullet missed.

While the hunter tried to sight in on the cub again, I snatched my own rifle off the ground and fired a round in the man's direction. *That* got his attention.

By the time he had his rifle lowered and spotted me, I had jacked another round into the chamber and had the sights lined up on his chest. I yelled at him to drop his rifle; fortunately, he complied.

As soon as I lowered mine, he started cussing at me for ruining his shot. Although my .338 magnum was now cradled in my arms, it was still pointing in his general direction as I closed the distance to him. Once more, he tried to reach for his rifle, but backed off at my command. With both of us boiling mad, I was glad to have the upper hand.

At first, all he could think about was killing Ontak, who was clearly visible high in a large spruce tree. When I demanded that the guy leave my cub alone – that Ontak was tame – he defended himself by claiming that he had seen the cub in the tree above me and thought he was just about to jump down and attack me.

"And just how did the cub get into the serviceberry tree in the first place?" I countered. Obviously, Ontak would have had to climb the trunk near where I had been napping, which would have probably awakened me. Scratch one excuse.

Then the guy threatened to call the state troopers, claiming that he had a legal right to kill any bear he saw, and that I had no authority whatsoever to stop him, tame bear or not.

He was perfectly, damnably correct. Any person carrying a valid hunting license – which could cost as little as $1 for an Alaska resident hunting just for subsistence – had a legal privilege to kill any black bear, whereas I had no right to keep that same bear alive. And certainly, by the warped logic of some hunters, the cub had no right to his own life.

As much as that infuriated me, it was a fact of life I had to live with and to which I had to adjust. Continuing to argue with the man would just make more trouble. Rather than try to sort out the hassle, Fish & Game would demand that I kill all three cubs or let someone like this yokel do so.

It was Alatanna who saved the day. Having heard the gunshots, she came running, bursting out of the woods sixty yards away and calling out. Beside her came Chrislee and Jonjoanak, who immediately took fright when they saw the hunter. They raced up a tree and remained there as my lovely lady joined me, red–faced and panting from her run.

As soon as I assured her that Ontak was okay, she turned toward the hunter. Instead of yelling at him, she thanked him for sparing "her baby." His anger melted into contriteness. He apologized, explaining that he had no idea anyone was raising cubs in the area.

By now, my gun was on the ground, too. Alatanna and I introduced ourselves to him and we all shook hands. We explained how the cubs had been orphaned and how we were trying to train them to fend for themselves. After making sure that all three cubs were still treed, we walked with the hunter a mile back to the road where he had parked.

Hopefully, his change of attitude was real, and we had converted a potential enemy into a budding friend who would do his hunting elsewhere, and refrain from telling any of his hunting buddies about our cubs ... hopefully.

That was our closest call with a hunter, but certainly not our only one. Keeping the cubs alive required keeping them so wary that they would remain at least a few hundred yards from all humans except Alatanna and me.

Some people talk as though increasing bears' fear of people minimizes the danger that bears pose to people. But anyone who thinks the matter through should realize that there is some level of fear that causes a bear to attack, rather than to flee, when it encounters someone at close range. Behavioral scientists call this range the "attack distance" or "critical distance." They hypothesize that the animal is afraid that turning its back on an enemy to flee will expose itself to attack by that enemy; so it instead attacks the enemy. Animals with little fear attack this way only if approached very closely; animals with intense fear have a longer attack distance – which elevates the risk that a close encounter will occur within this distance.

So, although I wanted our cubs to fear people enough to avoid them, I didn't want them to panic if they were ever surprised at close quarters. I can't claim to have achieved that balance by design, since I simply didn't know how to do it. But it happened anyway, perhaps as a consequence of their affection and trust for Alatanna and me.

On the few occasions when someone did show up at the cabin unannounced, the cubs sped away either into the forest or up into a tree. In no case were they ever aggressive – aside from making fear threats by woofing, pant- huffing, jaw-popping, and perhaps pounding a tree with their hands. On only two occasions, when surprised at close range, did a cub even make a short hop-charge by bounding forward a few paces and slapping the ground powerfully.

*   *   *

I could accept the fact that everything has its price, and that the survival of robust bear populations has been bought by allowing hunters to harvest "surplus" individuals. But I could not then, and I cannot now accept a situation where there is *no* place where even a few people can develop deep, intimate companionship with a few bears and other North American "big–game" species comparable to what Jane Goodall achieved with chimpanzees and Dian Fossey with gorillas.* About the only place bears are not hunted legally is inside our national parks – where companionship with wildlife is strongly discouraged. Outside of parks, hunting pressure keeps bears so afraid of people that intimate companionship becomes too difficult and perhaps too dangerous.

In a continent this large and a nation as progressive and creative as America, it is not reasonable that *every* bear outside of a national park or a few other kinds of refuge is an open target. Yet there is no mechanism for protecting companion bears from harvest. Anyone with a hunting license has more right to kill a bear like Ontak, Chrislee, or Jonjoanak than the animal has to live, or than people have to enjoy it alive.

A more enlightened perspective might place less value on producing meat, trophies, sport, and bragging rights than on producing science, education, and art from a diversity of perspectives.

Does this mean that I am anti-hunter? No, not even anti-hunting. When I lived in the deep bush, far from any grocery store, where the

---

In 2009, my friend Charlie Vandergaw was arrested for feeding black and grizzly/brown bears in Alaska, even though "his" bears never bothered anyone,. Now, most have been killed by authorities in a misguided attempt to assure human safety.

ghost of starvation was a guest at every meal, I did hunt. I loathed turning beautiful animals into meat, but I had no choice' without hunting, we would have died. Life is often a tangle of loves and hates.

Like bears and wolves, I enjoyed the thrill of hunting. I loved the intense satisfaction of providing meat for the table. Even more satisfying than the flavor of wild game was the knowledge that I was functioning as a part of the ecosystem. It nourished me, and someday my body would nourish it – but not quite yet.

Let me tell you, the excitement of winning a million-dollar lottery could not begin to compare with the joy of knowing that you will not starve; that you just may live through the bleak and terribly cold winter; that beyond whatever you have achieved with your own guts, determination, and skill, most of your success was a matter of luck, a gift from God, a sign of His favor. I have looked upon game I have taken with deep affection, knowing that I would not live if its life had not been surrendered. However reluctantly, it had died that I might live. Like my Native neighbors, I did not take that gift for granted, but with the deepest appreciation and reverence.

Do animal predators ever feel gratitude toward prey? Ontak and his sisters never displayed any detectable affection for their prey. However, there are times when wolves or African lions and their kin seem to treat prey with great affection, as Elizabeth Marshall Thomas has described so eloquently in her book *Tribe of Tiger* – although a felid licking prey probably has less to do with affection than with using the rasp-like surface of the tongue to remove hair from the prey's body.

Like my cubs, I took great pleasure in the excitement of the hunt. It added a critical zest to the arduous process of garnering meat and protein. I can understand why other people relish the thrill, and see nothing immoral or evil in this. It is simply nature's way of motivating predators, including humans, to get on with making a living, despite the effort and pain required.

I also recognize the critical role sport hunters have played in the conservation and sometimes restoration of game populations – including bears – and their habitat.

Yet having said all that, I consider it deeply immoral to kill animals just for trophies and for bragging rights. Although I delight in my collection of hides, skulls, antlers and horns, having one larger than the next guy does nothing for my ego. My own collection of such "trophies" comes strictly from animals which died of natural causes, with the exception of hides from two animals killed for meat. (On the other hand, I'm not immune to the short-lived satisfaction of owning a bigger faster computer than my friends).

Trophy hunters such as Sarkis Atamian[4] accuse opponents of a kind of penis envy – stating that everyone really wants trophies, but most of us simply lack the "balls" or skill to kill them . Personally, though, I'm not terribly impressed by people who "face charging bears" with a .400 Weatherby Magnum elephant rifle, given that my colleagues and I have often faced them bare-handed. Our lives don't lack for excitement or opportunities to test our nerve. Consider the following examples:

*   Bear biologists commonly crawl into bear dens to tranquilize black bears for research purposes. Few of the biologists carry a weapon, and I know of none who has ever been attacked. On the contrary, if the black bear awakens, it is most likely to flee if possible or otherwise to merely threaten, perhaps by bluff-charging. Personally, I once faced a sow that woke up from hibernation with her nose 4 inches from mine. On another occasion, I was sitting astride a black bear when his dose of tranquilizer wore off and he stood up.

*   The boar I called Mallic must have been one of the biggest black bears in North America. He stood over four feet tall at the shoulder, taller than any other black bear I have ever seen and taller than many grizzlies. Although he probably weighed no more than 400 to 500 pounds at the time I saw him, in the spring, he could well have exceeded 600 or 700 pounds by late fall. Had I wanted to shoot him, I could have easily done so; indeed, I considered it. He was eating another bear when I found him and soon appeared to be sizing me up for dessert. Worse, we might have met again sometime when I was not so well prepared to defend myself. Nevertheless, I chose to spare Mallic and was able to climb into my pickup and leave without harm to either of us.

*   I study some of the largest grizzly/brown bears in the world, a few of which approach 1,500 pounds. I watch and film the boars, often from as close as fifty yards and sometimes within ten yards, even during rut. So long as they never try to harm me, I will never harm them. Indeed, staying close to dominant boars sometimes keeps the more aggressive adolescent males at bay. Far from being a hazard, some big boars provide an invaluable safety zone. The excuse that big boars have to be killed to protect people or even cubs just doesn't hold water, judging from extensive research I and various colleagues have done on the subject.

In any event, my biggest objection to hunting is that it is so ubiquitous; that so many hunters feel that their sport should have precedence over all other uses of wildlife, in virtually all locations. [Some anti–hunters are just as extreme in wanting to ban all harvest of game.] Rogue hunters complain bitterly about being denied access to trophy animals within national parks or refuges; some even bait the animals outside these sanctuaries or poach within them.

On the contrary; we need more refuges where people can enjoy animals freely, without so much bureaucratic restriction and without risk of the animals being harassed or killed. Whether these refuges should be large or small should depend on how many people want to hunt versus how many people want to enjoy animals that are unhunted. In Alaska, where a high proportion of the populace hunts for meat or sport, I can see allowing hunting over most of the landscape. But we should prohibit hunting, trapping, etc. in areas especially well suited for watching wild-life such as bears, or perhaps for getting to know the animals personally or even rearing orphans.

We need areas dedicated to wildlife-human companionship – if not for the general public, then at least for select *wildlife ambassadors* like Charlie Vandergaw who have the knowledge and resources to get to know animals deeply and personally, and to convey what they have experienced to the public so that everyone can enjoy this, at least vicariously.

Chapter 13
CALL OF THE WILD

I awoke with Chrislee's cool nose pressing against my foot. Although Alatanna and I easily slept through the 4 A.M. alarm buzz, the cubs always took it as the signal to awaken us. They had no intention of letting us leave for work without first giving them a good tussle. After wrestling with the youngsters, we caressed and massaged each of them in turn, a treat that transported the cubs into momentary bliss. As my fingers brushed lightly through Chrislee's sleek inch-long summer pelt, I felt the powerful vibration of her purring, with no premonition that we would never again hug any of the cubs.

When we returned to the cabin that evening, there was no sign of the youngsters. They still hadn't shown up by morning. Although they were commonly gone overnight, they normally returned by morning to play with us, then to snooze in the security of the cabin. But not this day, or the next.

Had an adult boar, another predator, or a moose killed the cubs? Had the guy who had tried to shoot Ontak, or one of his buddies, returned and killed them all? Were they gone forever?

Fall arrived with blazing colors. Amid hillsides luminescent with chartreuse or golden aspen were patches aflame with mountain ash, blueberry, and fireweed in multitudinous shades of orange, red, and purple. Even as the fireweed stems and leaves burned scarlet, their pods burst open, releasing seed puffs of purest white that temporarily muted the scarlet into something softer and more pastel before the seeds took wing and scattered on the wind like billions of tiny feathers.

Yet for all that beauty, we hardly took notice. Weeks had passed since our last sign of the cubs. We were despondent, but fortunately too busy to mope.

Suddenly, one afternoon, our deep-woods serenity was shattered as the cabin door slammed open. There stood Jonjoanak. Rather than entering the cabin, she stood in the doorway, threatening us. Just what motivated this, I didn't know. Perhaps Ontak and Chrislee had been killed by someone, alienating Jonjoanak to all people, even us.

Jonjoanak's face was nearly vertical, upper lip puckered as though preparing to bite or bawl in fury. Her cheeks were sucked in so far that her head appeared elongated. Hunching her shoulders, she began clawing at the burlap insulation on the doorsill, then at the soil outside the sill, slamming her hands down forcefully before raking backwards – much as a bull might paw the ground before charging a matador. Jonjoanak did this while staring at us and inhaling with unusual deliberation and power, at intervals of about one second – about twice the length of a normal inhalation.

After raking several times, Jonjoanak shook herself vigorously. Woofing and huffing repeatedly, she stalked into the cabin, forelegs as stiff and pigeon–toed as those of a silent film cowboy as she continued to stamp her forepaws against the ground with each step – a gait I named the *cowboy walk*.

Recalling the cubs' preference for darkness, Alatanna blew out the kerosene light, hoping that this would calm Jonjoanak. She talked softly to the cub and tried to pet Jonjoanak, but her affection was rebuffed. Jonjoanak remained inside only long enough to assure herself that Ontak and Chrislee were absent and no food was available. Stalking outside again, she climbed a tree from which she refused to descend until ready to sleep for the night. Finally at rest in her usual spot behind the stove, she kept a wary and baleful eye on us. Her foul temper continued unabated day after day. Each time the cabin door slammed open again, we looked up to see Jonjoanak there alone. Then suddenly, after two weeks, we were astounded to see her accompanied by Chrislee and Ontak. Where had they been since late July?

And how big they were! Even with all the rich food Jonjoanak had obtained with our help, she hadn't grown as fast as her two siblings. All now weighted at least fifty pounds. Although Ontak had originally been smaller than his sisters, he was now noticeably larger.

How had they fared so well? What had they been eating that put on so much bulk? Although boletus mushrooms were now incredibly abundant, they contained few calories and the cubs fed on them only sparingly. Worse, berries had been scarce for the past month. The only reasonable explanation was that the cubs had been fishing. Yet I had found no trace of their tracks along Catlin Creek, and more distant creeks were generally usurped by larger black bears or even grizzlies.

To have survived fishing among those other bears, the cubs would have needed the protection of a mentor. Could they have had help – perhaps from Jeen To? Prior to the disappearance of my own cubs, two of Jeen To's youngsters had been lost, at least temporarily. From mid- to late July, I never saw her accompanied by any cub but her largest son, Pee Tee, suggesting that his two siblings had died. Yet on two occasions more recently, I had again seen her with at least three cubs. I wasn't close enough for an exact count, much less to identify the individual cubs. Although they had looked suspiciously like my own foundlings, they had fled too quickly for me to be sure that these were not just PeeTee's missing siblings.

At first, the idea that a bear might adopt orphaned cubs sounded far fetched. Then I recalled Robert Leslie's report, in *The Bears and I*, about an old barren female who had temporarily adopted three orphaned cubs – before supposedly bequeathing the cubs to him. Grizzly bears in Yellowstone National Park also adopted cubs, according to John and Frank Craighead, whose data were to later become the focus of my doctoral dissertation.[1]

Although any mother tends to maximize her genetic fitness by raising her own offspring, she can gain to a lesser degree from rearing offspring of close relatives – according to theories of *kin selection* just published at that time by Robert Trivers and Edward Wilson.[2]

Could this explain adoption in bears? As Lynn Rogers and other colleagues had recently discovered, a young female black or grizzly bear often establishes her home range in or near her mother's domain. Females with overlapping or adjacent domains *are* likely to be close kin.[3]

Any orphaned cubs found by a female could well be her own descendants or those of a sister, daughter, mother, or cousin. By rearing the cubs of close kin, a female could help perpetuate her own genetic lineage.*

JeenTo could very well have been closely related to Doddy. Had she adopted Ontak, Jonjoanak, and Chrislee when they disappeared in late July, thereby saving their lives?

No matter how much we wanted to hug Ontak and Chrislee on their miraculous return, we dared not. The cubs' separation from us had already begun, and had to be completed if they were to survive despite a death sentence recently issued by Fish & Game. From now on, they would need to avoid all people.

Each time the cubs returned to the cabin, we threw stones or banged pots and pans to drive them away. It broke our hearts. Tears filled Alatanna's eyes; mine misted. But we had no choice. "Bear hugs, little ones, bear hugs," was the thought with which we saw them flee.

After a few days of confusion about our abrupt hostility, the cubs disappeared for good. The last time we saw them, they were indeed accompanying JeenTo and PeeTee. Like the dog Buck in Jack London's famous story, our cubs had answered *the call of the wild*.

I realize now that we had answered it too. By inviting these intelligent, joyful and fierce creatures into our hearts, our lives, and our family, and by adapting to them as much as possible, we had simultaneously extended ourselves into their "family," their world. We had ceased being alien tourists in nature and become fellow participants. We too had found our way home.

Preview of Sequel

GRIZZLIES AMONG GLACIERS

I stand calf-deep in sedgegrass, on the Pacific coast of the Alaska Peninsula. Wind roars down volcanic peaks and over a glacier, spattering me with numbing rain. Clouds as dark and heavy as basalt hang overhead. My heart thunders, my palms grow slick. The grizzly sow has all my attention. She and her cub were the first mother–infant pair I saw this year; so I gave them names beginning with "a": "Alba " for the mother, "Abelar" for the cub. He is the size of a large house cat.

Alba is ten body lengths away, and her son so close that I can see the gleam of moisture on the amber of his eye. Alba grazes, but Abelar is consumed with curiosity. Too bold to heed his mother's warnings, he has approached to within twenty–five feet. I sit, then lie belly–down, facing the bears. Alba relaxes. She quits looking up every minute or so. She no longer stares in my direction, not even when Abelar comes closer. Weeks of effort have gone into achieving this trust.

Abelar's approaches are always touch–and–go, like waves on a rising tide–advance and retreat, then advance a bit farther before retreating again to the safety and comfort of his mother.

Abelar lies down twenty feet away, black, hairless foot soles splayed out behind him, "hands" resting under his chin. He watches me lazily for several minutes before rolling over onto his back. Knees and elbows thrust limply into the air, belly exposed to the mist, he is asleep.

Alba is still grazing, but now she too has settled down, five yards beyond her cub, facing away from us. Lying on the slick, wet sedgegrass, she crops off all the sedge and goosetongue within reach of her mouth. Then, using just "hands" and forearms, she pulls herself along without ever standing up.

With each bite, she grasps plants in her incisors, then yanks her head back or sideways, ripping the sedge apart or tearing it out by the roots. After five to ten bites, she slows briefly to chew, occasionally grinding her teeth together so forcefully that I briefly fear she is threatening me. But no, she is just chewing the tough, fibrous plant.

Most of the sedge is now too mature to be palatable; but here and there I find fresh protein-rich sprouts, just a few inches tall, with bright green blades. I pluck them by the handful and relish their nutty flavor–a perfect compliment to the more salty and succulent goose-tongue plants, and the razor clams which abound here on the sea coast. I not only watch the bears forage through this natural smorgasbord of delicacies; I join them–a tiny first step in experiencing life as bears do–in what my Native friends call *becoming bear.*

Epilogue
BENEFITS AND HAZARDS OF ACCLIMATING BEARS TO PEOPLE

I wrote **Beauty** both to give you an idea of what I have experienced knowing bears personally, and to help preserve the opportunity for a few of you to do the same. I have taken pains throughout my story to depict the real challenges of hand-rearing, companionship, and general coexistence, as well as how I coped with these challenges, including mistakes made and wisdom gained. Nevertheless, if any of you are to attempt companionship, to say nothing of fostering orphans, you will need a great deal more insight into the benefits and hazards than I have provided so far. To better prepare yourself, you might want to read this epilogue and eventually my other books, including *When Bears Whisper, Do You Listen?*, *The Language of Bears*, *Bear Aggression*, and *Grizzlies Among the Glaciers:*, as well as books by Ben Kilham and Charley Russell who wild-reared orphans a few decades after I did – which was a few decades after Robert Leslie wild-reard three cubs in British Columbia. [1] Also visit our website *www.bear-viewing-in-alaska.info.*

* * *

Once our triplets left with JeenTo and PeeTee, Alatanna and I dared not linger lest the cubs try returning. The time had come to permanently sever their bond with us. We packed up and left the cabin, never to return. We spent the next two years in the Tirolean Alps of Austria where I researched the behavior of European mountain goats (chamois), elk (red deer), and roe deer.

How much I missed Ontak and his sisters! They had provided many opportunities to study behavior in ways that were impossible with animals that were afraid of people, such as the black bears I had investigated in Northern California or the grizzlies I had researched on the Alaska Peninsula. My mind kept returning to the cubs, both amazed at how much they had revealed in so short a time, and regretful that our opportunities to keep on learning from them had not continued for many years into the future, in keeping with the precedent set by Jane Goodall with chimpanzees.

I had planned on following the cubs' development from infancy through adulthood, watching how their personalities and social relationships changed with experience and maturation. I wanted to understand the intricate roles played by learning, self-awareness, and cognition in innovative adaptations by bears – goals which I have since pursued with fully wild grizzly/brown bears.

COMMUNICATION AND AGGRESSION

In particular, I have sought deeper insight into the psychology and language of bears – into the system of postures, gestures, facial expressions, vocalizations and other signals by which bears express their moods and intentions, or by which they inform or manipulate other individuals. Such knowledge is not only fascinating scientifically, but potentially critical to safety during close encounters. It can make the difference between life and death for both man and bear.

Although attacks are uncommon, threats are not. Believing "better safe than sorry," most people are willing to respond by shooting when in doubt. I have been in that situation myself and never want to repeat it.

Even back in the early 1970s, I knew that making decisions that were right for myself and a bear would be much easier if I could discern whether the bear was angry, afraid, or calm – not how it *felt*, but how it would probably *behave*. I needed to be able to anticipate whether the bear was likely to attack, either offensively or defensively, and how my own behavior might affect this likelihood. Behavior that could reassure a fearful animal might encourage attack by one determined to dominate or eat me. If a bear charged, I needed to judge whether it was just trying to intimidate me or whether it was intending to maul or kill me, and how my behavior might change its mind for better or for worse. I wanted to know how my own actions and reactions could alter the course of an encounter – what I could do to keep myself safe, and what could get me hurt. I wanted to be able to distinguish when a bear's mood was playful or curious, and when that mood minimized my danger or accentuated it. I had no desire to be a bear's chew toy.

Compared to my at-a-distance observation of grizzlies on the Alaska Peninsula during 1972, living with the cubs taught me far more towards answering those questions. Most of this was novel information, without precedent in the literature. I had also learned a great deal new about ursid diets and habitat preferences. These data were stored in the home of Alatanna's sister when we left for Europe. Before my data could be shipped to me, however, they were destroyed by fire. A decade passed before I could pick up where I left off researching ursid communication and aggression.

By that time, considerable information had been published by a host of other investigators, beginning with captive work by Gordon Burghardt and his students (Ellis Bacon, Rober Jordan, Cheryl Pruitt, and Jeanne Ludlow), and by David Henry, as well as fieldwork by Derek Stonorov and his successors (Mike Luque, Al Egbert, and Tom Bledsoe) at the McNeil River sanctuary, where grizzlies were so acclimated to people that some individuals walked, fished or rested within a few yards of people. [2]

Since then, research has continued as quickly as possible given constraints on funding and research permits. Dozens of scientific papers have been published by colleagues. Personally, I have now documented thousands of interactions involving black or grizzly bears in natural habitat or at garbage dumps in Alaska, California's Sierra Mountains, Montana's Rocky and Bitterroot Mountains, New York's Adirondack Mountains, and Vermont's Green Mountains. (Although anything but aesthetic, dumps are utilized by bears in much the same manner as natural food concentrations. Any kind of food concentration can be an invaluable window on ursid social behavior, especially communication and aggression.)   While our efforts have not answered all of the questions I posed three decades ago, we are close to major breakthroughs, as will be summarized my succeeding books.

Critical to virtually all research on ursid communication and aggression has been the opportunity to make close range observations of the same individual bears day in and day out – just as I first did with moose, following in the steps of Goodall with chimpanzees and Val Geist with mountain sheep. [3]

FOOD HABITS

I have already explained the limitations of classical methods for assessing what bears eat. Scat analysis, for example, is effective for quantifying amounts of berries and other foods that leave easily identifiable remains; but such analysis reveals little about items such as mushrooms and meat, the residues of which are excreted as formless dung.

The insights about foraging provided by studying my cubs were, of course, just first steps. To learn more, I had planned to more systematically compare what they ate with the contents of their dung – contrasting input to output. I could have qualitatively and quantitatively documented how diet changes as bears mature and learn, and as supplies of each major food rise and fall seasonally and from year to year. While the diet of hand-reared bears might not duplicate that of mother-reared bears, there ought to be a lot of similarity, judging, for instance, by how much my cubs had learned by trailing their fully wild kin. In any event, whereas I never had opportunity pursue this farther, other colleagues have, particularly Lynn Rogers, Greg Wilker, Sue Mansfield, and Terry DeBruyn.

HABITAT PREFERENCES

Given that bears spend most of their time eating, and are usually found near prime food sources, understanding diets is essential to understanding how habitat is used. One needs to know (a) how the distribution of various foods and other factors affect where animals spend most of their time, (b) which kinds of habitat are most important to them under various sets of conditions – for instance wet versus dry years – and (c) thus how much of each kind of habitat is needed over the long run, and (d) which kinds of habitat must be protected or regenerated when scarce. If we can't prioritize our efforts to protect habitat according to the value of that habitat to bears, the best habitat is likely to be lost – for instance to degradation by recreation, logging or oil exploitation. Protect too little, and wildlife populations could crash, eliminating animals from which people could otherwise benefit. Protect too much, and people could lose jobs without achieving any benefit for nature. It is a difficult balancing act.

Success depends on reliable information on where animals actually spend their time. This is typically done by equipping animals with radio transmitters that periodically reveal the animals' location. My observations on moose had already revealed that the primitive radiotelemetry apparatus available in the early 1970 s sufficed only for distinguishing which coarse-grained areas an animal was in. It could not provide reliable data on those fine-grained areas known as *microhabitats* such as meadows, wetlands, and ponds within the forest. This became obvious when I happened to read estimates by a senior state biologist of where certain moose had been on certain days, at specified times. Having been with those moose at those times, I knew that some of his estimates were several hundreds of yards off. In one case, for example, a moose that the state biologist had thought was in dense forest had instead been feeding in a shallow lake. Although such errors were minor on a landscape scale, they tend to overlook the importance of certain microhabitats.

I had planned similar ground-truthing for telemetric monitoring of bears, using the cubs as guinea pigs. Alatanna and I would have teamed up for combining close observations with distant radio-tracking, one of us doing one job, one doing the other, then comparing results. With luck, we would have been able to learn how differences in topography, habitat type, and other factors affected the accuracy of radio-locations, so that errors could be anticipated in the future and corrective measures taken.

In fact, it was not until the summer of 1976 that I began working on these problems with bears, while serving as a field assistant to Chuck

Jonkel on the North Fork of Montana's Flathead River. During the interim, however, I had plenty of opportunity to learn the intricacies and frustrations of radio-telemetry monitoring in other mountainous terrain, the Tirolean Alps, while studying European elk and mountain goats. In addition to knowing which areas were or were not used by bears, we needed to learn why. Even prime food sources may be avoided if they don't provide sufficient escape cover, or if they are also used by enemies. Habitat of little value during normal conditions may prove critical during droughts. And so on.

Since about 1961, the "Jane Goodall approach" – of using acclimated animals to study social behavior, foraging, and habitat preferences – had been employed on wild sheep by Valerius Geist, caribou by Peter Lent, European elk (red deer) by Anton Bubenik, and moose by Val Geist and myself. Derek Stonorov, Al Egbert, Mike Luque, Tom Bledsoe and I applied it to grizzly and black bears during the 1970s. In the late 1980s, it was picked up by a series of fellow bear biologists who carried their studies of acclimated black bears to heights of rigor and innovation beyond what had been possible with Ontak and his sisters. Chief among these investigators have been Lynn Rogers and Greg Wilker in Minnesota and Terry Debruyen in Michigan. Terry now works here in Alaska on polar bears. Lynn's several TV movies and Terry's book *Walking With Bears,* along with their scientific papers, are fascinating and highly informative.[4]

ENDANGERED SPECIES

At the time that I was *"bearenting"* Chrislee and her siblings, America's *Endangered Species Act* had not yet worked its way through Congress. Few people had an inkling of how rapidly most of the world's bear populations were declining. But enough was known about the plight of the panda bear that it was adopted as the symbol of the World Wildlife Fund. Yet not until 1980 were field studies of the panda begun in China – conducted by the renown biologist George Schaller, along with Ken Johnson and Howard Quigley with whom I had worked on black bears while we were grad students at the University of Tennessee.[5]

Meanwhile, captive breeding and rearing programs were established in China and America. These programs offer great hope. But success has been limited so far. Some of these difficulties may have arisen because the panda's phenomenal popularity exaggerated its apparent taxonomic uniqueness. Few keepers realized how much insight into pandas might be gained from information on other bears. Indeed, I write these words just hours after suggesting to Don Lindburg, panda bear Team Leader at the San Diego Zoo, specific ways in which knowledge on black and grizzly bears might be applied to improve captive breeding of pandas and augmentation of wild populations.

For example, the lackluster breeding attempts by some boar pandas may reflect a lack of social stimulation. In many mammals, male virility is heightened by rivalry with other males – an example of *social facilitation*. This is one reason why males in some species gather in so-called *leks*. I have likewise seen boar and estrus sow grizzlies form breeding concentrations. Ben Kilham told me that he has found evidence of the same thing among black bears. (Lek sites might be critical habitat for bears.) If virility is similarly facilitated among pandas, perhaps a captive boar could be stimulated by sensing other boars nearby. If other boar pandas are unavailable in person, one might simulate that with video projections or substitute male brown or black bears, possibly colored to resemble pandas. The projections or surrogates and their pens might be anointed, as appropriate, with urine, feces, saliva and other scent- (pheromone-) laden "secretions" collected from boar pandas elsewhere.

To date, most success with rearing captive pandas has depended critically on winning the cooperation of the animals through gentleness, affection, and bonding with their keepers. I suspect that close relationships with people will also prove essential for returning pandas to the wild – both to assure success for the cubs and to learn as much as possible from each attempt.

There are basically two schools of thought in bear reintroduction. The *"bearenting"* school holds that proper contact with human mentors can greatly enhance success (as I did with Ontak and his sisters) by introducing the cubs to new kinds of food; guiding them to new sources of food, water, and other necessities; alerting them to hazards; and providing the emotional security needed to explore novel situations, face enemies (such as predators or dangerous prey), and socialize with other bears. By contrast, the *isolationist* school contends that contact between humans and orphans should be minimized. This is based on the belief that bears which do not fear people, and especially those used to getting food from people, are likely to become dangerous as adults – a controversy to which I will return below.

Although pandas may indeed be the least aggressive of all bruins, the difference is not as great as is commonly thought. People have been mauled by pandas, whereas even grizzly and polar bears can be quite benign when food is abundant and the animals have learned tolerance for one another and for people. More importantly, all ursids have the capacity for friendship and affection, not only with each other, but also with humans. Some bears simply enjoy watching people and perhaps even befriending us.

At the time I wrote this book, pandas were so rare and vulnerable that no one had dared attempt reintroducing them. I thus suggested that panda biologists might do well to study what has been learned by reintroducing black and brown/grizzly bears, and then try the same thing. Although there are major differences between pandas versus other Eurasian bears, there should be enough similarities for the experience to substantially reduce the risks faced in eventually reintroducing pandas. Chinese biologists accepted my idea and Ben Kilham mentored them.

Pandas eat little except bamboo in the wild; yet they consume a variety of fruits and vegetables in captivity. A nearly exclusive diet of bamboo is apparently not due to either a lack of edible wild plants or an inability to digest them. One must wonder why pandas don't supplement their diet of bamboo with more of the same foods as Eurasian brown and black bears, with whom they have historically shared habitat? Although bamboo is available year-around, with little searching, most edible parts of the plant are lower in energy than foods typically consumed by black and brown bears. Are these other plants and prey instinctively less palatable than bamboo, or don't pandas recognize these other species as food?*

---

* Limited use of other wild foods is described by G. Schaller *et al.* 1985.

More broadly: is there some common denominator – such as unpalatability or ignorance – that underlies (a) pandas "ignoring" these other foods, as well as (b) grizzly or black bears in some areas ignoring certain foods that are highly prized in other areas?

Given that periodic flowering of bamboo could lead to mass starvation of pandas, wouldn't these animals benefit greatly from learning to eat other foods which could sustain them?

One of the things that panda biologists might learn from experienced "bearents" is how to introduce cubs to novel foods. Then, as these novel foods begin appearing in the scats of fostered-cubs, and these scats are examined by fully wild pandas, the trait might spread, broadening the population's diet and the realized carrying capacity of its habitat.

Were purists to complain that broadening the diet is unnatural, I would counter that the current isolation of pandas in tiny isolated islands of habitat is also unnatural; the animals can no longer cope with local bamboo famines by emigrating to areas where bamboo still flourishes. Unless a better alternative can be found, one unnatural situation may have to be countered by another. Obviously, dietary expansions should initially be attempted with only a few pandas, which are monitored closely so that any adverse effects can be quickly detected and alleviated.

Insights about "bearenting" can be found not only in my own report, but also in those of several colleagues. Little is known about James Capen Adams who was accompanied by hand-reared grizzly/brown bears while capturing animals for zoos and circuses, during the mid-1800's. We have much better documentation from half-a-century later when Robert Leslie raised a litter of black bears in the wilds of British Columbia, and when Peter and Gertraud Krott reared brown bear cubs in the Italian Alps. Now, over the past decade, Ben Kilham has raised black bears in the wilds of New Hampshire, while Charley Russell and Maureen Enns reared orphaned brown bear cubs on the Kamchatka Peninsula of Siberia. Further insight has been provided by Gordon Burghardt and his students, as well as numerous other colleagues, who have reared and studied bears in captivity.[6]

We can only wonder how much farther along recovery of pandas and other rare bears would be now if government agencies and the public had been quicker to see bears as something more than living targets for their sport, or as demons for their nightmares. Instead of focusing exclusively on problems which have arisen from familiarizing some bears to people, more attention should be paid to cases where familiarization has not led to problems, so that the causes of failure and success could be distinguished.

The popular attitude of *"guilty until proven innocent"* tends to block attempts to objectively test "innocence," and to learn ways of gaining the benefits of *acclimating* bears to people without suffering the detriments of having the bears *habituate* to people or become *food-conditioned*. It is long past time that the fallacies of conventional "wisdom"– that habituation and food conditioning are inevitable consequences of familiarization – are exposed to the harsh light of rigorous observation, analysis and experimentation. Agencies need to grant research permits and to facilitate funding – not only for investigators with a history of opposition to familiarization, but also to those with a history of success.

OF BEARS AND APES

Even before such research is completed, we can learn much by looking at comparative information on other species, for instance great apes, especially gorillas and chimpanzees – for whom the public tends to have high tolerance, affection, and fascination. I see no reason other than bad propaganda why people should have less interest in or kindness towards bears than toward apes.

"What," you might ask, *"do apes half-way around the world have to do with bears in North America, South America, or Eurasia? Don't divergent ancestries preclude evolutionary convergence?"*

Actually, no. There are several critical parallels between bears vs. apes – as was first detailed by Gordon Burghardt.

1. Some of the ecological niches occupied by apes in Africa overlap niches occupied by bears on other continents – which may be why there are no longer both apes and bears in any ecosystem except in southeast Asian habitat shared by sun bears and orangutans.

2. Chimpanzees, gorillas and most bears are omnivorous forest-dwellers who obtain much of their nutrition from fruits, nuts, succulent forbs, and invertebrate prey.

3. Apes and most bears take refuge in trees, where they make similar "nests," although for different purposes.

4. Most apes and bears have black pelts.

5. All are semi-bipeds, with great manual dexterity of their fingers, and with similar structures in the brain that function in complex dexterity and in sequences of behavior and memory.

6. All apes and bears have keen intelligence and

7. binocular (3D) color vision, as well as

8. prolonged maternal care and training of youngsters.

9. Mother apes and mother bears carry infants on their bodies, clinging to their hair; while this is not common in North American bears, it is typical of sloth bears in the vicinity of India.

10 Both bears and chimpanzees throw violent tantrums when frustrated, and both fight with each other over food or rank.

"But bears attack each other and occasionally eat their victims; they also sometimes attack and rarely eat people; chimpanzees and gorillas don't," you might say.

Ah, but chimpanzees do, as Jane Goodall eventually learned from African Natives who had long lived around these apes. [7]

Neither bears nor apes attack people very often, but it does happen, especially during a close encounter when the animal is afraid for itself or its young, or when there is competition for food. Both bears and chimpanzees (as well as baboons and elephants) are fond of some human foods and will, at times, take these foods violently. Rarely, a human child is killed and perhaps eaten.

"Then I should be more afraid of chimpanzees, not less afraid of bears?" you ask? No. The horror of tragedies should never blind us to how rarely they occur, whether the tragedies arise from animal attacks, plane crashes, or automobile accidents.

Because attacks can be so traumatic, they are remembered for many years. Stories are told and retold, sometimes with embellishments and variations that can make one attack sound like several. Tales of "close calls" further exaggerate the apparent frequency of "attacks."

A point never to be forgotten is that the risk of such tragedy can be minimized with proper precautions. Goodall and her family and colleagues lived for decades amidst scores of human-acclimated chimpanzees, who often spent hours each day in her camp, with few or no serious injuries to any person. Dian Fossey did something similar with gorillas, as recounted in her book *Gorillas in the Mist*.

Approached correctly, people can also safely coexist with acclimated bears – as was amply demonstrated by Stan Price and his two successive wives, who lived for decades among grizzly bears on Alaska's Admiralty Island. A few of these bears occasionally visited Stan inside his cabin. Charley Vandergaw had even closer relationships with grizzly/brown and black bears. Likewise, a number of other people, including Jim Faro, Will Troyer, Tom Smith, Tim Treadwell Kent Fredriksson, Buck Wilde and I have camped or resided in the midst of numerous black or grizzly bears for months or weeks without being attacked. Nikita Ovsyanikov has spent montjhs walking among the polar bears he studied.[8] And thousands of people, with no interest in bears, have lived safely in regions where bears abound – just as large numbers of Africans have lived around chimpanzees and gorillas while rarely suffering significant harm.

If people are willing to give chimpanzees and gorillas the benefit of the doubt, why not bears? The fact that gorillas and chimpanzees live on another continent where they are someone else's problem is one reason for a different attitude towards apes vs. bears in North America, but certainly not the only reason. What should matter most to us is that bears are here, they are *our* responsibility, they are as fascinating as apes, and in some situations, just as safe to view, acclimate, and perhaps even befriend. We might have less problem with North American bears if we gave them as much benefit of the doubt as we would give pandas, gorillas, and chimpanzees.

Jane Goodall's research is recognized as one of the crowning achievements of twentieth century science. Even 30 years ago, it had already yielded a wealth of new insights into the depth of understanding that can be achieved about animals – and thus about ourselves – through intimate long-range studies of acclimated individuals and social groups. That is essentially what my colleagues and I have been doing with bears, within the limits of available funding and research permits.

MANAGEMENT ATTITUDES TOWARD BEARS AS VERMIN, TROPHIES, OR COMPANIONS

Up until a "few" years before I reared Ontak and his sisters, bear "managers" across North America sought to exterminate bears as potential marauders. Bears sometimes killed livestock or attacked people. Even experienced woodsmen, without a gun in hand, tended to be terrified of bears, and were determined to return the favor. Most carried a gun and some shot at many a bear so unwary or unlucky as to be within rifle range. No one wanted to tangle with a ferocious bear, much less to have one invade his camp or home. Many people even resented bears competing with them for fish and game.

At that time, most opposition to exterminating bears, to say nothing of lobbying to maintain robust populations, came from people who wanted bears available to kill for meat, fur, sport, or trophies. It was mainly through their efforts and cash investments that bears were finally elevated from the official status of "vermin" to that of "game." No longer could bears be poisoned, trapped, or shot on sight by anyone with an itchy trigger finger. Except in defense of human life or property, bears could not be killed except during certain seasons, within specified bag limits, according to the rules of *fair chase*. Moreover, hunters now paid a license fee that could be applied to preserving critical bear habitat and to otherwise conserving, managing, and researching bears. This was an enormous step forward.

For these and other reasons, wildlife management focused on maintaining game populations at high enough vigor to produce a "surplus" of animals that could be harvested each year. There was little interest in protecting individual animals and sometimes opposition to rearing orphans.

* If an animal is eventually going to be harvested anyway, why spend many thousands of dollars and months of effort rearing it? (This is a perfectly valid argument with which I agree; it is only where humanitarian values or scientific insights are also at stake that "bearenting" is worthwhile.)

* In particular, why take the chance that familiarity with humans would predispose an animal to seek food from us, and possibly end up in a situation where the bear might injure someone? (With proper techniques, in the right situation, this can be avoided)

Wildlife management agencies have also learned the hard way that few people have the knowledge, resources, and commitment to properly rear wildlife. Far too many animals end up in tiny cages or chained to a tree, slowly going mad with boredom, frustration, loneliness, and neglect. The animals suffer and some become dangerous, especially once they reach adulthood and become much more assertive.

Before you seriously consider "bearenting" orphaned bear cubs, reread this book and try to imagine what it is like to have to spend 8 to 12 or more hours a day, 7 days a week, out in the field with cubs, no matter how foul the weather, how nasty the bugs, or how daunting the terrain. This is the kind of commitment that only a fanatic should make – preferably a research fanatic. For every minute of fun, you may spend an hour of brutally hard, uncomfortable work, and then more hours (and all winter) doing data processing and theoretical analysis. Worse, as the bears mature and become more assertive, your ability to keep them under control may depend on having established a life-long history of firm, consistent discipline and affection. Except for researchers, nearly everyone can best get to know bears by viewing fully wild ones under the supervision of an bear guide. (To learn of viewing opportunities, visit the website of the Bear Viewing Association *www.bear-viewing-in-alaska.info* or read my book *Bear Viewing in Alaska*. Advice on how to act during bear encounters is provided in the *Alaska Magnum Bear Safety Manual* and in *When Bears Whisper, Do You Listen?*

CHANGING ATTITUDES
& THE RISE OF BEAR VIEWING

In recent years, fortunately, attitudes towards bears have begun changing worldwide, including Alaska. As our own population has grown and become more "civilized," there have been declines in the proportions of the populace (a) dependent on hunting and fishing for sustenance, (b) hunting "big game" for sport, or (c) venturing far afield carrying a high-powered firearm. More people have learned how rarely bears actually attack anyone, and how to keep it that way (e.g., by avoiding surprise encounters, and by proper disposal of garbage and storage of food). Simultaneously, faster transportation from outside Alaska has minimized the need and profitability of raising livestock locally, and thus occasions when predators can justifiably be killed to protect domestic animals.

Interest in bear viewing has grown more quickly among the general public and among tourists than it has within our legislature or Department of Fish & Game. Both have long been dominated by predator-control and harvest-oriented philosophies. Indeed, many of our legislators and at least one governor have been fishing/hunting guides whose businesses have brought a lot of money into the state, and whose clients have had the wealth and power to support political campaigns.

Nevertheless, a succession of politicians and biologists, including Jim Faro, achieved the revolutionary step of establishing a sanctuary – at McNeil River –outside of a national or state park where bears are completely protected so that people can enjoy them and learn from them.

Unknown to me until recently was how much backlash was provoked by protecting McNeil. Although few hunters were against protecting bears in that small area, some feared that this would be just the first of many such set-asides that would gradually eliminate hunting opportunities over broad areas of Alaska (Actually, the total area suitable for prime viewing is minuscule). It was into this political hornet's nest that I stumbled with my idealistic vision of having areas where my cubs and other bears were not only protected, but available for acclimation – where there would be freedom for at least a few people to develop personal relationships with bears, whether for research, art, or spirituality.

Protection of McNeil and a few other areas came none too soon. The worldwide increase in ecotourism and nature documentaries on TV have sparked public interest in meeting bears "up close and personal" for observation, a sense of kinship, and photography. Pack Creek on Admiralty Island was once nearly deserted except for Stan Price and his wife; it now receives roughly 1400 visitors during each summer season. In the early 1970s, when I began research at Katmai National Park on the Alaska Peninsula, it was rare for even a dozen people a day to visit Brooks River to view bears; since then, visitor numbers have jumped to hundreds per day. Over the past decade, the number of bear-viewing guides at Katmai has increased many-fold. Each year, there is a long waiting list of people who want to see grizzlies at McNeil River State Game Sanctuary. Even garbage dumps are popular bear viewing sites; some have drawn hundreds of visitors a day. As the numbers of bear viewers and guides increase exponentially, the challenges of protecting people and bears from each other grow apace.

Government agencies dread the prospect of an epidemic of maulings–which could trigger retaliatory pogroms against bears. To prevent both tragedies, agencies are on the verge of drafting new regulations strictly limiting bear viewing and perhaps forbidding companionship – another reflection of the confusion between acclimating bears versus habituating and food-conditioning them, as I will explain later.

Balancing public demands for free access to wildlife against needs for protection is not an easy challenge for any government agency.

Agencies are constantly wary of making decisions that could leave them vulnerable to legislative censure or litigation. If a bear – especially one with a history of familiarity with people – mauls someone, the victim might sue an agency for not having killed the animal before it could do harm. Armed by the misconception that familiarity breeds contempt and aggression, some attorneys treat these tragedies as taps into the cash casks of government. Such litigation puts enormous pressure on agencies to take no chances with any bear that frequents areas around people – a dilemma which has only worsened over time.

Few of us would deny that restrictions on the public's relationships with bears are appropriate to the extent needed to protect people and bears from each other. But which of us would readily surrender our right to go a little "wild" in wilderness? Protective measures should not unnecessarily sacrifice the scientific or "re-creational" benefits which can come from a few people's close companionship with bears, and from the public viewing bears less intimately – benefits such as those alluded to in my verse *Renewal.* So long as proper techniques are used, and the number of people attempting this is not too great, acclimating bears can be done with reasonable safety and minimal impact on the animals, as well as with wonderful rewards to humanity.

HOW MUCH RISK IS TOO MUCH?

I have emphasized the important scientific insights about bears which can be gained only with acclimated individuals. Nevertheless, some critics argue that such knowledge – no matter how great its contribution to science, bear management, or keeping people safe – isn't worthwhile so long as there is the slightest chance that acclimated bears might harm someone.

I respond that any bear – or horse, cow, dog or cat – poses some risk (one of my wife's friends nearly died from cat scratches which became infected). The real issue is whether acclimating bears makes them significantly more dangerous than other bears. Frankly, I know of no evidence for this. On the contrary, I believe that properly acclimated bears are especially safe.

DOESN'T FAMILIARITY BREED CONTEMPT?

While there are certainly circumstances where companionship with bears, even fostering cubs, can make bears dangerous, this is only one possible outcome. Results depend on the techniques used, personalities of the individual people and bears, and environmental circumstances. These distinctions are easiest to understand if we first clear away a morass of confusion about proper use of terms such as contempt, respect, familiarity, habituation, food conditioning, and acclimation.

CONTEMPT

I equate contempt with confidence that an opponent cannot retaliate effectively against insult or injury. Insulting or demeaning an opponent is done by acting superior/dominant/disrespectfully towards it; ignoring the opponent's own dominance displays or threats; provoking attack, then easily warding it off; displacing the opponent (such as from a bed or fishing site); or usurping its food or mate.

FAMILIARITY

Victorian British high society feared that any servant allowed to get away with laxness in displaying subordinance was likely to begin acting as an equal, then to try dominating his master. Such insubordination was the kind of *familiarity* that *breeds contempt.*

Nothing but confusion arises from equating familiarity in that sense with familiarity in the sense of *familiarization,* "becoming accustomed to," or "acquainted with." I have spent thousands of hours around bears that were highly familiar with me and sometimes with people in general, and only a few of these bears have ever subjected me to aggressive or provocative disrespect; and none has done so repeatedly. On the contrary, bears which have not been taught contempt for humans tend to treat us with the level of deference warranted towards potentially dangerous peers – i.e., with "politeness."

PREDICTABILITY

In many cases, the more familiar bears are with humans – with the places and times where we are likely to be found, what we are or aren't likely to be doing (for instance, hunting), and how we are likely to react during close encounters – the less the bears are stressed by encounters, which minimizes the likelihood of defensive aggression. The more accustomed bears are to being "polite" to people, the more likely they to continue doing so without challenge.

At McNeil River, for instance, Alaska Department of Fish & Game biologists such as Larry Aumiller consider the predictability of bear viewers to be a prime reason why no viewer has ever been mauled in that area. Indeed, an apt motto for McNeil might be *"Familiarity breeds predictability, which fosters safety."* [9] Nevertheless, the importance of predictability should not be exaggerated. So long as bears can predict how you will behave toward them, most are very tolerant of variations in where, when and how they encounter people.

HABITUATION

Ethological and psychological glossaries commonly define "habituation" in terms of a response (especially an unlearned/unconditioned response) that loses its sensitivity to a specific stimulus due to lack of reinforcement. A classic example is waning of fear towards potential hazards (such as enemies). For example, my cubs were initially all afraid of dark stumps which, at first glance, could be mistaken for other black bears. Such mistakes waned rapidly over the three months they were with me. By contrast, a timid young grizzly whom I called Spooky kept fleeing from some of the same stumps day after day, week after week. My cubs quickly habituated to stumps; Spooky did not.

So too, an animal might quit fleeing from people who do not pursue it or attack. The animal might quit acting as a subordinate to people if we do not reinforce our dominance. Such progressive disrespect is essentially what most people have in mind when they refer to bears becoming *habituated*.

Unfortunately, using "habituation" and other key terms this way implies that

(a) "habituation" refers only to decay of respect/fear for humans into contempt,
(b) all such decay is the result of "habituation," and
(c) any familiarity with humans leads to contempt for us.

That is invalid, in part because it confuses *process* with *product*.

(a) Habituation is only *one* form of learning by which respect can be replaced with contempt.
(b) Respect and fear are only two of many kinds of behaviors which can habituate. For example, whereas a wide variety of novel odors initially arouse a bear's curiosity, most are soon ignored.
(c) Familiarization does not necessarily lead toward contempt.

A lot of confusion, and thus a lot of trouble, could be avoided by referring to the end result of respect-decay as "disrespect" or "contempt" rather than as "habituation."

FOOD CONDITIONING

To make matters worse, many people also confuse "habituation" with "food conditioning"– as when bears learn that they can obtain food from people, and begin expecting to do so, a kind of learning that seldom includes true habituation.

Confusion arises because food conditioning and loss of respect can occur together. All too often, when a bear is attracted to scents associated with humans (such as citronella insect repellent, coconut shampoo, peach hair conditioner, or floral perfume), or to our food, we surrender and flee. Acting submissively does not enhance wariness or respect.

Despite this common link between food conditioning and loss of respect toward people, there are also cases where the phenomena are quite separate.

* Bears that meet people at garbage dumps or salmon streams may learn to associate food and people, without ever having to intimidate people to get the food, and thus without learning contempt for the people. At dumps, most bears discover that patience is more effective than aggression toward people for yielding food.

* People can sacrifice a bear's respect of us simply by acting submissively even when there is no food involved, as when people flee from a bruin they meet on a mountain trail.

ACCLIMATION

Confusion over the various meanings of *familiarity* and *habituation* has compounded to the point where many wildlife managers believe that contempt for people and marauding for our food are nearly inevitable consequences of close contact with people, especially with human companions or foster parents.

Granted, there are cases where this has been true. But this is by no means inevitable. Proper behavior by people can enhance both respect and trust –the process which I call *acclimation* – for lack of a better alternative. There are also ways of providing bears with food without causing food conditioning – as Robert Leslie, Charley Russell, Maureen Enns, Ben Kilham, and I have done with our cubs.

Although I have already discussed several aspects of acclimation in the chapter on *Temper, Trust and Respect*, I would like to now add a few more points.

TRUST

According to Steve Herrero, author of the 1985 book *Bear Attacks: Their Causes and Avoidance,* a substantial proportion of all attacks are *defensive.* This proportion is far higher for grizzly bears than for black bears, and highest of all for sow grizzlies with infant cubs. Defensive aggression can be minimized by winning trust.

Any time that I encounter a nervous sow with cubs, I try to set her at ease *immediately*, for instance by acting submissively and withdrawing. Although some yearlings or two-year-old cubs have responded by briefly becoming more aggressive, none of the sows has ever done so. Instead, several of these sows have quickly come to trust me. An hour after one sow with two defensively-aggressive yearlings backed me down, she returned and nursed them nearby – exploiting the "zone of sanctuary" around me to "shield" her cubs from disturbance by other bears. Once she was at ease with me, her yearlings were too. Other sows have frequently left her infants within 100 yards, and sometimes within 5 yards of me, as though I were their baby sitter, while momma foraged up to a quarter-mile away. One of these sows once happened upon me while I was filming chum salmon partly stranded in shallow water. Rather than barge in and take the salmon, she and her cubs sat on a river bank about 50 yards away, waiting until I was done.

As bears learn to trust more and more people as individuals, they seem to gain greater trust for people in general – which is sometimes good, and sometimes bad. Although it is far better for bears to greet strange people with curiosity and friendliness than with aggression, some strangers may not be receptive. Even the most friendly and benign bear could be shot for walking up to an armed stranger who was unsure of the bear's intentions.

As you will recall, I took considerable precaution to keep Ontak and his sisters from generalizing their trust for Alatanna and me to other people. For that same reason, when I acclimate fully wild bears, I try to dress and behave distinctively, and confine my activities to select areas. This generally works well. Although certain individuals have been friendly wherever we have met, most have tolerated my proximity only at specific sites. Put differently, the more areas where individual bears become acclimated to me, the more trusting they are when meeting me in a new location. To keep acclimation localized, stay put.

RESPECT

Winning trust is the biggest, most critical challenge with the average bear. But trust alone is not enough. There are situations where approaching a bear could be as suicidal as walking through certain areas of Los Angles, San Francisco or New York. Although we are not yet fully certain of all the circumstances which determine the tolerance of bears for people, five factors stand out:

a) Don't draw bears to you with the scent of food, petroleum distillates, or other attractants.

b) If possible, confine your viewing of grizzly bears to the coasts of Alaska, Kamchatka, and perhaps British Columbia, where the animals tend to be very well fed on salmon, herbs and berries. These bears tend to be highly tolerant of one another and of people. Be much more cautious in inland habitats where   (a) prime foods are sparsely distributed, (b) bears may regularly prey on large mammals such as deer or moose calves, and (c) the bears are less tolerant of one another.

c) Although both grizzly and black bears are highly tolerant toward humans in areas where prime foods are both abundant and concentrated, grizzly bears can be especially touchy where prime foods are scarce or highly dispersed.

d) Bears which are tolerant when well fed and in a good mood may be less tolerant when famished or after being insulted or attacked by another bear – *redirected aggression*. Never assume that just because a bear was tolerant yesterday, that it will also be tolerant today. Some bears are as moody as people and should be treated at least as judiciously. Moreover, it is easy to mistake one bear for another, and bears which look nearly identical may have very different temperaments.

e) A very small minority of bears are either "sadistic" or predatory towards other bears and/or towards people.

Without weapons, your best protection from grouchy, sadistic, or predatory bears is winning and maintaining their respect. This is done, in part, by treating bears as equals or subordinates. Although people might feel safest among bears that act as extreme subordinates, and flee in fear every time someone approaches, this can drive bears away from areas that they must share with people. Long-term coexistence requires being just dominant enough to assure "politeness" without denying bears access to essential habitat. Attempts to powerfully intimidate a bear should be reserved for extreme situations where nothing less will keep people safe. Remember that excessive aggression can provoke defensive attack!

We don't want to let any bear believe that it can injure us without being met with swift retaliation. As Jim Faro put it, respect comes from the potential for "mutually assured destruction." Bears can do so much damage to one another that similar-sized individuals seldom dare fight unless battling over something especially valuable – prime food, a mate or vulnerable cubs. Respect for us depends on convincing bears that we can retaliate at least as harshly as they can.

Fear without trust makes bears defensive. Trust without respect is equally dangerous. So long as John and Joan deferred to Doddy, they were reasonably safe. But how much danger did John and I put ourselves in when we refused to surrender the trash? What if we or someone else had refused to defer or tried to fight back?

Trust doesn't work without respect to back it up. While you don't necessarily have to outrank every bear, you must seem capable of retaliating so effectively that attacking you isn't worth it.

"Just how do you win a bear's respect without violence?" you might ask.

Winning respect depends on the circumstances. After the cubs had bonded to me, I could exert discipline in ways that wouldn't work with other bears. Although I once wrestled my cubs down, one at a time, in a futile attempt at physical domination, I never punished them with anything harsher than a light "message" slap to the paw or muzzle – quickly followed by displays of affection, to maintain the bond between us and help them distinguish discipline from foul temper. (Some bears, such as Jonjoanak, seem to carry grudges.) I also applied affection after each session teaching cubs not to bite people. (I grabbed each unruly cub by its muzzle, then used my thumb and fingers tips to push its cheeks between its molars, so that it could not bite down without biting itself.

Instead of punishing the cubs, I maintained their respect by wrestling playfully and in other ways. When the cubs transgressed, I warned them to cease and desist. I did this by using human signals (for instance, yelling "No!") as well as by mimicking ursid threats such as jaw pops. This usually worked. Their growing respect, in combination with their trust and deepening affection for Alatanna and me, became very effective for controlling their aggression and winning their cooperation. Whenever my cubs encountered a stranger or his/her spoor, I also tried to warn the cubs with human and imitation ursid alarm signals.

In his book *The Bears and I,* Robert Leslie revealed nothing about disciplinary problems with his cubs even into their third year; on the contrary, one became increasingly emotionally dependent on him and ever more eager to please him; a second preferred the company of other bears; and the third was killed for meat by a passing hunter. Until Ontak and his sisters left with JeenTo, we were approaching a comparable depth of kinship, which I had hoped would make them increasingly cooperative.

I have known a number of gentle adult bears, including two very large boars. Najuna was so fierce when challenged that only the alpha male dared antagonize him; yet with bears that treated him with reasonable respect, and with me, Najuna was extraordinarily tolerant and playful. The other boar, Cubby, was so trusting and gentle that people put their children on his back, whereupon Cubby typically sat down so that the kids slid off. He never harmed anyone, even when kids ended up hanging from his fur, which may have been painful. Najuna and Cubby were no more atypical on the gentle end of the temperament scale than infanticidal or cannibalistic bears are at the brutal end.

During his many years sharing Pack Creek with numerous grizzly bears, Stan Price learned that his best defense was often a tall walking stick. When a curious bear approached too closely, he pressed the tip of the stick against the "offending" bear, which quickly taught the animal to maintain a minimum distance from him. Charley Russell and Maureen Enns have done the same thing with grizzly/brown bears on the Kamchatka Peninsula, and I have accomplished this with grizzly and black bears using a camera monopod or tripod, or a ski pole. (The first time I used the ski pole on a large boar black bear whom I called Najuna, he hooked a claw in the basket and jerked the pole out of my hands. I cut the basket off and tried again, whereupon he gripped the pole between his claws and jerked it away again. Never again did I use the pole on him, and never again did he crowd closer than five feet. We had both learned a lesson.)

I have driven off many fully wild black and, occasionally, grizzly bears by walking toward them in a determined manner or by charging them. Although some of these bears, such as the yearling that looked into our bedroom window, returned again and again, most have not.*

> * Charging a bear is not something you should try on your own, without proper training, unless you're part of a group of at least four people, all within about three to five feet of one another. Even then, it's a last resort unless you've had professional training and carry a weapon as backup.

Steve Searles, bear manager for the town of Mammoth, in the Sierra mountains of California, is affectionately known as a "bear bully." Instead of killing problem bears, he dominates them by rushing and yelling at them, or by employing deterrents such as shotgun blanks, popper shells (which fly through the air toward the bear before exploding), and canned aerosol pepper spray. In some states (but not California) it is legal to deter bears by shooting them with rubber/plastic bullets. or "beanbags". These and other nonlethal methods of managing bears have been reviewed in a booklet by Sylvia Dolson, which is available for download at bearsmart.com.[10]

There is no indication that pepper spray – unlike gunshot or arrow wounds – has ever provoked or intensified an attack. On the contrary, spray which reaches the lungs, causing the bronchi to spasm, can supposedly halt even the most ferocious bear. There is nothing like suddenly being unable to breathe to distract an animal from committing mayhem. Additional deterrents may be the pain of getting pepper juice into the eyes, nostrils and mouth, as well as the snakelike hissing made when pepper is sprayed–a "hot" topic for future research.**

> ** In addition to Capsicum pepper, most bear sprays contain vegetable oil, which is highly attractive to certain bears. Some enthusiastically chew on items which have been coated with pepper spray. Anyone anointing himself this way in the mistaken belief that this will repel bears might just as well be inviting them over for a Mexican fiesta, with himself as the main dish – *Yo quiero* Taco Bell!

Large, aggressive dogs can be even more intimidating to bears than are people. I have seen grizzly and black bears chased off by leashed German shepherd, husky, malamute and Great Pyrenees dogs. Kurilian dogs are especially effective, and have been used systematically to intimidate bears in various parts of Europe and North America – fostered by the dedicated leadership of Carrie Hunt.***

*** Unless your dog has been professionally trained for intimidating bears, never let it run free, unless the bear is just about to attack the dog and/or you. Otherwise, the dog could approach the bear and provoke attack, then flee to you for protection, with the bear hot on its heels. Preferably use at least 2 or 3 dogs so that a bear can't focus attack on any one of them, and so that you have backups in case one dog fails or dies. For detailed information on use of dogs, consult Carry Hunt or perhaps *Bear Attacks II - Myth & Reality* by Gary Shelton.

The use of leashed dogs and other nonlethal deterrents magnifies the intimidating quality of a human's threats, much as banging metal cans together magnified threats by the chimpanzee Mike, as Goodall described in *In the Shadlow of Man*. When bears flee from such threats, they are responding to us much as if we were dominant bears.

Bears that reside near people without endangering us or our property may, in fact, protect us by excluding potential troublemakers. The social vacuums left by removal of resident adults is often filled by immigrants, especially preadolescent and adolescent males, who may be much less suited to coexisting with people. This side-effect of removing acclimated bears was first documented by Jane Tate in her doctoral research in the Great Smoky Mountains National Park, and has since been confirmed by a variety of managers including Steve Searles. Removal of acclimated bears may also backfire by genetically selecting against the very traits that facilitate coexistence with people. These are two more reasons why harvest of bears may, under some circumstances, can make bears more aggressive, not less so.

I have long believed that learning how to control aggression through respect and trust is especially valuable in areas such as Katmai National Park and McNeil Falls where bear-watching is rapidly growing in popularity – an idea the merits of which have been thoroughly confirmed by McNeil biologists such as Derek Stonorov, Larry Aumiller, Cauleen Matt, and Polly Hessing. [9]

HUNTING

The various, sometimes contradictory, ways in which hunting affects the danger bears pose to people will be systematically addressed in my book *Grizzlies Among the Glaciers*. For now, let it suffice to address just the notion that fear of hunters (human predators) increases respect by bears for people, reducing our risk of being mauled. (For example, see James Gary Shelton's book *Bear Encounter Survival Guide* and its sequels.) [11]

Although I have high regard for the discipline of Shelton's thinking, on this point I am skeptical. It contradicts my first-hand experience that coastal Alaska brown bears are much more defensively aggressive where they are hunted than where they are protected. It also contradicts logic. While it makes sense for animals to submit to dominants, so long as submission increases safety, submission to a predator would be suicidal. Even where enhancing fear of predation by humans makes bears avoid us by a wider margin, it seems to also make the animals more defensively aggressive when chance encounters do occur. And they occur with surprising frequency. Neither bears nor people pay enough attention to much besides members of their own species. Also, both bears and people spend a lot of time intensely preoccupied.

"BEARENTING" WITHOUT FOOD CONDITIONING

There are certainly situations where some bears become dangerous once they have gotten food from humans and have lost respect for us (assuming they ever respected us in the first place). Doddy was a good example. After finding garbage behind the cabin, then being fed and befriended by John and Joan, Doddy became so aggressive and bold that she had to be killed – illustrating all too well the saying that *"a fed bear is a dead bear."*

In theory, Doddy's cubs could have become just as dangerous, given that they too had raided the cabin for food and had intimidated John and Joan. However, one week of raiding does not constitute a "habit." The cubs and Doddy plundered John's cabin no more than half a dozen times, over the space of several days. They got a significant amount of food only on the first couple of raids. No one else in the area reported losing food to a bear at that time. After Doddy's death, the cubs raided our food supply only a few times, and were fed indoors for merely a week or so. Subsequently, they did no raiding and were fed only outdoors, except when nursing from the baby bottle.

In theory too, any problem with Doddy's cubs would have been aggravated by feeding and acclimating them to us over the next three months. However, so far as we know (from our own experiences and reports by John and Joan Purdy who returned to the cabin after we left) that didn't happen. Why not? Presumably because of how we raised the cubs.

Granted, bears which become accustomed to being fed by people do sometimes become demanding, even violent if treats are withheld or just unavailable. Bears reared in captivity and then released are no exception. If all the food a bear has ever eaten has come from people, you should not be surprised if they come back to people when they can't forage profitably, either because they don't know where to find wild foods or how to harvest them efficiently, because they are harassed by other bears, or simply because wild foods are scarce.

The *isolationist* approach probably works best with bears that already have enough maturity and experience in the wild to fend for themselves. Where that is not possible, future conflicts with humans are more likely to be avoided by instead "bearenting" orphans – raising the cubs in the wild while training them to forage and helping them to socialize, as Robert Leslie, Ben Kilham, Charley Russell, Maureen Enns, and I have done.

As quickly as possible, I weaned my cubs off of human foods by feeding them wild foods and especially by teaching them to forage for themselves. I never gave the cubs any meat except salmon. They never tasted candy or other sweets except for the Karo syrup or honey mixed into their mush when we first adopted them. Aside from the occasional fruit, about the only groceries I ever gave them were rice and oatmeal – not exactly the kind of fare for which bears normally become aggressive. In any event, during their last month with us I gave the cubs no human food except occasional snacks of peanuts and raisins, which I doled out in such small amounts that the cubs never aggressively tried to steal these treats. They had long since discovered that they could get no other food from us or from our cabin; and they didn't need to do so.

Ontak and his sisters had learned a wide variety of wild foods and where these could be found in a diversity of habitats. These cubs had been trained to forage effectively and seemed to have an even more diversified diet than fully wild bears. They were unusually skilled for their age at catching salmon.

Our cubs should have also been able to hold their own in competition with peers. They were about twice the size of fully wild cubs like JeanTo's youngsters of equal age. This was the result of the supplemental foods we had provided during their first month with us, and of the abundance of salmon and berries which we had helped them obtain.

Ontak, Jonjoanak and Chrislee all respected humans and avoided everyone but Alatanna and me, with the initial exception of Zak. Even Chrislee did not trust other people enough to approach them or to allow approach. Yet the cubs were not so afraid of people they would be likely to respond violently to surprise close encounters.

Neither experience nor logic revealed any evidence that our cubs were likely to ever become even as dangerous as mother-reared black bears – which are really not very dangerous at all, under most conditions.

Indeed, I've found no evidence of any "bearented" cub ever becoming a dangerous marauder. Although a few of Kilham's male cubs have raided neighborhood bird feeders or otherwise gotten into minor mischief, apparently none has ever seriously threatened a human. Nor did any cases of human injury by bear foster-reared before being turned loose turn up when John Beecham did a world-wide survey onthe subject.

To be on the safe side, however, even those risks can be minimized by rearing orphans in areas so isolated from other people that the cubs would never have much opportunity to bother anyone – which is why I had wanted to transfer Ontak and his sisters to into the Wrangle Mountains or to an offshore island.

*   *   *

Now, having done my duty of addressing potential hazards of "bearenting,"close companionship, and other forms of acclimation, let me refocus attention where it should be: on the wonder of these fascinating beings. Like Ontak and his sisters, bears in general are remarkable animals, deserving of our interest, respect, kindness and tolerance. Although it may not be desirable to acclimate all bears, the more we learn about our ursine kin, the more ways we will find to safely acclimate some of them, and to enjoy the *beauty within the beast*.

Renewal

In part because bears can be so dangerous,
they force you to pay attention.
The awe of being in their presence
strips away the chaos of thoughts and distractions
that normally dominate your consciousness.
They focus your attention on the moment.
They flood your blood
with adrenaline and endorphins.
They introduce you to terror, awe,
amazement and ecstasy.
They connect you to the deepest pulses of life.
This is their gift.
The power to take your life,
or to renew it;
to re-create who you are,
if only for a moment,
and perhaps for a lifetime.

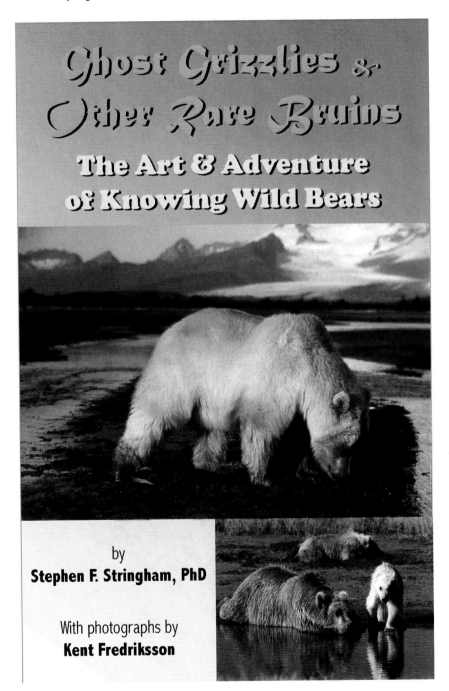

Ghost Grizzlies & Other Rare Bruins

The Art & Adventure of Knowing Wild Bears

by
Stephen F. Stringham, PhD

With photographs by
Kent Fredriksson

WHICH BEAR IS THAT?

Author Steve Stringham has had over 10,000 close encounters. He has gotten to know scores of bears and befriended a few. This book relates his experiences with some of those bears. And it explains the art that makes this possible for him -- and perhaps for you. Learn how to distinguish a white (Ghost) grizzly from a white (Spirit) black bear from a polar bear; or a Basalt griz from a blackie, or a Lava griz from a Cinnamon black bear. Learn how tell a male from a female; or an adolescent from a prime adult. Learn traits that distinguish a trophy boar from a dominant sow. If a sow isn't accompanied by cubs, how can you tell whether she has recently nursed--in which case, her cubs may simply be out of sight? Ethical sportsmen don't shoot sows with cubs; and everyone knows the danger of getting between cubs and their mother -- at least in the case of grizzly/brown bears. Best of all if you are a viewer, how can you distinguish individual bears? Suppose that you visit the same viewing site repeatedly. You see a bear that resembles one you enjoyed watching before, perhaps one that was comfortable with people nearby? Don't jump to conclusions that it's the same bear or that it will react the same way. Look carefully, using tips taught in this book. With care and luck, you too may have the privilege of seeing past the superficiality of generic bruins and glimpse the wonder of these magnificent beings with an intelligence to rival those of dolphins, chimpanzees (and some people). This book contains a unique selection of images of bears from around the world by amazing photographers such as Kent Fredriksson.

WildWatch
Publications Division
39200 Alma Ave.
Soldotna, AK 99669
wildwatch.llc@gmail.com

ISBN: 978-0-9796782-2-6

9 780979 678226

90000

BEAR VIEWING IN

ALASKA

Expert Techniques for a Great Adventure

STEPHEN F. STRINGHAM
PHOTOGRAPHY BY KENT FREDRIKSSON

**What's the best way to see bears up close
and in the wild?**

Where can you take the best photographs?

**How do you avoid making a bear nervous
and defensive?**

Thousands of people travel to Alaska each year specifically to view wild bears—one of the fastest growing outdoor recreational activities in the world. Dr. Stephen F. Stringham, a naturalist, biologist, and professional viewing guide, tells you where to find the best viewing locations, when to make your trip, and what conditions to expect. How do you know when a bear is becoming agitated and aggressive? What questions should you should ask when hiring a viewing guide? And perhaps most importantly, how can you avoid disturbing the animals you're viewing?

Enlivened by personal stories and Kent Fredriksson's gorgeous photographs, this invaluable resource is for anyone interested in experiencing firsthand the majesty and grace of Alaska's wild bears.

Stephen F. Stringham, PhD, is director of both the Bear Communication and Coexistence Research Program and the Bear Viewing Association. He has studied bears since 1969, teaches at the University of Alaska, and is the author of *Beauty Within the Beast: Kinship with Bears in the Alaska Wilderness.*

FALCON GUIDES®
falcon.com

Cover photo by Kent Fredriksson
Cover design by Todd Grosser

P.O. Box 480
Guilford, CT 06437
www.falcon.com

FalconGuides® is an imprint of
The Globe Pequot Press

$12.95

ISBN 978-0-7627-3953-0

9 780762 739530

51295

0 24933 01295 4   03953

Available at   **www.bear-viewing-in-alaska.info/Books_and_Videos.html**

ALASKA MAGNUM
BEAR SAFETY MANUAL

Don't Risk Your Life
to Live Your Dreams
of Fishing, Hunting, Hiking, Camping,
or Watching Wildlife in the Far North

Stephen Stringham
author of
BEAUTY WITHIN THE BEAST
BEAR VIEWING IN ALASKA

Photographs by
Kent Fredriksson,
Amy Shapira and others
Illustrations by **Gerald Trombley**

Do you dream of wilderness adventure ?

Do you hunger for the battle of landing a giant King salmon,
bagging trophy moose and caribou,
walking where no one has walked before,
or seeing a grizzly teach her cubs to outwit wolves?

If you love wildlife and wilderness, Alaska may be as close to Heaven as you are ever likely
to get while alive. At least it can be Heavenly, if you are not mauled by a bear. There is no
way to eliminate all attack risk. But risk can be drastically reduced if you select the right
times and places to have adventures, and if you follow the advice in this book.

At last, a bear safety manual tailored to the unique challenges
of hiking, camping, fishing, hunting and watching wildlife
in Alaska and western Canada.
And finally, definitive advice (*Ten Golden Rules*) for safe bear viewing.

There is almost no place in this vast region that you can go without a good chance meeting
bruins. Most bears just want to live and let live. But what if you accidently frighten
a mother with cubs? What if you surprise a bear feasting on a moose carcass or one that
hates anyone trespassing on its fishing site? What if a bruin demands the prize King you
have just landed? How can you avoid conflicts like these or cope with them?

For decades, such questions have been asked of Dr. Stephen Stringham, a renown authority
on bear psychology, communication and aggression. For decades, he has been providing
effective answers. Now, he is sharing them with you.

Safety begins with wisdom. The more you know about an animal, the more predictable
it will become to you, and the better you will be able to avoid encounters -- your first
line of defense. If avoidance fails, and an encounter occurs, your second line of defense is
trying to appease the animal to curb any defensive aggression, or to intimidate it to curb
bullying or predatory aggression. Intimidation can be enhanced by combining alpha body
language with a deterrent such as pepper spray or a flare. Only as a last resort should you
play dead or shoot. This book tells you exactly how to stop even a charging bear.

Bear behavior, including body language, and safety techniques are illustrated with over 100
photos and diagrams. Each technique is described in careful detail, based on decades of field
experience by Stringham and by other wildlife biologists, animal control technicians, guides,
and rangers. What worked for them could also work for you to assure that adventuring in bear
country is everything you dreamed it could be -- and more.

Cover photos: Front: large **Kent Fredriksson**
small **Lena Summers**. Back: **Amy Shapira**

WildWatch Publications
@WildWatch LLC
39200 Alma Ave.
Soldotna, AK 99669
wildwatch.llc@gmail.com

ISBN: 978-0-9796782-0-2

5 1995

9 780979 678202

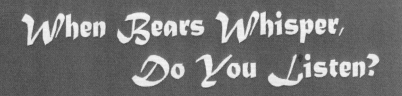

When Bears Whisper, Do You Listen?

Negotiating Close Encounters With Wild Bruins

Stephen F. Stringham

author of
Bear Viewing in Alaska
Alaska Magnum Bear Safety Manual
Beauty Within the Beast
The Language of Bears

Photographs by Kent Fredriksson
Illustrations by Gerald Trombley

A must-read guide for every bear viewer and anyone else who might face close encounters.

Whispers are subtle signs of a bear's moods and intentions – signals by which bears win the cooperation of their fellows, often without having to "shout," much less attack.

Those and other signals are detailed in a companion volume *The Language of Bears.* *This* book explains how communication forms the cornerstone of diplomacy – of minimizing aggression by building mutual trust and respect.

Trust minimizes defensive aggression; respect minizes offensive (predatory or bullying) aggression.

We humans can mimic ursine diplomacy to minimize our own risk of attack and to gain the cooperation of bears.

Learn the secrets of this esoteric art from renown *whisperer* Dr. Stephen Stringham. Learn how he has won the trust and respect of hundreds of grizzly/brown and black bears, and the "friendship"of a special few. Based on decades of field research and over 10,000 close encounters, Stringham reveals unique insights into the mind of these amazing beings whose ecology and psychology are so much like our ancestors.'

This book, like his previous works, is a masterful blend of practical wisdom, spellbinding adventure, and delightful humor. Popular science at its best.

WildWatch Publications
@WildWatch LLC
39200 Alma Ave.
Soldotna, AK 99669
wildwatch.llc@gmail.com

ISBN: 978-0-9796782-1-9

9 780979 678219

BEAR AGGRESSION
Why Bears Attack & How to Minimize Risk

by
Stephen F. Stringham, PhD
Author of
**ALASKA MAGNUM BEAR SAFETY MANUAL
WHEN BEARS WHISPER, DO YOU LISTEN?
BEAR VIEWING IN ALASKA
BEAUTY WITHIN THE BEAST**

Photos by Kent Fredericksson

Does your heart beat faster when you venture into bear country? Does your skin turn cold and prickle when you find fresh tracks or scat so new it's still steaming? What do you do when you actually meet a bear – shoot the animal or blast it with pepper spray? Did you know that neither the most powerful gun nor the hottest spray is as critical to your safety as your brain – as what you know about bears and how you apply that knowledge?

You can learn something from bear attack stories – from cases (like Tim Treadwell's) where safety precautions were either ignored or failed. But you can learn far more from cases where precautions worked. That's exactly what you'll find in this book – the third in a bear safety trilogy by Dr. Stephen Stringham, wildlife biologist, viewing guide, and veteran of over 10,000 close encounters.

     1. Alaska Magnum Bear Safety Manual
     2. When Bears Whisper, Do You Listen?
     3. Bear Aggression

Bear Aggression analyzes statistics on how attack risk differs according the speies of bear, its motivation, and the context of any encounter. Then it explains methods of minimizing your risk in each situation – usually without having to shoot the bruin.

Stringham's defensive tactics rest on an unprecedented exploration of bear aggression – of the motives that drive bears to intimidate, injure or occasionally kill peers – motives like defending cubs, competing for food, or cannibalism. Understanding those scenarios provides critical insights for handling situations where its you that a bear sees as a threat, a rival, or a potential meal. After reviewing case after case where he or someone else successfully handled such encounters, Stringham provides step-by-step instructions for how you too might succeed.

Like Stringham's other books, Bear Aggression is filled with his signature blend of piercing analysis, practical advice, high adventure, and low humor. As entertaining as they are informative, these books are a must for everyone daring enough to meet bears face to face on their own turf.

WildWatch Publications
@WildWatch LLC
39200 Alma Ave.
Soldotna, AK 99669
wildwatch.llc@gmail.com

ISBN: 978-0-9796782-1-9

9 780979 678219

Available at   www.bear-viewing-in-alaska.info/Books_and_Videos.html

GRIZZLIES AMONG GLACIERS

Stephen F. Stringham, PhD

Stringham's first book *Beauty Within the Beast* told the warm and wonderful story of his experiences raising three orphaned black bear cubs in the Alaska wilds. Later books (e.g., on bear viewing techniques and safety precautions) provided glimpses of his experiences while studying the behavior and ecology of grizzly/brown bears. But only now is his full story emerging, and along with it the story of some very remarkable animals and their home -- a sea coast dominated and shaped not only by the ocean, but also by terribly cold winters, titanic glaciers, and erupting volcanos. The ecology and behavior of coastal bears are compared and contrasted with those of bears in Interior Alaska, as well as other parts of North America.

Like Stringham's other books, *Grizzlies Among Glaciers* is filled with his signature blend of piercing analysis, practical advice, high adventure, and delightful humor. As entertaining as they are informative, Stringham's books will carry you into a world of scientific adventure that few other people have more than glimpsed.

WildWatch Publications
@WildWatch LLC
39200 Alma Ave.
Soldotna, AK 99669
wildwatch.llc@gmail.com

ISBN: 978-0-9796782-1-9

9 780979 678219

90000

Available at   www.bear-viewing-in-alaska.info/Books_and_Videos.html

The Language of Bears

Communication is the Key to Coexistence

Stephen Stringham

Photos by Kent Fredriksson & others

WHY LEARN BEAR BODY LANGUAGE?

Suppose you meet a bear, perhaps while hiking in the woods or fishing along a stream. How will it respond? That depends on its mood and intentions – e.g., on whether it's afraid, angry or perhaps even playful. It's response may also depend on how you react. Trying to intimidate a frightened or angry bear could trigger attack, whereas trying to appease the bruin could set it at ease. Yet, appeasement might encourage a predatory bear. So you'd better be able to tell the difference -- between these and numerous other possibilities.

Granted, you might simply shoot the bear, if you happen to be carrying an adequate firearm and are expert in its use. But a lot of people lack that option, especially inside a national park where firearms are forbidden. And people who just wound a bear are often mauled a lot worse than people who don't shoot. In any event, why shoot a bear that might be just curious or even friendly?

In many situations, assessing risk and selecting your best response requires reading the bear's mood and intentions from its body language – its vocalizations and other sounds, as well as its facial expressions, gestures, and postures.

The art of communiating with bears to through body language to achieve mutual cooperation, has previously been known to only a handful of people. Now, for the first time, the "language" of bears is made public. Based on decades of scientific research and over 10,000 close encounters, animal *communicator* Dr. Stephen Stringham summarizes the findings of fellow experts and combines them with his own insights in a narrative that is highly informative and wonderfully entertaining.

Understanding the "language" of bears is, of course, only the first step in peaceful coexistence. The next is applying that knowledge to negotiating close encounters – the subject of a companion volume *When Bears Whisper, Do You Listen?*

WildWatch Publications
@WildWatch LLC
39200 Alma Ave.
Soldotna, AK 99669
wildwatch.llc@gmail.com

ISBN: 978-0-9796782-1-9

9 780979 678219

Available at   www.bear-viewing-in-alaska.info/Books_and_Videos.html

Endnotes

Chapter 6
1. Burghardt and Burghardt 1972.

Chapter 7
1. Leslie 1968; Krott 1961; Krott and Krott 1963.
2. Burghardt and Burghardt 1972.
3. Leyhausen 1979.
4. Nelson 1969.
5. Beck 1980.

Chapter 8
1. Wright 1909; Mills 1919.
2. Murie

Chapter 9
1. Mealey 1980.

Chapter 10
1. Wright 1909.
2. Rogers and Wilker 1995.
3. Debruyen 1999.
4. Kilham

Chapter 11
1. Luque and Stokes 1974.
2. Bledsoe 1987.
3. David Garshellis, Minnesota Department of Natural Resources, Grand Rapids.

280

Chapter 12

1. Leslie 1968.
2. Thomas 1994.
3. Owens and Owens 1984.
4 Atamian 1995.

RECOMMENDED READING

BEAR BEHAVIOR

Bacon 1973; Bacon and Burghardt 1974a.b; Henry and Herrero 1974; Jordan 1974; Ludlow 1974; Pruitt 1974.

BEAR DIETS

Carlock *et al.* 1983; Eagle and Pelton 1983; Elowe 1987; Graber 1981; Hugie 1982; Leslie 1968; Mace and J. Jonkel 1986; Mealey 1977; McLaughlin et al. 1987; Rogers and Allen 1987; Treadwell & Clausen 2008; Willey 1979.

PLANTS WHICH ARE EDIBLE, MEDICINAL OR TOXIC FOR HUMANS

Anonymous 1985; Angier 1972; Buchman 1979; Densmore 1928; Erichsen-Brown 1979; Garibaldi 1999; Gibbons 1962; Harrington 1967; Jones 1983; Miller; Peterson 1977; Pojar and MacKinnon 1994; Underhill 1980; Viereck 1987; Vogel 1970.

BIBLIOGRAPHY

Angier, B. 1972. *Feasting Free on Wild Edibles.* Stackpole Books, Harrisburg.

Atamian, S. 1995. *The Bears of Manley: Adventures of an Alaska Trophy Hunter in Search of the Ultimate Symbol.* Publication Consultants, Anchorage.

Bacon, E. S. 1973. *Investigation on perception and behavior of the American Black Bear (Ursus americanus).* Ph.D. dissertation, U. Tennessee, Knoxville.

Bacon, E.S. and G. M. Burghardt. 1974. Ingestive behaviors of the American black bear. *Ursus* 3:13-25.

Bacon, E.S. and G. M. Burghardt. 1974. Learning and color discrimination in the American black bear. *Ursus* 3:27-36.

Beck, B. B. 1980. *Animal Tool Behavior: The Use and Manufacture of Tools by Animals.* Garland STPM Press, New York.

Beecham, J. 2006. Orphaned Bear Cubs: Rehabilitation and Release Guidelines. *Report to the World Society for the Protection of Animals.*

Bledsoe, W. T. 1987. *Brown Bear Summer: Life Among Alaska's Giants.* E. P. Dutton, New York.

Buchman, D. D. 1979. *Dian Dincin Buchman's Herbal Medicine: The Natural Way to Get Well and Stay Well.* Gramercy Publ. Co., New York.

Burghardt, G. M., and L. S. Burghardt. 1972. Notes on behavioral development of two female black bear cubs: the first eight months. *Ursus.* 2:207-220.

Carlock, D. M., R. H. Conley, J. M. Collins, P. E. Hale, K. G. Johnson, A. S. Johnson, and M. R. Pelton. 1983. *The Tri-State black bear study.* Pope and Young Club, Big Game Records.

Craighead, F. C., Jr. 1979. *Track of the Grizzly.* Sierra Club Books, San Francisco.

Craighead, J. J., F. C. Craighead, and J. Sumner. 1974. A population analysis of the Yellowstone grizzly bears. *Mont. For. and Cons. Exp. Sta. Bull. 40.* U. Montana, Missoula.

Craighead, J. J., J. S. Sumner, and J. A. Mitchell. 1995 The grizzly bears of Yellowstone: Their ecology in the Yellowstone Ecosystem, 1959-1992. Island Press, Corvelo, CA.

Craighead, J. J., F. C. Craighead, Jr., and J. Sumner. 1976. Reproductive cycles and rates in the grizzly bear, *Ursus arctos* horribilis, of the Yellowstone ecosystem. *Ursus* 3:337-356.

Debruyen, T. D. 1999. *Walking with Bears.* The Lyons Press, New York.

Densmore, F. 1928. *How Indians Use Wild Plants for Food, Medicine, and Crafts.* Dover Publications Co., New York.

Dolson, S. 2001. *Nonlethal Bear Management Guidebook.* Bear Smart, Whistler, B.C. Canada. bearsmart.com.

Eagle, T. C., and M. R. Pelton. 1983. Seasonal nutrition of black bears in the Great Smoky Mountains National Park. *Ursus* 5:94-101.

Egbert, A. L. and A. W. Stokes. 1974. The social behavior of brown bears on an Alaskan salmon stream. *Ursus* 3:41-56.

Elowe, K. D. 1987. *Factors affecting black bear reproductive success and cub survival in Massachusetts.* Ph. D. Thesis, Univ. of Massachusetts.

Erichsen-Brown, C. 1979. *Medicinal and Other Uses of North American Plants: A Historical Survey with Special Reference to the Eastern Indian Tribes.* Dover Publ., New York.

Garibaldi, A. 1999. *Medicinal Flora of the Alaska Natives.* U. of Alaska Press.

Giest, V. 1972. *Mountain Sheep: A Study in Behavior and Evolution.* U. Chicago Press, Chicago.

Geist, V. 1979. *Mountain Sheep and Man in the Northern Wilds.* Cornell U. Press, Ithaca.

Gibbons, E. 1962. *Stalking the wild asparagus.* David McKay Co., New York.

Goodall, J. van Lawick-. 1971. *In the Shadow of Man.* Houghton-Mifflin Co., Boston.

Goodall, J. 1990. *Through a Window: My Thirty Years with the Chimpanzees of Gombe.* Houghton Mifflin Co., Boston.

Graber, D. M. 1981. *Ecology and management of black bears in Yosemite National Park.* Ph.D. Thesis. Univ. California, Berkeley.

Harrington, H. D. 1967. *Edible Native Plants of the Rocky Mountains.* U. New Mexico Press, Albuquerque.

Heller, C. 1985. *Wild Edible and Poisonous Plants of Alaska.* Coop. Ext. Service, U of Alaska.

Henry, J. D. and S. M. Herrero. 1974. Social play in the American Black Bear: Its Similarity to Canid Social Play and an Examination of its Identifying Characteristics. *Amer. Zool.* 14:371-389.

Hittel, T. H. 1860. *The Adventures of James Capen Adams, Grizzly Bear Hunter of California.*

Hugie, R. D. 1982. *Black bear ecology and management in the northern conifer-deciduous forests of Maine.* Ph. D. Thesis, Univ. of Montana, Missoula.

Jones, A. 1983. *Nauriat Nigiñaqtuat: Plants That We Eat.* Maniilaq Association.

Jordan, R. H. 1974. Threat behavior of the black bear, *Ursus americanus. Ursus* 3:57-63.

Kilham, B. 2002. *Among the Bears.* Henry Holt and Co. New York.

Krott, P. 1961. Der gefährliche Braunbär (*Ursus arctos* L. 1758). *Z. Tierpsychologie,* 18:245-256.

Krott, P. and G. Krott. 1963. Zum Verhalten des Braunbären (*Ursus arctos* L. 1758) in den Alpen. *Z. Tierpsychologie,* 30:160-206.

Leslie, R. F. 1968. *The Bears and I.* E. P. Dutton & Co. New York, NY.

Leyhausen, P. 1979. *Cat Behavior: The Predatory and Social Behavior of Domestic and Wild Cats.* Garland STPM Press, New York.

Ludlow, J. C. 1974. Observations on the breeding of captive black bears, *Ursus americanus. Ursus* 3:65-69.

284

Luque, M. H. and A. W. Stokes. 1974. Fishing behavior of Alaska brown bear. *Ursus* 3:71-78.

Mace, R. D., and C. J. Jonkel. 1986. Local food habitats of the grizzly bear in Montana. *Ursus* 6:104-110.

McLaughlin, C. R., G. J. Matula, and J. H. Hunt. 1987. A draft habitat suitability index model for black bears in the conifer-deciduous forests of New England: its application in Maine. *East. Workshop Black Bear Res. and Manage.* **8:000-000.**

Mealey, S. P. 1977. The natural food habits of grizzly bears in Yellowstone National Park, 1973-74. *Ursus* 3:281-292.

Miller, D.S. *Berry Finder*. Nature Study Guild, Berkeley.

Mills, E. A. 1919. *The Grizzly*. Ballantine Books, New York.

Murie, A. 1981. *The Grizzlies of Mount McKinley*. U. S. Department of Interior, National Park Service, Scientific Monograph Series No. 14.

Nelson, R. 1969. *Hunters of the Northern Ice*. U. Chicago Press, Chicago.

Ovsyanikov, N. 1996. *Living With the White Bear*. Voyageur Press, Stillwater

Owens, M. and D. Owens. 1984. Cry of the Kalahari: An American Couple's Seven Years in Africa's Last Great Wilderness. Houghton Mifflin Co., Boston.

Peterson, D. and J. Goodall. 1993. *Visions of Caliban: On Chimpanzees and People*. Houghton Mifflin Co., Boston.

Peterson, L.A. 1977. *A Field Guide to Edible wild plants: Eastern and Central North America*. Houghton Mifflin Co., Boston.

Pojar, J. and A. MacKinnon. (ed). 1994. *Plants of the Pacific Northwest Coast: Washington, Oregon, British Columbia, and Alaska*. Lone Pine Publ., Vancouver, B.C.

Pruitt, C. H. 1974. Play and agonistic behavior in captive black bears. *Ursus* 3:79-86.

Rogers, L. L. 1987. Effects of food supply and kinship on social behavior, movements, and population growth of black bears in northeastern Minnesota. *Wildl. Monogr.* **97**. 72pp.

Rogers, L. L., and A. W. Allen. 1987. *Habitat suitability index models: black bear, Upper Great Lakes Region.* U. S. Dept. Int., Washington D. C. Biol. Rep. 8200.144).

Rogers, L.L. and G. W. Wilker. 1995. How to obtain behavioral and ecological data from free-ranging, research-habituated black bears. *Ursus* 8:321-327. *bears.org* or *bearstudy.org*

Russell, C. 1994. *Spirit Bear.* Key Porter Books, Toronto.

Russell, C. and M. Enns. 2002. *Grizzly Heart.* Random House, Toronto.

Schaller, G. B. 1993. *The Last Panda.* U. Chicago Press, Chicago.

Schaller, G. B., H. Jinchu, Pan Wenshi, and Zhu Jing. 1985. *The Giant Pandas of Wolong.*

Shelton, J.G. 1994. *Bear Encounter Survival Guide.* Pallister Publ, Hagensborg, B.C. Canada

Shelton, J. G. 1998. *Bear Attacks - The Deadly Truth.* Pallister Publ, Hagensborg, B.C. Canada.

Shelton, J. G. 2001. *Bear Attacks II: Myth & Reality.* Pallister Publ, Hagensborg, B.C. Canada.

Stringham, S. F. 1985. Responses by grizzly bear population dynamics to certain environmental and biosocial factors. Ph.D. dissertation, U. Tennessee, Knoxville.

Thomas, E. M.. 1994. *The Tribe of Tiger: Cats and Their Culture.* Simon & Schuster, New York.

Treadwell, T. & J. Palovak. 1997. *Among Grizzlies.* Harper Collins, New York.

Treadwell, E. M. & T. P. Clausen. 2008. Is *Hedysarum mackenziei* (wild sweet pea) actually toxic? www.ethnobotanyjournal.org/vol6/i1547-3465-06-319.pdf

Trivers, R. L, & D. E. Willard. 1973. Natural selection of parental ability to vary the sex ratio of offspring. *Science* 179:90-92.

Underhill, J. E. 1980. *Northwestern Wild Berries.* Hancock House Publ. Ltd. Surrey, B.C.

van Lawick-Goodall, J. (see Goodall, J. van Lawick-.)

Viereck, E. G. 1987. *Alaska's Wilderness Medicines Healthful Plants of the Far North.* Alaska Northwest Publ. Co.

Vogel, V. 1970. *American Indian Medicine.* U. Oklahoma Press, Lincoln.

Walker, T. and L. AuMiller. 1993. *River of Bears.* Voyageur Press, Stillwater

Willey, C. H. 1979. *The Vermont black bear.* Vermont Fish and Game Department.Montpelier.

Wilson, E.O. 1975. *Sociobiology, the new synthesis.* Belknap, Cambridge, MA.

Wright, Wm. H. 1909. *The Grizzly Bear: The Narrative of a Hunter-Naturalist.* Charles Scribner's Sons. New York. Reprinted by U. of Nebraska Press, Lincoln.

ABOUT THE AUTHOR

Dr. Stringham participated in the first study of black bear population ecology on the northern coast of California. That was just after completing his Bachelor's degree in Marine Ecology (Humboldt State University), during which he also researched effects of pollutants on the development of sea urchin embryos, as well as ecology of estuaries. From there, he journeyed to Alaska where he has spent much of the past 33 years studying the behavior of grizzly bears, black bears and moose.

Initially, his observations of Alaskan bears were just hit and miss encounters while he focused on learning how moose communicate and care for their calves, and especially how the calves are protected from predators such as bears, which are said to kill the majority of young moose in certain parts of Alaska. That research, done on the Kenai Peninsula, served as the basis for his Master's degree in Wildlife Management at the University of Alaska.

As part of his moose research, he raised orphaned calves. On the side, he has also raised Arctic foxes, red foxes, and wolves. His efforts to "know" animals don't stop at the generic level. He gets to know them as individuals and occasionally develops personal relationships with them. This was inspired by his adoptive Cherokee grandmother Teetzineela.

She instilled a deep respect for the way Indigenous peoples relate to Nature and a determination to integrate Indigenous, Western and Eastern "sciences" to better understand and steward wildlife. Steve has served as an advisor to several Native groups including the Sitka Tribe of Alaska and the Alaska Native Brotherhood. He taught in the Salish-Kootenai and Blackfeet Tribal colleges and was a founding Director of the Blackfeet Environmental Office.

Although Dr. Stringham saw bears occasionally during his moose research, these were just tantalizing glimpses and a few close calls which, though sometimes frightening, just whet his appetite to know the animals better, especially in terms of their communication, aggression and coastal ecology.

He went on to study grizzly bears on the Alaska Peninsula, at Katmai National Monument (now Katmai National Park and Preserve), and then black bears in various parts of Alaska. He has also studied bears in Montana, New York and Vermont.

Dr. Stringham's research on communication and aggression has been approached from the perspectives of both bear-human and bear-bear interactions. Much of his work has focused on aggression by adult males toward cubs and how the abundance of adult males in a population affects rates of cub production and survival. This was the subject of his Ph.D. dissertation in Behavioral and Population Ecology (University of Tennessee). Since then, Dr. Stringham's seminal work on bear population ecology and conservation has branched out to the roles of adult male mammals and to the application of risk assessment to conservation of Threatened and Endangered species.

Dr. Stringham still lives in Alaska where his research with bears and moose continues, and where he introduces students and ecotourists to bears "up close and personal." He and his wife Jackie jointly operate WildWatch LLC, producing educational media (books, videos, interactive software, etc), tutoring students, and doing environmental assessment and conservation. She is a former liaison to the United Nations and a multi-cultural educator.

288

Anyone interesting in joining one of Dr. Stringham's tours or enrolling in his field courses can contact him at gobearviewing@hotmail.com. or at *www.bear-viewing-in-alaska.info.*

Dr. Stringham is President of *WildWatch* (*Consulting, Research, Ecotourism and Other Educational Services*) Director of the *Bear Communication & Coexistence Research Program,* and Director of the *Bear Viewing Association.*

BOOK ORDERS: To order copies of this or other BVA books, go to the Bear Viewing Association website **bear-viewing-in-alaska.info >> Ground-breaking books ...** *All profits from sales directly from BVA are used to fund bear conservation, research and education.*